Political Science

Reference Sources in the Social Sciences Series
Lubomyr R. Wynar, Series Editor

POLITICAL SCIENCE
A Guide to Reference and Information Sources

HENRY E. YORK
Social Science and History Librarian
Cleveland State University

1990

LIBRARIES UNLIMITED, INC.
Englewood, Colorado

LIBRARIES UNLIMITED, INC.
P.O. Box 6633
Englewood, CO 80155-6633

Library of Congress Cataloging-in-Publication Data

York, Henry E.
    Political science : a guide to reference and information sources /
Henry E. York.
    xvi, 249 p. 17x25 cm. -- (Reference sources in the social sciences series ; no. 4)
    Includes bibliographical references and index.
    ISBN 0-87287-794-9
    1. Reference books--Political science--Bibliography.   2. Political
science--Bibliography.   I. Title.   II. Series.
Z7161.Y75   1990
[JA71]
016.32--dc20   90-41158
                                                              CIP

Contents

v

Foreword

This series, Reference Sources in the Social Sciences, is intended to introduce librarians, researchers, and students to major sources within the social science disciplines. The series covers the following disciplines: sociology, political science, history, economics and business, anthropology, education, psychology, and general social science reference sources.

The organization and content of each volume are shaped by bibliographic forms and subject structures of the individual disciplines. Since many subject areas within the social sciences are interrelated, some reference sections in the various volumes will have certain features in common (e.g., a section on general social science sources). Each volume in the series constitutes a unique reference tool stressing the informational subject structure of the discipline, major reference publications, databases, and other relevant sources, including serials, research centers, and major professional organizations.

It is hoped that *Political Science: A Guide to Reference and Information Sources* will fill an important gap in the professional social science literature and provide useful tools for research in political science. The volume is divided into six sections with many subheadings and has over 800 entries, including information on databases and computerized searching.

Henry E. York is the Social Science and History Librarian at Cleveland State University in Cleveland, Ohio, where he is responsible for the development of the reference collection in various social science disciplines, including political science. He contributes to *American Reference Book Annual* and other professional publications.

Lubomyr R. Wynar
Series Editor

Introduction

DEFINITION OF POLITICAL SCIENCE

The term "political science" is derived from the Greek word *polis*, city state, and the Latin, *scientia*, science. Political science, it follows then, is the study of politics and political behavior. Among the many contemporary definitions of political science is this one offered by David Robertson in his *Dictionary of Modern Politics*: "The study of the nature, distribution, and dynamics of power, usually at the national or international level, but sometimes at a very 'macro' level."[1] *The Blackwell Encyclopedia of Political Thought* defines political theory as the "systematic reflection on the nature and purpose of government, characteristically involving both an understanding of existing political institutions and a view about how (if at all) they ought to be changed."[2] The sections on dictionaries and encyclopedias in this guide will provide references to many sources of other definitions of political science, its subfields, and related disciplines.

SCOPE AND PURPOSE

Descriptions of more than 800 of the major resources for the study of political science, its subdisciplines, and related social science fields are provided in this guide, which is intended primarily for college students, librarians, and beginning researchers. Printed reference sources, including bibliographies, indexes, dictionaries, handbooks, statistical sources, and other categories, are covered for works published between 1980 and 1987. Many of the most important reference

---

[1]David Robertson, *A Dictionary of Modern Politics.* (Philadelphia: Taylor & Francis, 1985), 265.

[2]David Miller, ed. *The Blackwell Encyclopedia of Political Thought.* (New York: Basil Blackwell, 1987), 383.

sources in political science are serials; these have been included regardless of their beginning date, if they are still being published. The vast majority of the titles listed in this guide are in English, published in the United States or Great Britain. Cited for the specialist or advanced researcher are several other guides to the literature of this discipline that provide access to older monographs and foreign-language titles. A few important titles that have not gone out of date or been replaced by newer material have been included.

In addition to the reference works, this guide also considers computer data-bases, periodicals, organizations, and publishers useful for the study of political science. The entries follow the bibliographic format used by Libraries Unlimited in its *American Reference Books Annual* (*ARBA*). In the selection of main entries, if the *ARBA* entry was lacking, OCLC practice was followed. The prices cited were current as of 1988 or 1989.

The annotations are descriptive and usually critical. Titles considered generally not to be useful have been omitted. Inclusion, with whatever limitations noted, is therefore an implicit positive evaluation. The annotations range in length from approximately 80 to 200 words for the reference books; for other materials the annotations are briefer.

The scope of this bibliography has been defined to exclude legal publications; guides to government documents; guides to legislative and other governmental activity; bibliographies of government agency publications; directories and rosters of government officials; and texts of laws, treaties, and publications dealing with individual states.

ORGANIZATION AND COVERAGE

This guide is divided into six chapters. The first deals with general social science reference sources, that is, reference titles, such as *The Social Science Encyclopedia* (entry 15), that span the various social science disciplines. Selection here was necessarily limited to titles specifically useful in the study of political science. In some cases titles ranging beyond the social sciences have also been included if no other more specialized titles exist. The selected titles are grouped by category. Some of the standard categories used throughout the book are: atlases, bibliographies, biographical sources, chronologies, dictionaries and encyclopedias, directories, guides, handbooks, indexes, sourcebooks, and yearbooks. It should be noted that the distinctions between these categories are not always totally clear; this was especially apparent with some handbooks/directories and bibliographies/guides.

Chapter 2 deals with social science disciplines other than political science. The table of contents lists the 12 disciplines included. Here selection was severely limited to titles of greatest usefulness to political scientists who might need to access material in these other disciplines. The focus therefore has been on dictionaries, basic handbooks, and basic statistics sources. Guides to the literature have also been cited extensively for those who wish to have a more comprehensive introduction to these fields.

The third chapter lists resources that provide comprehensive coverage of political science, that is, all topics, time periods, and countries in general, without a specific, narrower focus. This part of the bibliography begins with a listing of printed reference sources, followed by the names of major publishers in the political science field. The next section identifies and describes the major English-language periodicals suitable for undergraduate study or reading by the general public. News and current events magazines are not included. This section is followed by a section on organizations, which contains four subdivisions: (1) scholarly and professional associations, (2) research centers, (3) associations of government officials, and (4) advocate organizations. In the concluding section on computerized searching, online searching and the use of CD-ROMs are discussed.

Chapters 4, 5, and 6 contain the selections of reference sources covering the various fields within political science. These have been arranged geographically in chapter 4, with divisions covering all of the regions of the world; four sections are reserved for the United States, since there are so many relevant publications. Chapter 5 is arranged topically and includes six subjects on which a large amount of material has appeared: international organizations; international relations; communism and Marxism; human rights; peace and conflict; and terrorism, espionage, and intelligence services. When the geographic and topical categories overlap, the subject category takes precedence. For example, the title *Brazil and Its Radical Left: An Annotated Bibliography on the Communist Movement and the Rise of Marxism (1922-1972)* (entry 687) is found in the section on communism, not in the geographical section on the Americas. Chapter 6 deals with public policy literature.

The arrangement of citations should make the location of material straightforward if the table of contents is used for guidance. The author/title and subject indexes provide additional access. Remember also to check the general reference sources in chapters 1 and 3 if more specialized titles are not found in the sections devoted to works with a specific focus.

The last four chapters form the core of this bibliography, as they provide comprehensive coverage of political science within the scope of limitations mentioned above.

ACKNOWLEDGMENTS

A number of persons have been helpful in the preparation of this bibliography. I would like to thank in particular Lubomyr Wynar, the series editor. Most of the titles cited here were reviewed in the main library at Cleveland State University, where its strong collection and the support of the library administration have been much appreciated. Also my thanks to Deborah and Benjamin for their continuing interest.

1

General Social Science Reference Sources

BIBLIOGRAPHIES

1. **Handbook of Latin American Studies: A Selected and Annotated Guide to Recent Publications.** Austin, Tex., University of Texas Press. 1935- . annual. index. $65.00. LC 36-32633. ISSN 0072-9833.

This major bibliography, covering all important publications on Latin American — including books, periodical articles, pamphlets, and documents — is a source of prime importance for the study of Latin America. Since 1964 the bibliography has alternated yearly between coverage of the humanities and the social sciences. The entries are classified by academic discipline, with subdivisions by countries. Each chapter is signed by the scholar responsible for its compilation and begins with a brief survey of the literature. The annotations are in English, though many of the entries are for Spanish or Portuguese publications. There are author and subject indexes.

2. **International Bibliography of the Social Sciences.** London, Tavistock; Chicago, Aldine. 1955- . annual.

This is not a publication itself, but a series designation for four annual bibliographies which together offer extensive coverage of journals published throughout the world. These services were the result of bibliographic studies initiated by the International Committee for Social Science Documentation, which received aid from UNESCO. The four series are the *International Bibliography of Social and Cultural Anthropology* (see entry 114), the *International Bibliography of Economics* (see entry 55), the *International Bibliography of Sociology* (see entry 102), and the *International Bibliography of Political Science* (see entry 104).

3. **A London Bibliography of the Social Sciences.** London, Mansell, 1931- . annual. price varies. LC 31-9970. ISSN 0076-051X.

Annual supplements provide current coverage for this standard bibliography of the social sciences, which is principally based on the extensive holdings of the British Library of Political and Economic Science at the London School of Economics. Books, pamphlets, and some government publications are included, and coverage is worldwide. The entries are arranged by subject. There are no author index, cross-references, or annotations, but this remains a major social science bibliography for the breadth of its current coverage and for its retrospective coverage in the early volumes, which reaches back to classic titles from the early 19th century. The German and French equivalents of this bibliography are:

Bibliographie der Wirtschaftswissenschaften. Göttingen, Vandenhoech & Ruprecht, 1968- . annual. price varies. LC 88-21210. ISSN 0340-6121. (This supersedes the *Bibliographie der Socialwissenschaften*, which began in 1906.)

Bulletin analytique de documentation politique, économique et sociale contemporaire. Fondation Nationale des Sciences Politiques. Paris, Presses Universitaires de France, 1946- . monthly. Fr.575. LC 49-51779. ISSN 0007-4071.

4. Rand Corporation. **Selected Rand Abstracts.** Santa Monica, Calif., Rand Corporation, 1963- . quarterly. index. $75.00/yr. LC 65-2088. ISSN 0037-1343.

This abstracting service is a guide to the publications of the Rand Corporation, an independent, nonprofit organization engaged in scientific research and analysis. Its research is funded by the United States government, state and local governments, and private sources such as foundations. Its work involves most disciplines, including the physical and biological sciences as well as the social sciences, where there is an emphasis on policy-making and planning.

Selected Rand Abstracts indexes the corporation's research reports in quarterly issues, which are cumulated annually. There are author and subject indexes to provide access to the abstracts. Broad headings are used in the subject index, such as arms control, government regulation, international relations, and the names of countries.

5. **Reading Lists in Radical Social Science.** Mark Maier and Dan Gilroy, ed. coordinators. New York, Monthly Review Press/Union for Radical Political Economics, 1982. 179p. $10.00. LC 81-86025. ISBN 0-85345-616X.

These reading lists were compiled to offer suggested resources for teachers or students seeking material not included in traditional social science courses. The publisher, the Union for Radical Political Economics, founded in 1968, is an educational association of socialist intellectuals and activists. The format employed provides a series of course outlines and accompanying reading lists. The materials are arranged in about 20 broad categories, including Marxism and methodology, the state, development and regional studies, revolution, history, women, labor, the corporation, racism, crime, education, and hunger.

Although intended for use in preparing course guides or reading lists, this source can also be helpful to those seeking to expand the perspective of books and journals they consult in researching social science topics.

6. **Subject Guide to Books in Print.** New York, Bowker, 1957- . 4v. annual. $79.95/set. LC 79-5579. ISSN 0000-0159.

These annual volumes are the standard tool for identifying books in all subjects currently in print in the United States. The information is based on the present stock of some 22,500 American publishers with listings of more than 750,000 books currently available for purchase. The entries are arranged by topic and include the date of publication, price, and ISSN number. There is an extensive section listed under "Political Science," which begins with a list of some 80 *see also* references that lead to the major topics and subtopics related to political science. Library of Congress subject headings are used throughout this set. A companion set, *Books in Print* (New York, Bowker, 1947- . 7v. annual. index.

$249.95/set. LC 79-5579. ISSN 0068-0214) provides the same information arranged by author or title. The title set also includes a directory of American publishers and distributors with addresses and phone numbers. This database is available online through DIALOG and BRS and on CD-ROM as *Books in Print Plus* from Bowker.

BIOGRAPHICAL SOURCES

7. **Biography and Genealogy Master Index.** 2d ed. Detroit, Gale, 1980. 8v. $925.00. LC 82-7034. ISSN 0730-1316.

As an index to over 3,300,000 biographical sketches, this publication is an apt example of the utility of computer-generated tools for facilitating reference work. This one source provides access to over 350 biographical dictionaries. Historical and contemporary persons from all nations are covered, including many obscure political figures. Fortunately, there have been a number of supplements, including annual volumes, to keep this recommended starting point for biographical searching up-to-date. This index is also available online through the DIALOG database service.

8. **Biography Index.** New York, H. W. Wilson, 1946- . quarterly, with annual cumulations. $75.00/yr. LC 47-6532. ISSN 0006-3053.

Biography Index is an index of biographical material, including obituaries, collections of letters, diaries, memoirs, and bibliographies. Works of collective biography are analyzed. The material is gathered from periodicals indexed by Wilson, from current books, and from other selected sources. The index is in two sections. The main section consists of the entries arranged alphabetically by the names of the biographees, with citations to sources; the second section is an index of these individuals by profession or occupation.

BOOK REVIEW SOURCES

9. **American Reference Books Annual.** Bohdan Wynar, ed. Englewood, Colo., Libraries Unlimited, 1970- . annual. index. $85.00. LC 84-42829. ISSN 0065-9959.

New reference books in all subjects are listed and evaluated in this important source of reference reviews; 1,693 titles are included in the 1989 volume. The entries are grouped in broad subject headings — general reference works, the social sciences, the humanities, and science and technology — which in turn are subdivided by discipline, topic, and format. There is a chapter for political science, which includes international relations and public policy as well as general works and United States government and politics. Related sections include area studies and law as well as the other social sciences. There are three cumulative indexes. The reviews are often critical and usually signed. Citations to major reviewing journals provide access to additional evaluations. For reviews of specific titles or for systematic information about new reference titles, this is an excellent source.

10. **Book Review Digest.** New York, H. W. Wilson, 1906- . monthly, with quarterly and annual cumulations. service basis. LC 6-24490. ISSN 0006-7326.

As an index of book reviews, this standard Wilson title indexes about 100 English-language periodicals. The entries are arranged alphabetically by author of the book reviewed, with subject and title indexes. Citations include author, title, publisher, date, price, Dewey and LC call numbers, ISBN number, and subject headings. Each entry also provides excerpts from some book reviews and citations to others, making this a very convenient source for quick evaluations. This title, however, has as its focus general periodicals; only a short list of social science journals is included. *Book Review Index* (see entry 11) provides access to more social science reviews.

11. **Book Review Index.** Detroit, Gale, 1965- . bimonthly, with quarterly and annual cumulations. $160.00/yr. LC 65-9908. ISSN 0524-0581.

⁎ Although it lacks the excerpts from the book reviews that make *Book Review Digest* so convenient, this title is very useful for its broad coverage: over 400 periodicals are indexed each year for book reviews. The 1986 cumulation included 114,000 review citations for 63,000 books. All the social science fields are included. The books reviewed are listed by author, with citations to the reviews. There is a title index. This is the most comprehensive source for book reviews.

12. **Booklist.** Chicago, American Library Association, 1905- . 22 issues/yr. $56.00/yr. LC 76-612708. ISSN 0006-7385.

Booklist has earned an excellent reputation over many years for providing timely, well-written reviews covering adult fiction, nonfiction, children's books, and books for young adults. There is also in each issue a section, "Reference Books Bulletin," that provides reviews of major reference works. Unlike *Choice* (see entry 13), which focuses specifically on academic titles, this source is suitable for the wider public interested in identifying or reviewing political science titles of a more general appeal.

Library Journal (New York, Bowker, 1876- . semimonthly. $55.00. LC 76-645271. ISSN 0363-0277) is another source of book reviews covering popular or general as well as academic titles in political science. Coverage is broad and timely but the reviews are brief.

13. **Choice.** Chicago, American Library Association, 1964- . 11 issues/yr. index. $120.00/yr. LC 64-9413. ISSN 0009-4978.

As a book review journal designed by the American Library Association to assist book selection in academic libraries, this monthly title comprehensively covers all disciplines. Its paragraph-length reviews are written, but not signed, by a large group of scholars and specialists. The reviews generally evaluate the work, comment on its suitability for various types of collections, and compare it with other related titles in the same field. The author and title indexes cumulate annually. *Choice* provides systematic information on new titles in a field as well as reviews of specific titles.

14. **Wilson Library Bulletin.** New York, H. W. Wilson, 1914- . monthly (September-June). $30.00/yr. LC 30-9093. ISSN 0043-5651.

Wilson Library Bulletin provides a monthly selection of book reviews covering all fields of current publishing. Children's books, adult fiction, computer software, and reference books are all included, as well as popular and scholarly nonfiction. The reviews are substantial, well written, and (for major titles) often provide considerable critical analysis as well as description. This source, which provides access to reviews in political science and all subjects, is suitable for a wide variety of interests in the general public.

DICTIONARIES AND ENCYCLOPEDIAS

15. Kuper, Adam, and Jessica Kuper, eds. **The Social Science Encyclopedia.** Boston, Routledge & Kegan Paul, 1985. 916p. $75.00. LC 84-27736. ISBN 0-7102-0008-0.

In one volume, more than 500 scholars have provided an up-to-date overview of the social sciences, with an emphasis on political science, sociology, economics, anthropology, and psychology, but also including history, education, law, and such fields as demography, communications, and women's studies. The editors have concentrated on major issues and subjects, but about 10 percent of the entries are biographies. While a few major articles run to five pages, most entries average less than a page. All are signed and conclude with bibliographies. There is no subject index, but cross-references are numerous. Treatment in this excellent encyclopedia is theoretical and historical rather than factual, which makes it an appropriate source for reviewing the current state of a discipline or obtaining an overview. For quick answers on factual matters, dictionaries and encyclopedias in specific fields would be more useful.

There is unfortunately no current multivolume encyclopedia of the social sciences. The *International Encyclopedia of the Social Sciences* (David L. Sills, ed. New York, Macmillan and Free Press, 1968. 18v. LC 68-10023.) remains a superior source for comprehensive reviews of major topics and concepts. Volume 18 is a biographical supplement.

16. Miller, P. McC., and M. J. Wilson. **A Dictionary of Social Science Methods.** New York, John Wiley & Sons, 1983. 124p. $55.50; $22.00 (pbk). LC 82-13681. ISBN 0-471-90035-4; 0-471-90036-2(pbk).

The terms and techniques involved in empirical research methods in the social sciences are concisely defined in this dictionary based on material developed at The Open University in Great Britain. Approximately 1,000 terms used across the various social science disciplines are defined in about 200-300 words each. The authors also attempted to "illustrate and set in context" (preface) the terms defined. Many of the terms (such as error variance, least significant difference, and cluster analysis) deal with statistics. The definitions, which include relevant mathematical formulas, are clearly written and free of technical jargon. The terms are arranged alphabetically with numerous cross-references. This dictionary will be a useful aid for social scientists involved in quantitative research.

DIRECTORIES

17. Gabrouska, Svobodozarya. **European Guide to Social Science Information and Documentation Services.** Compiled for the European Cooperation in Social Science Information and Documentation. New York, Pergamon Press, 1982. 234p. $35.00. LC 81-23500. ISBN 0-0802-8927-4.

This directory attempts to contribute to "gaining a satisfactory view of the European landscape in social science information and documentation" (introduction) by providing a directory of 215 institutions and libraries with social science information services in 22 countries, including the Soviet Union and Eastern European states. Great Britain is not included.

The services are grouped by country, then alphabetically by English name. Libraries, information centers, bibliographic units, archives, and the like are covered. For each entry there is information on the local name, address, chief executive, major fields of interest, library, and services available to the public. There is subject access that points to appropriate institutions specializing in various topics of interest to social scientists.

18.   **Irregular Serials and Annuals: An International Directory.** New York, Bowker, 1967- . biennial. $159.00. LC 67-25026. ISSN 0000-0043.

This annually revised title is the standard source for current information about serials, annuals, continuations, progress reports, yearbooks, proceedings, transactions, and all such publications issued annually or on an irregular basis. It includes many annual reviews of events and statistical compendiums of interest to political scientists, including many works published in foreign countries. The 13th edition (1987/88) provides information on 35,900 serials. The entries are arranged alphabetically within 490 broad subject categories. Each entry includes publication information, price, frequency of publication, ISSN, and where the title is indexed. There is a title index.

19.   Katz, William A., and Linda Sternberg Katz. **Magazines for Libraries.** 5th ed. New York, Bowker, 1986. 1,057p. $95.00. LC 72-171066. ISBN 0-8352-2217-9.

Unlike *Ulrich's International Periodicals Directory* (entry 21), the Katzes' work attempts to be a carefully selected list of the "best and most useful" (preface) periodicals for use in schools, colleges, and public and special libraries. The entries are coded to indicate the type of audience for which each title is appropriate. For each title included, this source provides publication information, including editor, publisher, price, circulation, and where the title is indexed. The 5th edition, 1986, contains 6,500 titles in over 100 subject lists. There is also a paragraph-length annotation describing the content and focus of each periodical. As a selected list of basic titles, this source is useful as an overview of periodicals in subject fields and could be helpful in identifying titles for reading or research, in developing library collections, or in exploring publishing possibilities.

20.   **The Standard Periodical Directory.** New York, Oxbridge Communications, 1964/65- . biennial. index. $295.00. LC 64-7598. ISSN 0085-6630.

The 10th edition (1987) of this title provides information on 65,000 periodicals published in the United States or Canada. "Periodical" in this instance refers to any publication appearing at least once every two years; therefore, many serials such as transactions, proceedings, and yearbooks are included. The entries are arranged in 246 subject categories, with a title index. Each entry includes: title, address, phone number, editor and other staff, price, circulation statistics, and other publication information. Unlike *Ulrich's International Periodicals Directory* (entry 21), this source has a one-line description of the content of each periodical, plus brief information on advertising rates.

21.   **Ulrich's International Periodicals Directory.** New York, Bowker, 1932- . 2v. annual. index. $159.95/set. LC 32-16320. ISSN 0000-0175.

Ulrich's is an indispensable tool for information about periodicals. Although its coverage for American titles is not as extensive as *The Standard Periodical Directory* (entry 20), it does include international periodicals. The latest edition, the 26th, 1987/88, includes 70,800 entries arranged in over 542 subject categories. Information about each periodical includes title, year of first publication, frequency, price, editor, address, and where the title is indexed. Ulrich's is more thorough on this last point than *The Standard Periodical Directory*. It also has an extensive subject listing of indexes and abstracting services. Ulrich's is also searchable online through DIALOG and BRS and using CD-ROM technology with Ulrich's Plus from Bowker. *Irregular Serials and Annuals: An International Directory* (see entry 18) is the Bowker companion volume for titles published less frequently than twice a year.

22. **World List of Social Science Periodicals.** 5th ed., rev. Paris, UNESCO; distr., New York, UNIPUB, 1980. 447p. index. $27.00. LC 67-51954. ISBN 92-3-001789-2.

The latest edition of this irregularly published directory appeared in 1980 through the joint efforts of UNESCO's Social Science Documentation Centre and the International Committee for Social Science Information and Documentation. It is an international listing of social science periodicals, especially scholarly and research titles, arranged by country. There is also a separate section for international journals. For each entry this directory provides information on title, name and address of publisher and editor, frequency of publication, content or focus, and length of typical issues. There are indexes by subject and title. While this is not a comprehensive list of all social science titles, as examination of national bibliographies will attest, it is, nevertheless, a valuable list with worldwide scope.

23. **World Meetings: Social & Behavioral Sciences, Human Services, & Management.** New York, Macmillan, 1977- . quarterly. index. $155/yr. LC 83-7117. ISSN 0194-6161.

This quarterly publication provides current information on future meetings in the social sciences and related fields. The main section is arranged by serial number within three-month segments based on the date of the planned meeting. For each entry there is information on the sponsor, address for inquiries, summary of content, expected attendance, and deadlines for papers, publications, and exhibits. This information is updated quarterly. There are five indexes to this main entry section: subject, date, location, deadline, and sponsor. The sponsor directory and index can be used as a source of information on social science associations and institutes.

GUIDES

24. Inter-University Consortium for Political and Social Research. **A Guide to Resources and Services.** Ann Arbor, Mich., Institute for Social Research, University of Michigan. 1977- . annual. index. $20.00. ISSN 0362-8736.

The Inter-University Consortium for Political and Social Research (ICPSR), founded in 1962, is a partnership between the Survey Research Center at the University of Michigan and over 300 members, mostly universities, throughout the United States and the world. ICPSR serves social scientists by providing a central repository for machine-readable data files in social science fields. The data archive contains holdings on a wide range of categories, including census materials, social behavior and indicators, economic behavior and attitudes, and such topics of particular interest to political scientists as governmental structures, mass political behavior and attitudes, and legislative bodies.

The *Guide* is an annual catalog of ICPSR data. The main section is an annotated listing of the available studies. There are also indexes by title, principal investigator, subject, and ICPSR study number. A list of available codebooks to accompany the data files, with ordering instructions, is also included.

25. Li, Tze-Chung. **Social Science Reference Sources: A Practical Guide.** Westport, Conn., Greenwood, 1980. 315p. index. $35.00. LC 78-54052. ISBN 0-313-21473-5.

This review of social science reference sources is the outgrowth of the syllabus Professor Li used in a course he taught in a library school. About 800 titles are reviewed in 3 sections. The first section, in 10 chapters, covers general sources common to all the social sciences, including bibliographies, dictionaries, encyclopedias, handbooks, yearbooks, government publications, and computer databases. This section begins with a brief essay on the nature of the social sciences. The second part contains eight chapters, which review the reference sources in eight disciplines: anthropology, economics and business, education, history, law, political science, psychology, and sociology. The last part consists of one brief chapter dealing with bibliographical services in the social sciences. Li's work has author and title indexes but lacks a subject index.

26.   Sheehy, Eugene P. **Guide to Reference Books.** 10th ed. Chicago, American Library Association, 1986. 1,559p. $50.00. LC 85-11208. ISBN 0-8389-0390-8.

More than 14,000 reference books in all disciplines are identified and described in the 10th edition of this standard guide, which has long been considered a fundamental aid to research. The arrangement is first by broad category: general reference works, the humanities, social and behavioral sciences, history and area studies, science and technology, and medicine. These are followed by detailed breakdowns by field, which in turn are arranged by the type of reference source.

Under political science one finds sections on general works, national politics and government, parliamentary procedure, public opinion, communism and socialism, armed forces, and arms control and peace research. The annotations are very brief and focus on content. Since Sheehy's work is comprehensive in subject scope, it cannot be, in one volume, inclusive. It is, however, an excellent guide to the most important reference sources in all fields.

27.   Walford, A. J., ed. **Walford's Guide to Reference Material: Volume 2, Social & Historical Sciences, Philosophy & Religion.** 4th ed. London, Library Association; distr., Chicago, American Library Association, 1982. 812p. index. $74.50. LC 80-489414. ISBN 0-85365-564-2.

The object of Walford's guide is "to provide a signpost to reference books and bibliographies published mainly in recent years" (introduction). Volume 2 of the 4th edition for the social sciences contains some 5,000 citations, plus 2,000 more subsumed entries. In many ways this title resembles Webb's *Sources of Information in the Social Sciences* (entry 28), though Walford cites only reference sources and contains no narrative information on the disciplines covered. Walford's scope is international but with an emphasis on English-language materials, especially British. He has highlighted some topics, such as the European Economic Community, Parliament, and British local history. The entries are arranged by subject within chapters for each social science discipline. There is a combined author/title/subject index.

28.   Webb, William H. **Sources of Information in the Social Sciences.** 3d ed. Chicago, American Library Association, 1986. 777p. index. $77.00. LC 84-20494. ISBN 0-8389-0405-X.

William H. Webb and his associates have produced an important guide to the social sciences literature that surpasses all others for scope, comprehensiveness, and authoritative comment. There is one chapter for general titles, then separate chapters for history, geography, economics and business administration, sociology, anthropology, psychology, education, and political science. Each chapter begins with a short essay discussing the origin and development of the discipline and a description of the major subfields. Each of these sections contains citations to standard titles, making this a guide to the literature of the disciplines as well as to reference titles. The reference sections systematically cite and review the most useful current titles. Major databases, journals, monographic series, and organizations are also listed for each discipline. The political science section contains over

1,000 citations. While none of the subject chapters is exhaustive, this title is in many ways the best available for an overview of the social science literature. The editor of the second edition of this important guide was Carl M. White.

HANDBOOKS

29. Bryfonski, Dedria, and Robert L. Brubaker. **Contemporary Issue Criticism.** Detroit, Gale, 1982- . irreg. $90.00. LC 83-641399. ISSN 0732-7455.

Contemporary criticism—commentary and analysis—of current issues is systematically reviewed in this unique source. Criticism is limited to living writers or those who have died since January 1, 1960. Entries are arranged by author and include a picture, a short biographical sketch, and comments on the focus or main ideas of the writer. Excerpts (from one to three pages) from major works and excerpts from critical essays and book reviews follow. The criticisms of each author's works are arranged chronologically to reflect changing responses. All excerpts are cited completely. There are subject and critic indexes. Ninety-two authors are covered in the two volumes published through 1989. Political science, economics, sociology, history, and other social sciences are included. While certainly not a definitive treatment, this source is interesting for browsing and very convenient for quickly reviewing the work of a social scientist or for obtaining an overview of an unfamiliar writer.

30. **Encyclopedia of Public Affairs Information Sources.** Paul Wasserman, James R. Kelly, and Desider L. Vikor, eds. Detroit, Gale, 1988. 303p. $125.00. LC 87-25902. ISBN 0-8103-2191-2.

Public affairs encompass a wide cluster of subjects drawn from various social science fields, including business and economics, education, government and politics, law, sociology, and urban studies. The aged, capital punishment, civil rights, drugs, gambling, illiteracy, organized crime, and poverty are among the approximately 290 specific public affairs topics covered in the volume. All are contemporary issues of general public concern. For each of these topics the guide provides unannotated citations to sources arranged by type (e.g., abstract services, indexes, and information systems; annuals and reviews; associations and professional societies; bibliographies; directories; encyclopedias and dictionaries; handbooks and manuals; online databases; periodicals; research centers, institutes and clearinghouses; and statistical sources). There is an extensive outline of contents, plus over 330 cross-references. Although certainly not comprehensive, this is a useful guide for beginning the research process.

31. Miller, Delbert C. **Handbook of Research Design and Social Measurement.** 4th ed. New York, Longman, 1983. 678p. $29.95. LC 82-15287. ISBN 0-58228-326-4.

Research methodology is the subject of this student handbook, which has now reached its fourth edition. Definitely practical in approach, it attempts to offer basic instruction and advice on the appropriate methods of conducting social science research. Research design, data collection, questionnaire construction, sampling, and statistical analysis are some of the topics covered. There is also information on sociometric scales and indexes, research funding, and the reporting of research in meetings and journals. This handbook will be useful not only to novice researchers, but also to students seeking explanations of the basic concepts of social science research and identification or definition of major elements. The author has succeeded admirably in explaining clearly matters that are often made abstruse.

32. **Political and Social Science Journals: A Handbook for Writers and Reviewers.** Santa Barbara, Calif., ABC-Clio, 1983. 263p. index. (Clio Guides to Publishing Opportunities, No. 2). $24.85; $15.00(pbk). LC 82-18455. ISBN 0-87436-026-9; 0-87436-037(pbk).

The purpose of this handbook is to provide a guide for writers and reviewers to 440 English-language journals in political science and related social science disciplines. This source can assist the author in finding journals with suitable editorial focus and readership for a proposed article or review; it also provides specific editorial requirements.

For each periodical entry, information is presented concerning focus, editor, readership, index/abstract coverage, and circulation; specific guidelines for the submission of articles and reviews are given. Also included is a subject index of the journal titles. A series of introductory essays on manuscript preparation and submission and on writing book reviews provide guidelines especially useful for the novice.

INDEXES AND ABSTRACTS

33. **ASSIA: Applied Social Sciences Index & Abstracts.** P. F. Broxis, ed. London, Library Association; distr., Birmingham, Ala., EBSCO, 1987- . bimonthly. $756.00/yr. ISSN 0950-2238.

ASSIA represents a major new indexing service in the social sciences. It provides an interdisciplinary coverage to the social and behavioral sciences, including political science. This new title most closely resembles in coverage the *Social Sciences Index* (see entry 50), though that title indexes some 350 titles, while *ASSIA* covered over 500 titles in its first year. *ASSIA* also has the advantage of providing abstracts of the indexed articles. About half of the titles indexed in *ASSIA* are American; the remainder are mostly British or European. While *ASSIA* cannot equal the depth of coverage of specialized indexes in specific fields, such as *Psychological Abstracts* in psychology, it is an excellent source of periodical literature across the social sciences.

34. **Alternative Press Index.** Baltimore, Alternative Press Center, 1969- . quarterly. $100.00/yr. LC 76-24027. ISSN 0002-662X.

As an index to alternative publications, this index provides coverage to over 200 radical, liberal, or "underground" periodicals and newspapers, most of which are not indexed elsewhere. Many of the titles deal with various aspects of politics or political science, especially efforts to promote or achieve political change or social justice. Many other topics, ranging from feminism to environmental issues, are also covered. There is a useful list of all the titles indexed with addresses and subscription rates. The entries are arranged in a subject classification without author or title access.

35. **American Doctoral Dissertations.** Ann Arbor, Mich., University Microfilms International, 1957- . annual. $75.00/yr. LC 73-20866. ISSN 0065-809X.

36. **Dissertation Abstracts International.** Ann Arbor, Mich., University Microfilms International, 1938- . monthly, with annual indexes. $155.00/yr.(pts. A and B); $345.00/yr.(pt. C). ISSN 0419-4209(pt. A); 0419-4217(pt. B); 0307-6075(pt. C).

These two related titles provide comprehensive coverage of American doctoral dissertations, with increasing coverage of foreign dissertations. *American Doctoral Dissertations* is the more inclusive, including all entries in *Dissertation Abstracts International* (*DAI*), plus others gleaned from information from universities. The entries are arranged by broad subject category first, then alphabetically by university, and finally by author. Entries include the title and date of the dissertation. In addition to this information, *DAI* also provides abstracts of dissertations submitted by cooperating universities. Part A covers the humanities and social sciences. The entries also include the order number for obtaining paper or microform copies from University Microfilms International. There are author and subject indexes in each issue as well as cumulated annual indexes. These indexes are also available online through the DIALOG database service. University Microfilms also makes available a CD-ROM version (see entry 314).

37. **American Statistics Index: A Comprehensive Guide and Index to the Statistical Publications of the U.S. Government.** Bethesda, Md., Congressional Information Service, 1973- . monthly, with quarterly and annual cumulations. $2,220.00/yr. LC 73-82599. ISSN 0091-1658.

38. **Statistical Reference Index: A Selective Guide to American Statistical Publications from Sources Other Than the U.S. Government.** Bethesda, Md., Congressional Information Service, 1980- . monthly, with quarterly and annual cumulations. $1,600.00/yr. LC 81-645886. ISSN 0278-694X.

39. **Index to International Statistics.** Bethesda, Md., Congressional Information Service, 1983- . monthly, with quarterly and annual cumulations. $995.00/yr. LC 83-644889. ISSN 0737-4461.

The subtitle of the first of these three titles succinctly identifies the scope of this important reference work as a comprehensive guide and index to the publications of the United States government. As such it is the most complete and best-indexed tool for locating specific statistics among the myriad produced by the federal government. The base volume published in 1974 covered the years 1960-1973, with succeeding volumes bringing the series to date.

The abstract sections of each issue provide complete bibliographic information, including Superintendent of Documents numbers, *Monthly Catalog* entry numbers, and a description of the publication and the available statistical data. The entries are arranged by publishing agency, and accession numbers are provided. The very complete index sections provide access points by subject, title, name, agency, report number, and an extremely useful set of categories that includes economic, geographic, and demographic breakdowns. These indexes greatly facilitate locating data by SMSAs, by industry, by race, or by any of the 21 other categories.

The *ASI* Microfiche Library includes almost all the publications cited in the index. It is available on a subscription basis from the publisher. *American Statistics Index* is also available online through DIALOG database services (see entry 310). Congressional Information Service also publishes *Statistical Reference Index* (SRI) for statistical publications of private organizations and state governments and *Index to International Statistics* (IIS) for the statistics of major international and intergovernmental bodies.

40. **Bibliographic Index.** New York, H. W. Wilson, 1937- . semiannual, with annual cumulations. service basis. LC 46-41034. ISSN 0006-1255.

Bibliographic Index regularly examines about 2,600 periodicals for bibliographic material. Separately published bibliographies and bibliographies in books are also included. For inclusion the bibliography must have at least 50 citations. The subject scope is comprehensive, and there is a considerable amount of foreign-language material. A detailed subject classification provides for rapid identification of bibliographies on specific topics. Political science subjects are considered under a multitude of headings and subheadings, such as the names of countries, regions, and states.

41.   **British Humanities Index.** London, Library Association, 1962- . quarterly, with annual cumulations. $375.00/yr. LC 63-24940. ISSN 0007-0815.

Despite the somewhat misleading title for American ears, this British index covers all fields of the social sciences, including politics and political science, as well as the humanities and arts. About 400 periodicals, mostly British, are indexed quarterly by subject. The annual cumulation adds an author index. The entries provide complete bibliographic citations with cross-references to related subject terms. In its coverage of political matters, this index highlights political history, current events, and commentary rather than theoretical studies or quantitative analyses.

42.   **Current Contents: Social and Behavioral Sciences.** Philadelphia, Institute for Scientific Information, 1969- . weekly. index. $283.00/yr. LC 79-3415. ISSN 0092-6361.

The table of contents pages from more than 1,300 periodicals are reproduced in this weekly current awareness tool. Coverage is international. There is an author index (with addresses) and a keyword title index to the articles cited. There is also an address directory of the periodical publishers. A cumulative index is published triennially. The social and behavioral sciences series, one of several published by the Institute for Scientific Information, provides a means of keeping current with the periodical literature before the appearance of the traditional indexing and abstracting publications.

43.   **Directory of Published Proceedings: Series SSH-Social Sciences/Humanities.** Harrison, N.Y., InterDok, 1968- . quarterly. index. $165.00/yr. LC 68-59460. ISSN 0012-3307.

This directory is a bibliography of preprints and published proceedings of congresses, conferences, symposia, meetings, seminars, and the like in all fields of the social sciences and humanities. Coverage is international and not limited to materials in English. The primary arrangement of the citations is chronological by date of the meeting. Each citation provides the location, title, and sponsoring organization. There are editor, location, and subject/sponsor indexes for each issue, plus annual cumulative indexes.

44.   **Human Resources Abstracts: An International Information Service.** Beverly Hills, Calif., Sage, 1966- . quarterly. index. $175.00/yr. LC 75-644409. ISSN 0099-2453.

Covering a wide range of social science topics, this index provides information "relating to problems facing our cities and our nation" (editor). These subjects include employment, economic policy, labor relations, aging, health services, social welfare, and minority issues. The index includes books, government publications, and research reports as well as periodicals. The entries are arranged alphabetically within subject categories. The author and subject indexes cumulate annually.

45.   **Index to Social Science and Humanities Proceedings.** Philadelphia, Institute for Scientific Information, 1979- . quarterly, with annual cumulations. index. $625.00/yr. LC 80-649461. ISSN 0191-0574.

Conference literature—the published record of the papers presented at conferences, seminars, symposia, colloquia, conventions, and workshops—is reported in this quarterly publication. *ISSHP* covers about 1,000 proceedings each year published in various formats: journal articles, books, preprints, or separate reports. The proceedings are listed by number in the main section with the following information: conference name, location, date, sponsors, and complete citation to published proceedings. Access is provided by six indexes: author/editor, subject category, permuterm subject, sponsor, location, and organizational affiliation of author. Copies of many of the papers indexed in this title are available from the Institute for Scientific Information.

46. **The Left Index: A Quarterly Index to Periodicals of the Left.** Santa Clara, Calif., The Left Index, 1982- . quarterly. $55.00/yr. LC 82-5102. ISSN 0733-2998.

All subjects, the humanities and sciences as well as the social sciences, are included in this periodical index of about 75 American and European titles. All periodicals included have a Marxist, radical, or left perspective. Some are academic or scholarly; others, such as *Mother Jones*, are more commonly known; and some are ephemeral or "little magazines."

The full bibliographic entries are in the author list. The subject index cumulates annually. There is also a fairly lengthy list of book reviews with full journal citations. This title duplicates in part *Alternative Press Index* (entry 34), though each covers many titles not in the other. Both are useful guides to theoretical articles as well as to articles about political conditions in specific countries written from a left perspective.

47. **PAIS Bulletin.** New York, Public Affairs Information Service, 1915- . semimonthly, with quarterly and annual cumulations. index. $295.00/yr. LC 82-1132. ISSN 0033-3409.

48. **PAIS Foreign Language Index.** New York, Public Affairs Information Service, 1972- . 3 issues/yr., with annual cumulations. $495.00. LC 86-64261. ISSN 0048-5810.

With good reason these publications have long been considered major resources for accessing social sciences literature. The editors do not aim for comprehensive coverage, but focus on issues of public policy with an emphasis on factual and statistical information. With this orientation in mind, editors select material from the fields of political science, government, law, sociology, economics, international relations, demography, business, and social work. The index covers books, pamphlets, government publications, and reports from public and private agencies as well as a wide range of periodicals. *PAIS*, as it is frequently cited, is a subject index. The annual cumulations contain author indexes. The foreign-language title offers similar coverage for materials published in French, German, Italian, Portuguese, and Spanish. These indexes are available online through the DIALOG database service (see entry 318). The publisher also provides a CD-ROM version (see entry 327).

49. **Social Sciences Citation Index.** Philadelphia, Institute for Scientific Information, 1973- . 3 issues/yr., with annual cumulations. $3,100.00/yr. LC 73-85287. ISSN 0091-3707.

As an international, interdisciplinary index to the literature of the social sciences, this title covers some 2,000 journals, providing the most comprehensive coverage of these disciplines. Its three main distinctive sections serve very different purposes: (1) The source index is arranged alphabetically by the authors indexed during the year with citations to their articles. This is an efficient means of identifying the publications of writers on an annual basis. (2) The permuterm subject index involves the permutation of all significant words in the title and subtitle to form pairs of terms. Searching these matched pairs is a valuable additional means of zeroing in on elusive topics. (3) The citation index is arranged alphabetically by cited author (regardless of when the work was written) with references to the articles indexed during the year that cited the author. This unique feature allows tracing forward in time the development of scholarship. There is also a corporate index which makes it possible to identify authors by their organizational affiliations. This index is also available online through the DIALOG database service as Social SciSearch (see entry 320).

50. **Social Sciences Index.** New York, H. W. Wilson, 1974- . quarterly, with annual cumulations. service basis. LC 78-1032. ISSN 0094-4920.

This standard index provides author and subject access to 353 English-language periodicals in a wide variety of social science fields, including political science, public administration, law, sociology, and anthropology. Though coverage of periodical titles is fairly limited (in comparison, for example, to the *Social Sciences Citation Index* [entry 49]), and there are no abstracts of the articles cited, this Wilson index provides easy-to-use current access to the basic social science academic journals. The generous use of cross-references facilitates subject searches. There is also a separate listing of citations to book reviews. This index is available online through the DIALOG database service (see entry 319). The Wilson Company also provides a CD-ROM version (see entry 328).

STATISTICS SOURCES

51. **Statistical Abstract of the United States.** U.S. Bureau of the Census. Washington, D.C., GPO, 1878- . annual. $27.00; $22.00(pbk). LC 04-18089. ISSN 0081-4741. C3.134:[yr.].

As a single-volume compendium of statistics, this title has long been an indispensable reference source. Summary statistics, gathered from government and nongovernment sources, are present on the political, social, and economic situation in the United States. Population, vital statistics, immigration, education, government finances, social and welfare services, national defense, employment and earnings, elections, and business and economic statistics are a few of the general categories included. There is also a section on comparative international statistics. Many of the tables provide historical statistics. There is a detailed subject index.

The chapter on statistics sources provides references to sources, as do the footnotes after each table. Together these references provide a guide to additional material for those requiring statistical information in greater detail than the selective summary statistics this publication provides.

52. **UNESCO Statistical Yearbook.** Paris, UNESCO; distr., New York, UNIPUB, 1963- . annual. $58.00. LC 85-22069. ISSN 0082-7541.

This annual statistical compendium provides a wide variety of information in the areas of education, educational expenditures, scientific research expenditures and manpower, radio and television, films and cinema, book production, libraries, newspapers, and related cultural indicators for countries around the world. Comparative data for about 200 countries, acquired from UNESCO publications and questionnaires, are available from this yearbook, though the data are not complete for all nations. Introductory sections and table headings are in English, French, and Spanish.

53. United Nations. Statistical Office. **Statistical Yearbook.** New York, United Nations, 1949- . annual. $60.00. LC 50-2756. ISSN 0082-8459.

Nearly 200 statistical tables are provided in this annual international statistical compendium, which covers population, agriculture, manufacturing, finance, trade, and social statistics. Many of the tables are quite specific, covering such topics as book production, the prevalence of television receivers, illiteracy, and educational establishments. For each table information is provided for over 200 countries around the world. In most cases, historical statistics are given for as far back as the early 1970s. The opening section presents world summary tables with statistics by major regions. More current statistics on an ongoing basis are available from the United Nations' *Monthly Bulletin of Statistics.*

YEARBOOKS

54. **Annual Register: A Record of World Events.** London, Longman, 1758- . annual. index. $100.00. LC 84-647452. ISSN 0060-4057.

With minor changes in title, this venerable publication has continued since 1758, when Edmund Burke served as the first editor. It features survey articles by specialists on the developments of the preceding year. While coverage is international, there is a definite emphasis on British and Commonwealth affairs. In addition to the main section, in which essays focus on nations or regions, there are surveys of various continuing topics such as science, law, arts, economics, and religion. Maps, charts, the text of major documents, and a chronology of world events supplement the surveys. There are name and subject indexes.

2

Social Science Disciplines

ECONOMICS

Bibliographies

55. **International Bibliography of Economics.** London, Tavistock; New York, Methuen, 1952- . annual. index. $110.00. LC 55-2317. ISSN 0085-204X.

Although slow in appearing, two or three years after the publication date of the material cited, this annual bibliography provides international coverage of economics material published in all major languages. It includes books, journal articles, and research reports. The material listed is arranged in a detailed classification scheme; 15 main categories and several hundred subdivisions facilitate scanning particular subject sections. History of economic thought, economic history, and social economics and policy are some categories of particular interest to political scientists. Access to specific citations is provided by the author and subject indexes.

Biographical Sources

56. **Who's Who in Economics: A Biographical Dictionary of Major Economists, 1700-1986.** 2d ed. Mark Blaug, ed. Cambridge, Mass., MIT Press, 1986. 935p. index. $115.00. LC 86-2837. ISSN 0-262-02256-7.

Over 1,000 living and 400 deceased economists are included in this biographical directory. The main criterion for inclusion was frequency of publication, as measured by the *Social Sciences Citation Index (entry 49)*. Each entry contains name, year and place of birth, career positions, professional awards and affiliations, major field of interest, major publications, and a paragraph summarizing the economist's principal contribution to the discipline. The biographees are indexed by place of birth, place of residence, and major field of interest.

Dictionaries and Encyclopedias

57. Auld, Douglas A. L. **The American Dictionary of Economics.** New York, Facts on File, 1983. 342p. $17.95. LC 81-22052. ISBN 0-87196-532-1.

This dictionary features clear and concise definitions written for general readers and students. It is fine for quick definitions of terms. Coverage is limited to English-language material, with an emphasis on American topics and usage. Terms (capitalized value), phrases (galloping inflation), individuals (Galbraith), organizations (Federal Reserve System), and statistics (least squares regression) are all included from the fields of economic theory, economic history, econometrics, international trade, statistics, and business finance. The short sketches of prominent economists are particularly useful for locating the subject in the overall picture of economics.

58. **Encyclopedia of American Economic History: Studies of the Principal Movements and Ideas.** New York, Scribner, 1980. 3v. 1,286p. $120.00/set. LC 79-4946. ISSN 0684162717/set.

This very useful overview of American economic history begins with the observation that the "United States has always found its sense of purpose primarily in materialism" (preface). This is indicative of the focus of this work, which is to provide a scholarly and analytical perspective of U.S. economic history rather than a compendium of facts and statistics.

The 3 volumes contain 72 signed articles by prominent scholars; these articles are grouped in 5 sections: "Historiography," "Chronology," "Framework of Growth," "Institutional Framework," and "Social Framework." The articles, which are each about 10 to 20 pages long, provide a beginning point for research or a nontechnical synthesis for the general reader. All articles have extensive bibliographies.

59. Greenwald, Douglas. **Encyclopedia of Economics.** New York, McGraw-Hill, 1982. 2,070p. $69.95. LC 81-4969. ISBN 0-07-024367-0.

This work is appropriately titled an encyclopedia rather than a dictionary as it provides overviews and analyses of concepts, such as urban economics or the accuracy of economic forecasts, rather than definitions of specific terms. There are some 300 signed articles written by 178 prominent economists. The articles deal with concepts (communism), institutions (Joint Economic Committee of Congress), historical events (Great Depression), research methods (operations research), and economic factors (money supply). There are no biographies. Each article ends with a short bibliography. An interesting appendix contains a chronology of economic events from 400,000 B.C.

60. **The New Palgrave: A Dictionary of Economics.** John Eatwell, Murray Milgate, and Peter Newman, eds. London, Macmillan; New York, Stockton; Tokyo, Maruzen, 1987. 4v. index. $555.00/set. LC 87-1946. ISBN 0-935859-10-1.

This *New Palgrave* is the successor to the classic reference work, *Dictionary of Political Economy*, edited by R. H. Inglis Palgrave in the 1890s. There have been various reprints and editions over the years, but this is the first substantial revision and expansion of the original work. This *New Palgrave* will also be a standard title for many years to come as an excellent comprehensive dictionary, or really encyclopedia, of economics. Its only deficiency is a certain concentration on the English-speaking and British worlds.

The 4 volumes contain 2,000 signed entries by over 950 distinguished contributors. The scholarly subject entries usually have bibliographical references to relevant literature. These essay entries range from a few paragraphs to a few pages and cover the entire range of economic thought and theory throughout all ages and countries. Historical background information, diverse interpretations, and mathematical formulas are included in many of the articles. Practical information for consumers or investors is not included. The 655 biographical entries discuss the lives and works of prominent economists throughout the world. This is the essential source for scholarly overviews of topics in economics.

Guides

61. Fletcher, John, ed. **Information Sources in Economics.** 2d ed. London, Boston, Butterworths, 1984. 339p. (Butterworth Guides to Information Sources). $65.00. LC 83-25230. ISBN 0-408-11471-1.

Although this title has a decided British emphasis, it is the most comprehensive current survey of economics literature. Most of the information is clearly relevant in American libraries. This guide, written jointly by British librarians and economists, provides introductory chapters on library research in economics, followed by chapters identifying basic titles arranged by type of reference tool—bibliographies, periodicals, indexes, government documents, statistical sources, and online databases. The last section consists of a dozen chapters on the most useful citations in various fields of economics, such as economic history, econometric theory, and monetary economics. All citations have brief descriptive and evaluative annotations, which are especially useful for those not familiar with the literature of economics.

62. Hutchinson, William Kenneth. **American Economic History: A Guide to Information Sources.** Detroit, Gale, 1980. 296p. (Economic Information Guide Series, Vol. 16). $28.00. LC 73-17577. ISBN 0810312875.

The purpose of this Gale guide is to provide information on economic history for the beginning student in economics. It is equally appropriate for persons in other fields who require a comprehensive overview of the literature of this discipline. It identifies the most useful titles in the field in 10 chapters. The first addresses methodology, and the remaining nine are devoted to such topics as population and labor force, international-interregional development, and industrial growth and structure. Chronologically this guide covers economic history from the colonial period to around 1960. Most of the citations have brief content annotations.

Indexes

63. **Index of Economic Articles in Journals and Collective Volumes.** Homewood, Ill., Richard D. Irwin, 1886- . annual. index. $50.00/yr. LC 61-8020. ISSN 0536-647X.

64. **Journal of Economic Literature.** Nashville, Tenn., American Economic Association, 1969- . quarterly. index. $105.00/yr. LC 73-646621. ISSN 0022-0515.

Articles, book reviews, and a periodical index with selected abstracts are all available in the *Journal of Economic Literature*. The periodical section serves as a major current index of economic literature in journals. It begins with copies of the table of contents of current economic periodicals. These articles are then listed in a detailed subject classification with 10 main categories and many subclasses. This section is followed by a section containing abstracts for some of the articles cited. There is a separate author index. After a considerable delay, the citations in the *Journal of Economic Literature* appear in the annual *Index of Economic Articles in Journals and Collective Volumes*.

Statistics Sources

65. **Business Statistics.** U.S. Bureau of Economic Analysis. Washington, D.C., GPO, 1951- . biennial. $13.00. LC 78-1633. ISSN 0083-2545. C59.11/3:[yr.].

The Bureau of Economic Analysis provides in this biennial publication data for approximately 2,000 statistical series. For the most recent years, the data is reported monthly or quarterly, then annually back to 1961. This compendium of historical statistics can obviously be of great use to historians and political scientists. The statistics cover income, industrial production, commodity prices, construction, domestic trade, labor force, employment, earnings, finance, foreign trade, transportation, and many other related business and economic indicators. These statistical series are updated monthly by the bureau's *Survey of Current Business.*

66. **Handbook of Labor Statistics.** U.S. Bureau of Labor Statistics. Washington, D.C., GPO, 1926- . irreg. $16.00. LC 127-328. ISSN 0082-9056. L2.3/5:[yr.].

As a compendium of statistics, this government document is a convenient starting point for locating data produced by the Bureau of Labor Statistics and other federal agencies. Selected foreign labor statistics are also included. The 1985 edition includes 138 tables, covering such topics as labor force, employment, employment by industry, earnings, productivity, consumer prices, work stoppages, and occupational injuries. Most tables provide historical data as well as the latest statistics available. Footnotes and technical notes provide assistance in understanding the tables, the methodology used in compiling them, and guidelines to sources of more detailed information.

EDUCATION

Dictionaries and Encyclopedias

67. Barrow, Robin, and Geoffrey Milburn. **A Critical Dictionary of Educational Concepts.** New York, St. Martin's Press, 1986. 274p. $25.00. LC 86-21953. ISSN 0312002297.

The authors of this dictionary did not intend to provide another collection of various meanings attached to frequently used educational terms. Several standard dictionaries with definitions of terms are listed in this section. As an alternative, the authors wished to offer critical assessments of some of the key concepts in education. Creativity, curriculum design, intelligence, and values clarification are examples of the 120 ideas and issues selected for inclusion. Each term has been scrutinized for various meanings or usages and for current controversies. Frequently found conventional or normative judgments are also considered in light of current research. This book is especially valuable for the judgments expressed by the authors. The entry for "mainstreaming," for example, includes this succinct statement: "Many educators now regard mainstreaming as an over-simple solution to a series of very complex problems related to the education of handicapped students" (p. 146).

68. Dejnozka, Edward L., and David E. Kapel. **American Educators' Encyclopedia.** Westport, Conn., Greenwood, 1982. 634p. $65.00. LC 81-6664. ISBN 0313209545.

The principal section of this 1-volume encyclopedia offers almost 2,000 short articles on names and terms frequently found in the literature of education. The articles, each averaging 100-200 words, cover all levels of education and were written and reviewed by a large group of scholars and specialists. A series of 21 appendixes provides such material as lists of officials of professional organizations and a chronology of important legislation affecting education. Not intended to be a definitive work, this encyclopedia succeeds admirably as a ready source of concise information with leads to additional sources in the references that follow each article.

69.   **Encyclopedia of Educational Research.** 5th ed. Harold E. Mitzel, ed.-in-chief. New York, Free Press, 1982. 4v. index. $315.00/set. LC 82-2332. ISBN 0-02-900450-0.

Published first in 1941 and now in its fifth edition, this encyclopedia, sponsored by the prestigious American Educational Research Association, remains the most convenient source for authoritative reviews of research at all levels of education. The signed articles by recognized authorities offer a "critical synthesis and interpretation of reported educational research" (preface). The 256 essays/review articles are arranged by subject. In nonspecialist language they provide scholars, students, educators, and those interested in education information on the history, current status, and contemporary trends and developments in education. Following each article is an extensive list of references, which is particularly useful because the articles are extensively documented. Volume 4 contains a detailed name/subject index for the set.

70.   **International Encyclopedia of Education: Research and Studies.** Torsten Husen and T. Neville Postlethwaite, eds.-in-chief. Elmsford, N.Y., Pergamon Press, 1985. 10v. index. $1,750/set. LC 84-20750. ISBN 0-08-028119-2.

The 10 volumes of this encyclopedia present an up-to-date overview of scholarship relating to educational practices, problems, and institutions throughout the world. Each of the 1,500 signed articles is several pages long and includes a bibliography of major sources. The articles offer a state-of-the-art overview of scholarly and professional work for the various topics in education. The country articles provide concise portraits of education systems. The index volume contains a classified listing of the articles, a detailed subject index, and an author index.

71.   Rowntree, Derek. **A Dictionary of Education.** Totowa, N.J., Barnes & Noble, 1982. 354p. $22.50. LC 82-206312. ISBN 0-389-20263-0.

Rowntree's short definitions of over 3,000 terms arranged in alphabetical order cover British and American educational vocabulary. Terms that reflect primarily British or American usage are identified. The definitions range in length from a few sentences to a paragraph. This dictionary is especially useful for those not familiar with educational terminology, new terms, or jargon. The names of prominent educators and educational theorists are also included, with brief biographies and lists of key works. An extensive use of cross-references facilitates effective use of this dictionary.

Guides

72.   Durnin, Richard G. **American Education: A Guide to Information Sources.** Detroit, Gale, 1982. 247p. index. (Gale Information Guide Library; American Studies Information Guide Series, Vol. 14). $68.00. LC 82-15387. ISSN 08103312654.

Durnin's bibliography attempts to cull from the mass of writings on education the titles of greatest significance. These selections encompass books relating to the background, theory, practice, and organization of the American system of elementary, secondary, and higher education. Most of the entries are for recent publications, though a few older titles that have become classics are also included. Journals and dissertations are not included.

The entries are arranged alphabetically by author within 107 subject chapters ranging from "Academic Freedom" to "Women, Education of." The annotations are only one or two lines in length, but they frequently indicate significance in the field of education as well as content. This work begins with an extensive bibliographic essay which provides a valuable historical overview of American education since the 17th century.

73. Woodbury, Marda. **A Guide to Sources of Educational Information.** 2d ed. Arlington, Va., Information Resources Press, 1982. 430p. index. $39.95. LC 82-80549. ISBN 0-87815-041-2.

As the title clearly indicates, this volume is a guide to sources of educational information broadly interpreted to include around 700 sources found in the library, in print or nonprint formats, or in locations such as research centers, government agencies, associations, or clearinghouses.

The section on library resources is arranged by form (dictionaries, bibliographies, handbooks, etc.). The citations all have evaluative annotations as do those on computerized information retrieval sources and on institutional sources of information. There is a combined author, title, and subject index.

Handbooks

74. Berry, Dorothea M. **A Bibliographic Guide to Educational Research.** 2d ed. Metuchen, N.J., Scarecrow, 1980. 215p. index. $16.50. LC 80-20191. ISBN 0-8108-1351-3.

While this guide was developed as an outgrowth of instruction given to students in an education course on the resources of the library, it can equally well serve others, including those outside the field of education. It provides a systematic listing of nearly 700 titles arranged by form—encyclopedias, handbooks, statistical sources, etc.—that are essential or useful for library research in all fields of education. Each reference work cited has a descriptive annotation. There are author, title, and subject indexes.

75. **International Handbook of Education Systems.** New York, John Wiley & Sons, 1983/84. 3v. $245.00/set. LC 82-17375. ISSN 0-471-90078-8(v.1), 0-47-190079-6(v.2)., 0-471-90214-4(v.3).

The first volume of this three-volume set on education around the world covers Europe and Canada; the second sub-Saharan Africa, North Africa, and the Middle East; and the third Asia, Australasia, and Latin America. The United States, Great Britain, and the Soviet Union are omitted because they are "dealt with in many other publications" (introduction). The country chapters vary in length from 20 to 40 pages. Each offers a profile of the country's education system and covers such topics as educational administration, educational finance, development and planning, and curricula; other information is also provided in the form of charts and statistics. In addition, each country has a background section with information on geography, population, culture, history, politics, and the economy. The introductory chapter contains statistics and much tabular and comparative information.

Indexes and Abstracts

76. **Current Index to Journals in Education**. Phoenix, Ariz., Oryx Press, 1969- . monthly, with semiannual cumulations. $362.00/yr. LC 78-1463. ISSN 0011-3565.

77. **Resources in Education**. Washington, D.C., U.S. Department of Education, 1966- . monthly. $86.00/yr. LC 75-644211. ISSN 0098-0897.

CIJE, a monthly guide to current periodical literature in education, indexes some 780 educational and education-related journals. It is published in cooperation with the U.S. Office of Education's Educational Resources Information Center (ERIC). The main section arranged the entries by accession number in 16 subject categories corresponding to the ERIC Clearinghouse. Each entry has a brief abstract of contents. There are author, subject, and journal contents indexes.

The companion to this index, *Resources in Education* (*RIE*), provides indexing and abstracts for educational research reports, conference proceedings, professional papers, and other nonperiodical material. There are subject, author, institution, and publication type indexes to the main section, which is arranged by accession number. *RIE* material is available in hard copy or microfiche from the ERIC Document Reproduction Service. Many libraries have purchased microfiche sets. Since 1979, an annual cumulation has been published by Oryx Press (ISSN 0197-9973). This information may also be searched online through DIALOG and BRS and by using CD-ROM technology with products available from OCLC and DIALOG.

78. **Education Index**. New York, H. W. Wilson, 1929- . monthly, except July and August, with quarterly and annual cumulations. service basis. LC 78-574. ISSN 0013-1385.

Education Index is a cumulative index to educational literature published in English. It is primarily a periodical index with about 300 titles covered, but it also includes yearbooks and some monographs. All fields of education are indexed, including elementary, secondary, higher, adult, and special education. Subject and author entries are arranged in one alphabet. There is also an extensive listing of citations to book reviews. This well-known, easy-to-use Wilson title is a fundamental research tool in education. It is not as comprehensive as *Current Index to Journals in Education* (see entry 76), which covers twice as many periodicals.

Statistics Sources

79. **Digest of Education Statistics**. National Center for Educational Statistics. Washington, D.C., GPO, 1975- . annual. index. $13.00. LC 82-5029. ISSN 0502-4102. ED1.113:[yr.].

Data from many governmental and nongovernmental sources have been gathered to constitute this most useful compendium of educational statistics, which covers all aspects of education from kindergarten through graduate school. Some of the main topics examined are enrollment, teachers, graduates, number of schools, finances, federal funds, libraries, and research and development. While the data collected over the years have varied, many of the tables feature historical statistics. The volumes conclude with guides to additional sources and detailed subject indexes.

HISTORY

Atlases

80. **Atlas of American History.** 2d rev. ed. New York, Scribner, 1984. 306p. maps. index. $50.00. LC 84-675413. ISBN 0-684-18411-7.

The revised edition of this atlas contains nearly 200 maps, fulfilling its aim to be a "concise, easy to use, authoritative atlas of American history" (introduction). The maps are arranged in 11 sections, beginning with "America at the Time of Discovery" and working through the colonial, revolutionary, Civil War, and contemporary periods to the last section, "Current Issues, 1978-1984," which includes social and economic as well as historical data. The maps, which are black and white, have legends and explanatory notes but no narrative text. The index contains some 5,000 entries to places and events, with references to the appropriate maps. This atlas is an excellent companion to American history texts.

81. Barraclough, Geoffrey, ed. **The Times Atlas of World History.** rev. ed. Maplewood, N.J., Hammond, 1984. 360p. index. $75.00. LC 84-675088. ISBN 0843711299.

The editor of this atlas has attempted to present a graphic overview of history that is "world-wide in conception and presentation and which does justice ... to all people in all ages and in all quarters of the globe" (introduction). The maps are divided into seven categories: (1) the world of early man, (2) the first civilizations, (3) the classical civilizations of Eurasia, (4) the world of divided regions, (5) the world of the emerging west, (6) the age of European dominance, and (7) the age of global civilization. This revised edition pays particular attention to developing countries, the United States census and other recent statistical data, and current trouble areas such as Palestine and Lebanon. The volume concludes with a glossary and an index of historic place names. All of the maps, which are beautifully done in color and clearly portray the information discussed, are accompanied by excellent narrative essays. This atlas is equally suitable as a ready reference and as a source of summaries of historical periods.

Bibliographies

82. Beers, Henry Putney. **Bibliographies in American History, 1942-1978: Guide to Materials for Research.** Woodbridge, Conn., Research Publications, 1982. 2v. $260.00/set. LC 81-68886. ISBN 0-89235-038-5.

With nearly 12,000 entries, this is an extensive bibliography of bibliographies in American history. The extensive subject coverage includes areas of interest to political scientists, such as political, diplomatic, and military history. Archival material, manuscript collections, government documents, books, and periodical articles published between 1942 and 1978 are included. Volume 2 is organized by state, providing a state-by-state listing of bibliographies. This is a valuable resource for identifying bibliographies related to all aspects of the political history of the United States.

83. **International Bibliography of Historical Sciences.** New York, K. G. Saur, 1926- . annual. index. $41.00. LC 31-15829. ISSN 0074-2015.

Each volume of this annual series provides a selective unannotated bibliography of book and periodical articles broadly interpreted to include relevant political, cultural, social and economic works. All geographical areas and time periods are covered. From a political science perspective, the sections on legal and constitutional history and the history of international relations are especially useful. The general classification scheme by period and region serves as the table of contents. There is no subject index, but there are name and geographical indexes. There is an unfortunate time lag of about four years between the year covered and the appearance of the volume.

Biographical Sources

84. **Concise Dictionary of American Biography.** American Council of Learned Societies. 3d ed. New York, Scribner, 1980. 1,333p. $75.00. LC 80-13892. ISBN 0-684-16631-3.

This title is a convenient 1-volume summary of the authoritative *Dictionary of American Biography* (*DAB*) which has 20 volumes plus supplements. The *Concise Dictionary*, with 17,000 entries, covers individuals who were deceased by 1960. These entries attempt to retain the essential information from the longer original biographies in the *DAB*, but for extensive commentary, the original set would have to be consulted. *The Concise Dictionary* is a good source for identifying and obtaining basic facts on prominent Americans who died before 1960. The British equivalents to our *DAB* are the *DNB*, *Dictionary of National Biography*, and the *Concise Dictionary of National Biography*.

Dictionaries and Encyclopedias

85. Cook, Chris. **Dictionary of Historical Terms: A Guide to Names and Events of Over 1,000 Years of World History.** New York, Bedrick Books; distr., New York, Harper & Row, 1983. 304p. $15.95. LC 83-13377. ISBN 0-911745-16-5.

The author has attempted to bring together in one volume as many as possible of the historical terms frequently encountered by students and others in the history literature. Approximately 2,000 terms are included, with definitions that vary in length from a few lines to half a page. All time periods and geographical areas are covered, but there is an emphasis on British, European, and American terms. Cook has included many technical terms (de jure recognition), foreign-language terms (Dieu et mon droit), new terms (free fire zone), plus names of various political movements (Mensheviks). Names and events are included but not persons and places. Though certainly not comprehensive, this is a useful source for identification or clarification of historical terms.

Guides

86. Frick, Elizabeth. **Library Research Guide to History: Illustrated Search Strategy and Sources.** Ann Arbor, Mich., Pierian Press, 1980. $25.00; $15.00(pbk). LC 80-83514. ISBN 08-7650-119-6; 08-7650-123-4(pbk).

This slim volume serves primarily as a useful guide for college students involved in writing history papers. It offers advice on choosing topics, using libraries, refining search strategies, and evaluating sources. The instructions are illustrated with many helpful examples. For those not interested in such assistance, this volume also provides an extensive unannotated list of basic reference sources in history, classified in 21 categories based on time units (ancient, medieval, modern history) or regions and countries.

87. Fyfe, Janet, comp. **History Journals and Serials: An Analytical Guide.** New York, Greenwood, 1986. 351p. index. (Annotated Bibliographies of Serials: A Subject Approach Series, No. 8). $46.95. LC 86-9986. ISSN 0313239991.

This guide, which contains 689 periodicals and serials in the field of history, includes most of the major general journals, plus a wide selection of specialized journals and newsletters. Foreign-language titles were excluded. The entries are arranged under subject headings such as "Cultural History" and "History of Science." In addition to the standard bibliographic entry information, each annotation provides a paragraph or two describing the contents of the journals. These paragraphs, which focus on the particular contents of each of the titles, will be the most useful feature for researchers, for acquisitions librarians, and for those seeking publishers for articles. Four indexes — geographical, title, publisher, and subject — conclude the guide.

88. Prucha, Francis Paul. **Handbook for Research in American History: A Guide to Bibliographies and Other Reference Works.** Lincoln, University of Nebraska Press, 1987. 289p. index. $21.95; $9.95(pbk). LC 86-30871. ISSN 0803236824; 0803287194(pbk).

The first 17 chapters of this guide cover reference works in American history in such general categories as periodical indexes, book review indexes, manuscript guides, encyclopedias, handbooks, and other standard reference sources. Government documents and databases are also included. The first chapters provide an introduction to libraries and library catalogs. The second part of the guide contains 15 chapters dealing with various subject specialties, including political history, foreign affairs, and military history. Each category of material is introduced with background information, followed by a description of major titles with additional titles listed. This bibliography would be most useful for American history students seeking an orientation to the library and to research tools.

Handbooks

89. Morris, Richard B. **Encyclopedia of American History.** 6th ed. New York, Harper & Row, 1982. 1,285p. $30.72. LC 81-47668. ISBN 0061816051.

Now in its sixth edition, this work has long been considered the standard source for the essential facts about American history. The information is divided into three major sections. The first is a basic chronology of political and military events from precolonial times to 1981. While the material is arranged sequentially by date, the commentaries can be read through as a narrative summary. The second part is a topical chronology presenting information on such nonpolitical subjects as population, immigration and ethnic stock, the American economy, thought and culture, science, invention, and technology. The third section contains 500 brief biographical sketches of prominent Americans. There is also a listing of presidents, cabinet members, Supreme Court justices and the texts of the Declaration of Independence and the Constitution.

90. Schlesinger, Arthur M., Jr., ed. **The Almanac of American History.** New York, Putnam, 1983. 623p. $24.95. LC 83-3435. ISBN 039912850.

This handbook, basically a chronology of American history, contains an introduction by Arthur M. Schlesinger, Jr., general editor, and five chapters by other prominent history scholars. The chapters are: "Founding a Nation (986-1787)," "Testing a Union (1788-1865)," "Forging a Nation (1866-1900)," "Expanding Resources (1901-1945)," "Emerging as a World Power (1946-1982)." Each chapter features a series of short entries arranged in chronological order that summarize the most important political, military, and cultural events of the period. Interspersed with the chronologies are many fact boxes, biographical sketches, and numerous illustrations and maps. Each chapter begins with an essay that provides an overview of the details that follow.

91.   Steinberg, S. H. **Historical Tables, 58 BC-AD 1985.** 11th ed., updated by John Paxton. New York, Garland, 1986. 277p. $27.50. LC 86-18326. ISSN 0-8240-8951-0.

Through the use of the "bare bones of historical tables" (foreword), this title attempts to provide a chronology of the major facts of world history, beginning with Caesar subduing Gaul in 58 B.C. The emphasis, especially for the earlier centuries, is European, particularly British. With certain variations, the page format consists of 6 parallel columns for each time period (usually from 5 to 10 years), with political history divided into geographical columns followed by columns for economic, ecclesiastical, and cultural events. This is a very handy source for determining the dates of events or for identifying the main historical activities of a year or period.

92.   Wetterau, Bruce. **Macmillan Concise Dictionary of World History.** New York, Macmillan, 1983. $39.95; $18.95(pbk). LC 82-24952. ISBN 0-02-626110-3; 0-02-082410-66(pbk).

As a comprehensive reference work for world history, this one-volume title is a convenient key to a vast accumulation of facts. It contains 10,000 alphabetically arranged entries plus 7,000 chronologically arranged items. The aim of the editor was to provide maximum accessibility to the "specific bits of historical information" (preface). The entries proceed alphabetically through important events, people, and places, with 136 detailed chronological breakdowns interspersed for major countries or topics, such as the Reformation.

Indexes and Abstracts

93.   **America: History and Life.** Santa Barbara, Calif., ABC-Clio, 1964- . 3 issues/yr., with semiannual and annual cumulations. service basis. LC 84-640889. ISSN 0002-7065(pt. A); 0097-6172(pt. B); 0363-1249(pt. C); 0002-7065(pt. D).

As the companion volume to *Historical Abstracts, America: History and Life* is the leading abstracting service for the history of the United States and Canada. It abstracts relevant articles from nearly 2,000 serial publications, of which about 700 are published in the United States and Canada. Journals of state and local historical societies are included. The journal citations are arranged in part A by country, chronological period, and broad topic. There is a detailed subject index as well as an author index. These are cumulated annually in part D. Part C, an annual bibliography, includes citations to books, dissertations, and listings of the articles in part A. Part B, issued twice a year, is an index to book reviews. This index is also available online through DIALOG database service (see entry 311).

For extended searches of the periodical literature of history, see *The Combined Retrospective Index to Journals in History, 1838-1974.* Washington, D.C., Carrollton Press, 1977. 11v. LC 77-70347. ISBN 0-8408-0175-0.

94.   **Historical Abstracts.** Santa Barbara, Calif., ABC-Clio, 1955- . quarterly, with cumulative indexes. service basis. LC 56-56304. ISSN 0363-2717(pt. A), 0363-2725(pt. B).

Together with *America: History and Life*, this index by ABC-Clio provides comprehensive coverage of the world's historical literature. *Historical Abstracts* covers all of the world except the United States and Canada. It is published in two parts: A, which includes modern history from 1450 to 1914, and B, which includes 1914 to the present. Each part is arranged by a detailed classification scheme which begins with general works in such categories as historiography, methodology, and the teaching of history. The second section is a breakdown by topic; the third is by area or country.

Historical Abstracts contains citations and abstracts from approximately 1,800 journals published in over 80 countries. Selected books are included. References are also made to *Dissertations Abstracts International* (see entry 36). There are author and subject indexes which cumulate annually. This index is also available online through the DIALOG database service (see entry 315).

95. **Writings on American History: A Subject Bibliography of Articles.** American Historical Association. White Plains, N.Y., Kraus, 1974- . annual. index. $45.00. LC 75-22257.

The new series of this publication began in 1974, published by Kraus. With various imprints and policies, previous series extend coverage back to 1903. The American Historical Association's bibliography covers current periodical literature, with entries from 535 journals in the 1985/86 volume. The unannotated citations are listed in three broad chronological, geographical, or subject sections. Political science researchers will find of particular interest the sections that deal with constitutional history; administrative history, structure of politics, and political parties; diplomatic history, foreign policy, and foreign relations; and comparative studies. There is no subject index, but an author index is provided.

PSYCHOLOGY

Dictionaries and Encyclopedias

96. **Encyclopedia of Psychology.** Raymond J. Corsini, ed. New York, John Wiley & Sons, 1984. 4v. index. $249.95/set. LC 83-16814. ISBN 0-471-86594-X.

The 4-volume *Encyclopedia of Psychology*, written by more than 500 expert contributors, is generally considered the best up-to-date encyclopedia in the field of psychology today. The first 3 volumes contain over 2,000 signed entries, including 1,200 major topics and 600 biographies. Major psychological tests, psychology in foreign countries, and the major subject fields of psychology (arranged in 10 topical groupings) are all covered. The entries range from 200 to 7,000 words in length. The fourth volume contains the bibliography of 15,000 citations for the books and journal articles noted in the text and a subject index. This encyclopedia, written for "average intelligent laymen" (preface), is admirably suited for researchers and practitioners throughout the social and behavioral sciences.

An abridged one-volume version of this encyclopedia, also edited by Corsini, is the *Concise Encyclopedia of Psychology*, (New York, Wiley, 1987. $89.95. LC 86-22392. ISBN 0-471-01068-5). It contains a "maximum amount of information about a maximum number of relevant topics in a minimum of words" (preface). It is suitable for nonspecialists and persons outside the field of psychology.

97. Harre, Rom, and Roger Lamb, eds. **The Encyclopedic Dictionary of Psychology.** Cambridge, Mass., MIT Press, 1983. 718p. index. $85.00. LC 83-920. ISBN 0-262-08135-0.

Over 300 well-known international academic experts contributed to this dictionary. It covers the bases of contemporary psychology—including cognitive psychology, psycholinguistics, and neuropsychology—and the three main fields of applied psychology—educational, occupational and clinical.

The signed entries range in length from a paragraph to over a page and end with brief bibliographies. Terms are defined briefly, while theories and concepts receive expanded treatment. There is a combined name/subject index and many cross-references. This source is appropriate for social scientists and students as well as for psychologists.

98.   **Longman Dictionary of Psychology and Psychiatry.** Robert M. Goldenson, ed.-in-chief. New York, Longman, 1984. 815p. $39.95. LC 83-13591. ISBN 0-582-28257-8.

A search of primary sources—research papers, journal articles, major textbooks—of the last two decades was conducted to form the basis of entries in this dictionary. The result is a dictionary of 21,000 entries covering the vocabulary of all the psychosciences and allied fields. There are many neurological, physiological, and medical terms. In addition to terms and phrases, there are over 1,000 biographical portraits. The entries are concise and clear, with many cross-references, making this an excellent choice for a general psychological dictionary with comprehensive coverage.

Guides

99.   Borchardt, D. H., and R. D. Francis. **How to Find Out in Psychology: A Guide to the Literature and Methods of Research.** New York, Pergamon Press, 1984. $24.00. LC 84-2827. ISBN 0-08-031280-2.

Although this work was written to assist those involved in research in psychology, it can also be very useful for those who need an overview of the discipline or guidance in identifying seminal works or major reference tools. This guide includes chapters on the history and background of psychology, special fields within the discipline, and the conduct of research. Three chapters identify and describe the major bibliographic tools used to find out about the literature of psychology. There is also a chapter on the profession, with information on education and training, careers, and organizations in psychology.

100.   McInnis, Raymond G. **Research Guide for Psychology.** Westport, Conn., Greenwood, 1982. 604p. index. (Reference Sources for the Social Sciences and Humanities, No. 1). $45.00. LC 81-1377. ISBN 0-313-21399-2. ISSN 0730-3335.

Over 1,200 information sources are discussed in this guide for psychologists and others interested in psychological research. The citations are grouped into 17 bibliographic essays centered on a classification of major topics based on *Psychological Abstracts* (see entry 101).

The opening chapter includes general reference sources in psychology. The topical section on social processes and social issues will be of broad interest to social scientists. Coverage is especially strong for bibliographies and handbooks, though there is coverage of a wide spectrum of reference sources. Full bibliographic information for the citations appears in a separate section at the end of the book. A general index includes authors, titles, and subjects.

Indexes and Abstracts

101.   **Psychological Abstracts.** Arlington, Va., American Psychological Association, 1927- . monthly. index. $750.00/yr. LC 29-23479. ISSN 0033-2887.

Nearly 1,000 journals, in addition to books, dissertations, and research reports, are indexed in this important abstracting service for psychology and related fields. *Psychological Abstracts* is without question the major guide to the literature of psychology and a model for abstracting services.

Each entry has a short, nonevaluative abstract. The 1987 volume included 33,000 abstracts. There are 16 major categories for the classification of entries and many subdivisions. The author and detailed subject indexes cumulate quarterly and annually. This database is also available online through DIALOG and BRS as PsychALERT and in CD-ROM format as PsychLIT on SilverPlatter from SilverPlatter Information, Inc.

SOCIOLOGY AND RELATED FIELDS

Sociology

Bibliographies

102. **International Bibliography of Sociology.** London, Tavistock; distr., New York, Methuen. 1952- . annual. index. $110.00. LC 57-2949. ISSN 0085-2066.

As one of the titles in the *International Bibliography of the Social Sciences*, this volume is the annual bibliography for sociology. It includes books, pamphlets, reports, government documents, and journal articles published in many languages. The list of periodicals reviewed is extensive and especially impressive for the foreign-language titles.

The unannotated entries are arranged in a classification schedule with 11 major categories and many subdivisions. There is an author index and a very detailed subject index. Though the time lag of two to three years in publication eliminates this tool as a source of current citations, it remains a basic title for comprehensive coverage of the literature of sociology.

Dictionaries and Encyclopedias

103. **The International Encyclopedia of Sociology.** Michael Mann, ed. New York, Continuum, 1984. 434p. $34.50. LC 83-15340. ISBN 0-8264-0238-0.

As a one-volume encyclopedia this title provides brief entries with information on basic terms, phrases, concepts, and theories. While not comprehensive or definitive, it is fine for concise overviews of important topics, for which it includes much historical and developmental information.

There are also biographical portraits of eminent sociologists, with emphasis on their contributions to the discipline. The 750 signed entries range in length from a paragraph to several pages. Entries include cross-references to related terms and references to important sources of additional information. There is, however, no index. The editor and contributors' affiliation with the London School of Economics perhaps accounts for the British orientation of this work.

Guides

104. Aby, Stephen H. **Sociology: A Guide to Reference and Information Sources.** Littleton, Colo., Libraries Unlimited, 1987. 231p. (Reference Sources in the Social Sciences, No. 1). index. $36.00. LC 86-27573. ISBN 0-87287-498-2.

As the first title in a series, Reference Sources in the Social Sciences, Aby's guide identifies and annotates over 650 reference works and sources for students, researchers, and librarians. The titles included are primarily English-language works published between 1970 and 1986, with some standards from earlier days.

After covering the important works in the social sciences and titles in other social sciences disciplines, the author reviews 376 reference tools and sources in sociology and its subfields. For each entry there is complete bibliographic information, plus well-written descriptive and critical annotations. In addition to reference works, Aby also considers online databases, journals, research centers, and organizations. This guide provides an excellent, systematic overview of reference sources in sociology.

Indexes and Abstracts

105. **Sociological Abstracts.** San Diego, Calif., Sociological Abstracts, Inc., 1953- . 5 issues/yr. index. $264.00/yr. LC 58-46404. ISSN 0038-0202.

Sociological Abstracts, the major indexing and abstracting service in the field of sociology, provides nonevaluative abstracts for the world's serial literature in sociology and related disciplines. It is cosponsored by the International Sociological Association. Serials in the field of sociology are abstracted fully, regardless of language. Titles in related fields are abstracted selectively for a total of over 1,000 titles indexed. Papers presented at meetings of sociological societies and book reviews are also indexed.

The entries are arranged in 33 major categories, often with numerous subdivisions. Political interactions, urban sociology, violence, demography, and social change and economic development are among the categories that would likely contain material of interest to political scientists. There are author and subject indexes that cumulate annually.

This information is also searchable online through DIALOG and BRS and using CD-ROM technology with Sociofile on SilverPlatter from SilverPlatter Information, Inc.

For the extended search of sociological literature, see: *The Combined Retrospective Index Set to Journals in Sociology, 1895-1975.* Washington, D.C., Carrollton Press, 1978. 6v. LC 77-70347. ISBN 0-8408-0194-7.

Criminology

Dictionaries and Encyclopedias

106. DeSola, Ralph. **Crime Dictionary.** New York, Facts on File, 1982. 219p. $22.50. LC 80-23348. ISBN 0-87196-443-0.

This dictionary, which includes a diverse collection of terms, provides brief definitions, from one to several lines. Abbreviations, medical terms related to drug addiction, criminal jargon and slang, historical and literary allusions, terms related to penal institutions and weaponry, legal and law enforcement terms, colloquialisms, and many other categories of terms related to the criminal justice and criminal subcultures are found in this dictionary, for a total of some 10,000 entries. The appendixes include a list of foreign-language terms and a bibliography of selected sources relating to crime.

107. Kadish, Sanford H., ed.-in-chief. **Encyclopedia of Crime and Justice.** New York, Macmillan, 1983. 4v. 1,790p. index. $300.00/set. LC 83-7156. ISBN 0-02-918110-0.

This four-volume interdisciplinary set attempts to draw together a summary of current knowledge about criminal behavior and the reactions of society to it. The encyclopedia examines the causes of criminal behavior, the prevention of crime, the punishment and treatment of criminals, the functioning of the criminal justice system, and the laws that define crime and the treatment of it.

These topics are explored by means of a series of 286 essays written by American scholars. The articles, which generally cover concepts, theories, research, and historical and current issues, are suitable for professionals and laypersons who wish to review a topic or obtain an overview. The essays end with short bibliographies of additional sources. A subject index and a glossary of terms for the criminal justice field are also included.

Guides

108. O'Block, Robert L. **Criminal Justice Research Sources.** 2d ed. Cincinnati, Anderson Publishing, 1986. 183p. $14.95. LC 85-18629. ISBN 0-87084-664-7(pbk).

As a guide for students involved in library research in the field of criminal justice, this title reviews in 17 chapters the use of the card catalog, interlibrary loan, online databases, and other useful resources. Several chapters deal with basic reference tools of the field such as abstracts, indexes, and bibliographies, as well as some more specialized sources for government documents and legal research. Many of the works cited are annotated. This guide provides an introduction to basic reference works in the criminal justice field for beginning researchers or for individuals approaching this subject from other fields.

Indexes and Abstracts

109. **Criminal Justice Abstracts.** Monsey, N.J., Willow Tree Press, 1968- . quarterly. index. $100.00/yr. LC 77-647645. ISSN 0146-9177.

This quarterly publication features lengthy abstracts of selected current publications in the fields of criminology, penology, and law. The several hundred abstracts in each issue include coverage of books, dissertations, reports, and periodicals. *Criminal Justice Periodical Index* has a similar subject focus but includes only journals. Most issues also include a bibliographic essay that reviews the literature and research of a topic of current interest.

The abstracts are arranged under subject categories with a detailed subject index for direct access. The subject and author indexes cumulate annually.

110. **Criminal Justice Periodical Index.** Ann Arbor, Mich., University Microfilms International, 1975- . 3 issues/yr., with annual cumulations. $195.00/yr. LC 76-649385. ISSN 0145-5818.

Currently this title provides indexing to over 100 U.S., British, and Canadian journals in the fields of corrections, criminology, drug abuse, juvenile justice, rehabilitation, and police studies. Each issue contains two separate sections of entries arranged by author and by subject. The subject section uses an expanded list of Library of Congress headings. There is also an extensive listing of book reviews. The citations specify the availability of photocopies and/or microform copies from University Microforms International. This index is also available online through DIALOG database services.

Statistics Sources

111. **Sourcebook of Criminal Justice Statistics.** U.S. Bureau of Justice Statistics. Washington, D.C., GPO, 1973- . annual. index. $15.00. LC 74-601963. ISSN 0360-3431. J1.42/3:SD-SB- .

The Bureau of Justice Statistics publishes this essential series in order to bring together in a single, comprehensive volume nationwide statistical data of general interest. The over 700 pages of statistical tables are arranged in several major sections, covering such topics as characteristics of the criminal justice system; public attitudes toward crime and criminal justice-related topics; nature and distribution of known offenses; characteristics and distribution of persons arrested; judicial processing of defendants; and persons under correctional supervision. These subjects are broken down into many subtopics. A detailed list of figures and tables and an index facilitate use of this excellent source of statistics on crime.

112. **Uniform Crime Reports for the United States.** U.S. Federal Bureau of Investigation. Washington, D.C., GPO, 1930- . annual. $13.00. LC 30-27005. ISSN 0082-7592. J1.14/7:[yr.].

As "a reliable measure of lawlessness in our society" (foreword), the *Uniform Crime Reports* for over 50 years has attempted to present a systematic overview of crime in the United States reported in a uniform manner. This book of charts and tables provides a multitude of crime statistics on types of offenses reported, offenses cleared, persons arrested, and law enforcement personnel. Much of the information is broken down by age, sex, race, and other variables. There are also data on crime and arrest trends. The introduction and appendixes explain the crime report program used by the FBI, with specifics on methodology and with definitions of key terms.

Cultural Anthropology

Annual Reviews

113. **Annual Review of Anthropology.** Palo Alto, Calif., Annual Reviews, 1972- . annual. $35.00. LC 72-82136. ISSN 0084-6570.

Description and evaluation of current literature is provided in this title by contributing specialists whose essays review recent research. The chapter-length essays are followed by extensive bibliographies with full citations. All subdivisions of anthropology are covered, but specific topics or regions are not covered on a regular schedule. In addition to the annual author and subject indexes, each volume also contains cumulative indexes for recent previous volumes. This review is international in scope, with an emphasis on English-language publications. Its predecessor, the *Biennial Review of Anthropology*, provides coverage for 1959-1971.

Bibliographies

114. **International Bibliography of Social and Cultural Anthropology.** London, Tavistock; New York, Methuen, 1955- . annual. index. $110.00. LC 58-4366. ISSN 0085-2074.

As one of the four annual volumes in the *International Bibliography of the Social Sciences* prepared by the International Committee for Social Science Information and Documentation, this title is dedicated to anthropology—specifically cultural and social anthropology. The unannotated citations for books and journal articles are arranged in a detailed classification scheme, with 10 major categories and many subdivisions. Ethnography, area studies, social organization, and folk traditions are among the many topics that focus on specific regions, nations, and societies and that could provide information on the cultural background in which political activity takes place. Coverage is international, with works in many languages cited. There are subject and author indexes. The time lag in publishing is currently about four years.

Directories

115. **Serial Publications in Anthropology.** 2d ed. Compiled by the Library-Anthropology Resource Group. F. X. Grollig, S. J., and Sol Tax, eds. South Salem, N.Y., Redgrave Publishing, 1982. 177p. index. $17.50. LC 85-122316. ISBN 8-913178-64-0.

This directory, which lists 4,387 titles, includes serials, journals, monographic series, newsletters, and similar publications containing contributions to the field of anthropology. The entries are arranged by main entry, with short annotations that include publisher's address, frequency of publication, date of beginning publication, and where the titles are indexed.

Although the information provided for each entry is minimal, this is an excellent source for obscure titles not found in the more general serial directories. The index includes subjects, geographical units, and corporate authors.

Indexes and Abstracts

116. **Abstracts in Anthropology.** Farmingdale, N.Y., Baywood Publishing, 1970- . quarterly. index. $190.00/yr. LC 77-20528. ISSN 0001-3455.

About 3,000 abstracts annually are provided by this quarterly reference service, which indexes about 100 journals to produce a worldwide survey of current journal literature in anthropology. The entries are arranged in four major subfields of anthropology: linguistics, cultural anthropology, archaeology, and physical anthropology, with many subdivisions. Cultural anthropology may be the portion of most interest to political science, with its subsections on political structure and process, urban studies, and minorities. There are author and subject indexes for each issue.

Population and Demography

Dictionaries and Encyclopedias

117. **International Encyclopedia of Population.** John A. Ross, ed. New York, Free Press, 1982. 2v. 750p. index. $145.00/set. LC 82-2326. ISBN 0-02-927430-3.

The Center for Population and Family Health has prepared this two-volume international encyclopedia of population, which includes all aspects of demographic phenomena. There are 129 signed topical articles that summarize existing knowledge and research in survey fashion. There are also articles on major countries and all regions. Third World concerns receive extensive coverage.

This scholarly work, which avoids excessive technicality, can serve admirably to introduce or review major areas of knowledge in the fields of population and demography. There are bibliographies at the end of most articles. A detailed subject index and an outline of the contents provide access to specific topics.

118. Pressat, Roland. **The Dictionary of Demography.** Christopher Wilson, ed. Oxford, England, New York, Blackwell, 1985. 243p. index. $75.00. LC 84-28407. ISBN 0-631-12746-1.

The whole range of demographic study is covered in this dictionary. There is an emphasis on technical concepts and statistical terms, which the editor concluded most often need clarification. Basic concepts, prominent individuals, specific techniques, and theories from historical and contemporary demography are all included in the signed entries, which attempt to place the terms "in the context of present thinking and research" (foreword). The entries, which resemble short articles, include cross-references and short suggested reading lists. The subject index provides access to terms found only within the entries.

Indexes and Abstracts

119. **Population Index.** Princeton, N.J., Princeton University, 1935- . quarterly. index. $60.00/yr. LC 39-10247. ISSN 0032-4701.

The Office of Population Research at Princeton University and the Population Association of America prepare this index, which includes not only books and journal articles but also proceedings of professional meetings, government documents, and reports of organizations. Publications that are basically statistical are cited in a special issue.

The citations for population studies are listed under broad subject categories with many subtopics. There is no subject index, but there are author and geographical indexes that cumulate annually. All entries have abstracts that indicate content and scope of the material cited. This international index is essential for demographic research.

Statistics Sources

120. Bogue, Donald J. **The Population of the United States: Historical Trends and Future Projections.** New York, Free Press, 1985. 728p. index. $75.00. LC 84-18688. ISBN 0-02-904700-5.

Over 700 pages of statistics provide comprehensive coverage of the population of the United States through 1980. This title is useful as a source of specific statistics, as a resource leading to more detailed studies, and as an overview that pulls together myriad statistics with information on long-term trends.

The data are arranged in five major categories: (1) overview of the United States population (size, growth, distribution, composition by race, ethnicity, sex, age); (2) dynamics of population change (marriage, divorce, mortality, fertility, migration); (3) social characteristics (ancestry, education, household composition); (4) economic characteristics (employment, occupation, income); and (5) special topics (poverty, religion, political demography). There is a subject index to all data. This is a well-organized, clearly written source for summary demographic data for the United States.

121. **Demographic Yearbook.** New York, United Nations, Statistical Office, 1949- . annual. index. $90.00. LC 50-641. ISSN 0082-8041.

Over 1,000 pages of statistics constitute this standard volume on worldwide population, with comparative figures for over 200 countries. The tables begin with a world survey of population, birth and death rates, age and sex ratios, vital statistics, and similar data. There follow detailed demographic tables published each year, which are excellent sources for data for historical or time studies. Most volumes also feature a special topic such as international migration. There is an introduction that discusses contents, methodology, reliability, etc., and a cumulative subject index to all statistical data in the current and previous volumes.

122. **1980 Census of Population. Volume 1, Characteristics of the Population.** U.S. Bureau of the Census. Washington, D.C., GPO, 1981-1983. LC 81-607950. C3.223/10:980/[vol.]/[pt.].

123. **1980 Census of Population. Volume 2, Subject Reports.** U.S. Bureau of the Census. Washington, D.C., GPO, 1984/85. C3.223/10:980/[vol.]/[pt.].

These two series are the major, basic titles in the decennial census of population conducted by the Bureau of the Census, which has many other products in paper, on microfiche, and in machine-readable formats as described in the Census Bureau catalog of publications. In addition to providing population and socioeconomic data useful for understanding American political activity, the census impacts directly on politics, since the configuration of congressional districts and the allocation of federal and state funds often depend on census data.

Volume 1 of the *Census of Population* consists of four separate series, each with reports for each state and territory, plus a national summary: (A) *Number of Inhabitants* (final population by place), (B) *General Population Characteristics* (household relationships, age, race, sex, marital status, etc.); (C) *General Social and Economic Characteristics* (nativity, citizenship, ancestry, education, income, poverty, etc.); and (D) *Detailed Population Characteristics* (part C data presented with more detailed geographical breakdowns). Volume 2 includes separate reports on various topics, including geographic mobility, marital characteristics, occupation, earnings, and poverty.

There are many published guides to census materials in addition to the Bureau's catalogs and the tables of contents and indexes published with these volumes.

Race and Ethnic Relations

Dictionaries and Encyclopedias

124. Cashmore, Ernest. **Dictionary of Race and Ethnic Relations.** Boston, Routledge & Kegan Paul, 1984. 294p. $28.00. LC 84-11730. ISSN 0710099045.

The author of this dictionary has attempted to clarify for practitioners, academics, and laypersons the basic concepts, schools of thought, historical events, and research related to race and ethnic relations. Inequality and discrimination are the specific issues of interest. Although labeled a dictionary, the entries, which run about two to three pages each, resemble articles in a handbook. Typical articles treat such subjects as affirmative action, immigration laws, the Ku Klux Klan, prejudice, segregation, and slavery. Each entry provides a historical overview and a brief bibliography for further reading. The book has a British emphasis, but it includes many topics relevant to the American scene.

125. Thernstrom, Stephen, ed. **Harvard Encyclopedia of American Ethnic Groups.** Cambridge, Mass., Belknap Press, 1980. 1,076p. $70.00. LC 80-17756. ISBN 0-674-37512-2.

The core of this encyclopedia is the 106 signed essays on American ethnic groups. These entries range in length from 3,000 to 40,000 words. All the major ethnic groups are covered as are minor ones such as the Maltese and the Frisians. Certain religious groups, such as Eastern Catholics, are also included. Southerners, Yankees, and Appalachians also have entries. The articles cover the origins of the groups, their social, political, and cultural life, and such matters as the degree of ethnicity present in the current population. There are numerous maps, statistical tables, and bibliographies of suggested readings at the end of each essay. This encyclopedia is an excellent source for portraits of American ethnic groups.

Handbooks

126.   Ploski, Harry A., and James Williams, comps. **The Negro Almanac: A Reference Work on the Afro-American.** 4th ed. New York, John Wiley & Sons, 1983. 1,550p. index. $97.00. LC 82-17469. ISBN 0-471-87710-7.

This handbook is virtually a one-volume encyclopedia on all aspects of black involvement in American history and contemporary life. The comprehensive treatment is divided into 34 major subject chapters, which begin with a chronology and cover historical, political, economic, and social information. There is a considerable amount of biographical information and statistical data, and numerous illustrations. There is also an extensive bibliography on Afro-Americans and a detailed subject index. This is an excellent source for overview articles and for ready-reference facts.

Indexes and Abstracts

127.   **Index to Periodical Articles by and about Blacks.** Boston, G. K. Hall. 1973- . annual. $79.50. LC 78-643647. ISSN 0161-8245.

This index now covers about 40 general and scholarly Afro-American periodicals, some on a selective basis. It is compiled by the staff of the Hallie Q. Brown Memorial Library at Central State University, Wilberforce, Ohio.

The author and subject entries are interfiled to form one alphabet. Subject headings are based on an expanded version of the *Library of Congress Subject Headings* with numerous cross references. While this index is a primary source for coverage of Afro-American periodicals, it is published annually with no supplements and with a delay of several years.

128.   **Sage Race Relations Abstracts.** Beverly Hills, Calif., Sage, 1975- . quarterly. index. $105.00/yr. LC 80-647565. ISSN 0307-9201.

Published on behalf of the Institute of Race Relations in England, this abstracting service includes some books, essays, and pamphlets, as well as American and European periodicals dealing with race relations and related topics, such as immigration, and relevant demographic and area studies.

The abstracts are arranged in a classification scheme under broad subject headings. The author and subject indexes unfortunately appear only in the final issue of each volume. Each issue also usually contains one or two bibliographic essays, plus a list of addresses of "elusive" organizations and publications.

Social Work

Dictionaries and Encyclopedias

129.   Timms, Noel, and Rita Timms. **Dictionary of Social Welfare.** Boston, Routledge & Kegan Paul, 1982. 217p. $21.95. LC 82-5385. ISBN 0-7100-9084-6.

This dictionary covers social work and social policy for practitioners and students. The definitions are clear, concise, and often include cross-references to other terms and elaborations designed to place the terms in a contemporary context in the field of social welfare. Historical origins, policy applications, and relevant controversies are also highlighted. Each entry ends with a short bibliography for further reading. Unfortunately, this dictionary has a marked British orientation, which will limit its usefulness in some situations.

Guides

130.   Conrad, James H. **Reference Sources in Social Work: An Annotated Bibliography.** Metuchen, N.J., Scarecrow, 1982. 201p. index. $16.00. LC 81-21219. ISBN 0-8108-1503-6.

Reference works published between 1979 and 1981 are comprehensively covered in this bibliography of social work. Major representative titles from related fields are also included, for a total of 656 citations. The entries are grouped in a classification scheme based on *Social Work Research and Abstracts.* The various fields of service — aging, child abuse, family, handicapped, poverty, suicide, women, and many more — are all covered. The listings of dictionaries, handbooks, indexes, and other relevant reference sources can serve as access points to the literature of the field. The appendixes contain lists of social work journals and organizations. There are author, subject, and title indexes.

Indexes and Abstracts

131.   **Social Work Research & Abstracts.** New York, National Association of Social Workers, 1965- . quarterly. $75.00/yr. LC 77-642178. ISSN 0148-0847.

The National Association of Social Workers, a major professional organization in the social work field, produces this index and abstract service. The abstracts are arranged in a classification scheme under six main topics: (1) fields of service (aging, alcoholism, crime, family, housing, etc.); (2) social policy and action; (3) service methods; (4) the profession; (5) history, and (6) related fields of knowledge (other social science disciplines). Dissertations and selected books, in addition to several hundred periodicals, are indexed. The author and subject indexes cumulate annually. *Social Work Research & Abstracts* is the basic access resource for current literature and research in the social service field. It is available as an online database through BRS.

Urban Studies

Indexes and Abstracts

132.   **Index to Current Urban Documents.** Westport, Conn., Greenwood, 1973- . quarterly, with annual cumulations. $250.00/yr. LC 73-641453. ISSN 0046-8908.

Local documents issued by 286 of the larger U.S. and Canadian cities and their counties and regions are indexed, with detailed bibliographic descriptions, in this quarterly index. Annual reports, audit reports, community development plans, environmental impact statements, policy statements, statistical tables, master plans, and many other types of publications are included, with an emphasis on those that deal with social, economic, and political matters. There are two listings of the documents: by geographic location and by subject. All documents cited are available on microfiche from the publisher.

133.   **Sage Urban Studies Abstracts.** Beverly Hills, Calif., Sage, 1973- . quarterly. index. $125.00/yr. LC 73-641964. ISSN 0090-5747.

Each issue of this quarterly index service contains about 250 abstracts of current urban studies literature. Periodicals, books, dissertations, pamphlets, government publications, major speeches, legislative research studies and "fugitive material" are all included. The entries are arranged under 15 major subjects, including trends, urban history, planning, theory and research, as well as such topics as housing, environment, crime and public services. Each entry has a paragraph-long abstract. There are author and subject indexes that cumulate annually.

134.   **Urban Affairs Abstracts.** Washington, D.C., National League of Cities, 1971- . weekly, with semiannual and annual cumulations. index. $275.00/yr. LC 74-645424. ISSN 0300-6859.

The National League of Cities publishes this index, which is valued for the current information its weekly supplements provide and for the convenience of its annual cumulations. The service indexes several hundred periodicals, journals, and newsletters. The citations and abstracts are grouped in about 50 major subject categories with many subdivisions. Government, law and legislation, municipal administration, politics, public administration, and public policy are some categories of obvious potential interest to political scientists. Coverage is international, but there is an emphasis on the United States, Canada, and Great Britain. There are indexes by author, subject, and geographic region.

Women's Studies

Bibliographies

135.   Chapman, Anne, comp. and ed. **Feminist Resources for Schools and Colleges: A Guide to Curricular Materials.** 3d ed. New York, Feminist Press at The City University of New York, 1986. 190p. index. $12.95(pbk). LC 85-10110. ISSN 0935312358.

Now in its third edition, this expanded bibliography discusses print and audiovisual resources in its two main parts. These parts are in turn divided into subsections corresponding to major subject areas commonly found in high schools and undergraduate college curriculums. The 445 annotated entries (310 print, 135 audiovisual) focus on material that is nonsexist and appropriate for classroom use. Multicultural perspective and sensitivity to forms of discrimination are also considered. This bibliography does not attempt to be a comprehensive guide to resources in general for women studies. Each entry has an accompanying annotation of from 50 to 250 words. These are descriptive and evaluative, drawn from reviews and publishers' catalogs. There are author/title and subject indexes.

For a comprehensive bibliography on all aspects of women's studies (with more than 1,200 entries), there is Catherine Loeb's *Women's Studies: A Recommended Core Bibliography, 1980-1985* (Littleton, Colo., Libraries Unlimited, 1987. 538p. $55.00. LC 86-27856. ISSN 0872874729).

Guides

136.   Terris, Virginia R. **Woman in America: A Guide to Information Sources.** Detroit, Gale, 1980. 520p. index. (American Studies Information Guide Series, Vol. 7; Gale Information Guide Library). $60.00. LC 73-17564. ISBN 0-8103-1268-9.

"The significance of woman's experience" (introduction) is the subject of this guide, which is designed to aid research into the lives of American women. It is intended for those beginning in this field as well as for experienced researchers. Almost all the 2,495 citations have content annotations, albeit very brief.

The entries, arranged under subject headings, begin with general sources and work through the women's movement and many aspects of the lives of women in the United States, including economic status, government service, fashion, women in prison, women in the arts, sexuality, sports, and many other topics. The items cited range from the early 19th century to the late 1970s. Appendixes list research centers, libraries, government agencies, organizations, periodicals, and newsletters relevant to women's studies. There are author, title, and subject indexes.

Indexes and Abstracts

137.   **Women Studies Abstracts.** Rush, N.Y., Rush Publishing Co., 1972- . quarterly, with annual index. $84.00/yr. LC 72-623243. ISSN 0049-7835.

Scholarly journal articles in over 300 periodicals are indexed in this title. Selected books, newspaper articles, and pamphlets are also included. Paragraph-length abstracts are provided for a wide range of topics of interest to women's studies, including subjects related to politics and government policies. The entries are arranged under broad subject categories. Book and media reviews and new reference works are also listed. Each issue contains a name/subject index which cumulates annually.

3

Political Science —
General Reference Sources

ANNUAL REVIEWS

138. **Annual Review of Political Science.** Norwood, N.J., Ablex Publishing, 1985- . annual. $35.00. LC 86-650007. ISSN 0748-8599.

The appearance of this series in 1985 marked the beginning of an annual review publication for political science, a type of publication with a stronger history in most other academic disciplines. The objective of this title is to provide a comprehensive literature review for recent years in selected topics within political science. These essays, seven in the second volume, cover major empirical and theoretical advances as assessed by experts in the various subdivisions.

The articles include an overview of the subject and bibliographies several pages in length. Annual reviews are useful particularly for those who wish to keep up-to-date with new developments and readings and for those who approach an unfamiliar subject area and need a general overview for orientation and/or a reading list for study in greater depth elsewhere.

INDEXES AND ABSTRACTS

139. **ABC Pol Sci: A Bibliography of Contents: Political Science and Government.** Santa Barbara, Calif., ABC-Clio, 1969- . 6 issues/yr. index. service basis. LC 70-6512. ISSN 0001-0456.

The table of contents pages of more than 300 journals, U.S. and foreign, are reproduced in this service, which covers political science, government, international relations, public policy, and related topics. It is valuable, as originally intended, as a current awareness service, and also now, with improved subject indexing and annual and five-year cumulations, as an essential research tool for retrospective searching of the political science periodical literature.

The subject index contains keyword access points, with two or more assigned as subject descriptors to each article to form the subject profiles. Each keyword is cited in the alphabetical index sequence, providing multiple points of entry. For many searchers, especially students, this current bibliography would be the preferred starting point for locating periodical articles relating to political science.

140.   **Annual Supplement, [year]: An Annual Supplement to the Universal Reference System's Political Science Series, Employing a Single Index and Catalog to Carry Materials Pertaining to the Ten Basic Volumes in the Series.** New York, IFI/Plenum, a division of Plenum Publishing, 1965- . 3v. (Political Science, Government, and Public Policy Series). $350.00/set.

These supplements update the original 10-volume set of the *Universal Reference System* published in the late 1960s. It was a computer-produced annotated bibliography covering books, articles, documents, and papers using a classification scheme developed by Alfred de Grazia. Each citation is indexed by keywords and assigned descriptors.

The coverage includes all the fields related to political science, including international relations, public policy, comparative government, and other less closely related subjects such as mass behavior, economic regulation, and administrative management. The annual supplements present a comprehensive coverage of current literature and provide an in-depth index. With its unique classification scheme and terminology, however, this resource will not be the first choice of researchers who need a modest number of citations readily available in more generally familiar indexes.

141.   **The Combined Retrospective Index Set to Journals in Political Science, 1886-1974.** Washington, D.C., Carrollton Press, 1977. 8v. index. $880.00. LC 77-70347. ISBN 0-8408-0186-6.

Sometimes referred to as C.R.I.S., this set offers author and subject access to 88 years of the periodical literature of political science. Some 200 major American and British periodicals are covered in this indexing project. The foreword refers to this effort as the "Great Leap Backward in retrospective indexing." Volumes 1-6 constitute the subject indexes. Volume 1 covers international affairs and organizations, volume 2 covers political behavior and research methodology, and volumes 3 through 6 cover public administration and government. These broad topics are subdivided by subject categories. Access is then by keywords drawn from the titles of the articles indexed. The last two volumes form the author index. For retrospective periodical searches in political science, this title offers the most efficient access.

142.   International Committee for Social Science Information and Documentation. **International Bibliography of Political Science; Bibliographie internationale de science politique.** Paris, UNESCO, 1954-1961; New York, Tavistock, 1962- . annual. index. (International Bibliography of the Social Sciences; Bibliographie internationale des sciences sociales). $112.00. LC 54-3623. ISSN 0085-2058.

This bibliography is a section of the UNESCO-sponsored series International Bibliography of the Social Sciences prepared by the International Committee for Social Science Information and Documentation. The extensive classified list (over 6,000 items a year now) includes selected books, periodical articles from over 500 titles, pamphlets, and government publications.

The unannotated citations are listed under six main headings: "Political Science," "Political Thought," "Political Systems," "Political Life," "Government Policy," and "International Life," with multiple subdivisions. There is an author and detailed subject index. Reference to articles analyzed in *International Political Science Abstracts* and to book reviews are useful. The three- or four-year time lag in publication limits the usefulness of this index for searching current political science literature.

143. **International Political Science Abstracts; Documentation politique internationale.** Paris, International Political Science Association, 1951- . bimonthly. index. $215.00 (institutions); $65.00(individuals). LC 54-3623. ISSN 0020-8345.

The International Political Science Association publishes this bibliography in cooperation with the International Committee for Social Science Information and Documentation and with the financial support of UNESCO. Each volume provides some 5,000 abstracts in English or French from over 600 political science periodicals.

The abstracts are arranged in large subject categories with detailed subject and author indexes that cumulate annually. Although there are various periodical indexes to current political science literature and abstracting services covering specialized fields, this title is the only comprehensive source for abstracts in all subject areas of political science.

BOOK REVIEWS

144. **Perspective: Reviews of New Books on Government/Politics/International Affairs.** Washington, D.C., Helen Dwight Reid Educational Foundation, 1972- . index. $45.00/yr. LC 72-620473. ISSN 0048-3494.

This quarterly publication provides over 300 reviews of political science books a year. The signed reviews are by political scientists from American colleges and universities. The reviews, usually about one column in length, are arranged in geographical categories based on country or region or in topical categories such as international relations or theory. There is an annual index to the authors of the books reviewed.

In addition to content, the reviewers typically comment on related works, the author's methodology, the significance of the title, and its appropriateness for classroom use. This title is widely used as a selection tool in libraries as well as a source for commentary on current titles of interest to the political science discipline.

Many journals have extensive book review sections as noted in the chapter on journals. The German and French equivalents of *Perspective* are:

Neue Politische Literatur: Berichte über das Internationale Schrifttum. Wiesbaden, F. Steiner, 1956- . quarterly. DM 80. LC 58-37179. ISSN 0028-3320.

Revue française de science politique. Paris Fondation Nationale des Sciences Politiques, 1951- . bimonthly. Fr.305. LC 55-41631. ISSN 0035-2950.

145. **Political Science Reviewer: An Annual Review of Books.** Bryn Mawr, Pa., Intercollegiate Studies Institute, 1971- . annual. $10.00. LC 73-64389. ISSN 0091-3715.

Unlike *Perspective*, which features short reviews that appear fairly soon after the books are published, *Political Science Reviewer* is an annual publication devoted to lengthy reviews of a limited number of titles. These titles are not necessarily recent publications but may be major or classic textbooks or studies. For these reasons, while this source is less useful for book selection in libraries, it is an excellent publication for in-depth critical and evaluative reviews by American academic political scientists. Each volume contains about 10 bibliographic essays, each usually dealing with several related titles.

DICTIONARIES AND ENCYCLOPEDIAS

146. **Blackwell Encyclopaedia of Political Institutions.** Vernon Bogdanor, ed. Oxford, England, New York, Basil Blackwell Reference, 1987. 667p. index. $55.00. LC 87-6571. ISBN 0-631-13841-2.

The purpose of Blackwell's encyclopedia is to provide a source of concise information on the central concepts used in the study of political institutions. The focus is on leading organizations, movements, and individuals found in the advanced industrial nations. It complements *Blackwell Encyclopedia of Political Thought* (see entry 147).

The 247 contributors from 13 countries have produced a series of signed articles which vary from half a page to several pages. The articles attempt to define each concept succinctly and to provide additional clarification through discussion and/or examples. The entries are followed by suggestions for further reading. There are numerous cross-references and a general index for names and subjects.

147. **Blackwell Encyclopedia of Political Thought.** David Miller, ed. Oxford, England; New York, Basil Blackwell, 1987. 570p. index. $60.00. LC 86-29972. ISBN 0-631-14011-5.

The entries in this encyclopedia range from one paragraph to almost five pages, from brief definitions or indentifications to substantial essays. All focus on political thought – the major ideas and doctrines that have influenced political theorists and politics currently and in the past. Key concepts in political thought, such as authority, freedom, justice, and central ideologies (for example, anarchism and nationalism) are defined and analyzed. Biographical entries are also provided for 120 political thinkers.

The entries are all signed by an international team of contributors drawn mainly from British and American academics. This one-volume encyclopedia is an excellent starting point for the user seeking a concise, to-the-point, but not simplistic, introduction to political thought. The extensive cross-references, the selective bibliographies following the entries, and the detailed index all add to its usefulness.

148. Plano, Jack C., Robert E. Riggs, and Helenan S. Robin. **The Dictionary of Political Analysis.** 2d ed. Santa Barbara, Calif., ABC-Clio, 1982. 197p. bibliog. index. (Clio Dictionaries in Political Science, No. 3). $19.75. $9.95(pbk). LC 82-4032. ISBN 0-87436-331-4; 0-87436-339-X(pbk).

Unlike other political science dictionaries that typically offer definitions of commonly used historical, descriptive, or institutional terms, this reference source concentrates on terms that relate to the contemporary behavioral approach to political study and research. Terms dealing with the analysis of data, especially statistical analysis, are emphasized.

For each of the approximately 200 entries there is first a paragraph of definition. There then follows a "significance" paragraph providing illustrations, examples, and applications for each concept. This format admirably clarifies, in plain English, terms that are often ambiguous or characterized by technical jargon. There is a subject index.

149. Riff, M. A., ed. **Dictionary of Modern Political Ideologies.** New York, St. Martin's Press, 1987. 226p. $37.50(pbk). ISBN 0-312-00928-3.

For readers desiring background information and analysis, this dictionary offers essay-length discussions of 42 "isms" or political ideologies. The essays average about 2,500 words, with some approaching 10,000. For shorter entries and quicker answers, *A Dictionary of Political Thought* by Roger Scruton (see entry 151) would be a good alternative.

The 43 concepts or ideologies covered in this title include communism, Zionism, anti-Semitism, African nationalism, Gaullism, and Islamic fundamentalism. The authors, generally British academics, describe the origins, historical developments, and current influence of the concepts. The entries end with a bibliography for further reading.

150.   Robertson, David. **A Dictionary of Modern Politics.** Philadelphia, Taylor & Francis, 1985. 341p. $34.00. LC 85-2728. ISBN 0-85066-320-2.

The author has attempted to compile a dictionary that would be useful for "those grappling with politics today" (preface). To this end he has chosen approximately 400 terms in current use dealing mainly with political ideals and philosophies. Only people and institutions identified with key creeds and ideologies are included. No events are included. The emphasis here is similar to that in Roger Scruton's *A Dictionary of Political Thought* (entry 151), though many items appear in only one of these sources.

Robertson's definitions range from a paragraph to two pages. The origins and contemporary significance of the terms are examined, especially the ambiguities relating to different usages or interpretations. The longer entries are short essays placing the terms in historical context for the reader. There is no subject index.

151.   Scruton, Roger. **A Dictionary of Political Thought.** New York, Macmillan, 1982. 499p. $19.95. LC 82-47532. ISBN 0-06-015004-0.

The focus of this dictionary is not on battles, treaties, prominent political figures, and the like. The emphasis here is conceptual, not factual. Events and individuals are included only if they help to explain a concept. Entries for proper names are limited to thinkers, e.g., Aquinas and Marx. The terms in this dictionary of concepts were taken from the actual practice of politics and from academic disciplines — political science, philosophy, sociology, and economics. These concepts constitute "the principal ideas through which modern political beliefs find expression" (preface).

The entries vary from a short paragraph to a page. The definitions successfully treat complex or abstract matters in a clear and concise manner. Asterisks are used to indicate cross-references to entries from terms used in the definitions.

DIRECTORIES

152.   American Political Science Association. **APSA Departmental Services Program: Survey of Departments.** Washington, D.C., APSA, 1971/72- . annual. $20.00. LC 74-646024. ISSN 0094-7954.

153.   American Political Science Association. **APSA Directory of Departmental Chairpersons.** Washington, D.C., APSA, 1972- . annual. $20.00. LC 73-647293. ISSN 0092-8658.

154.   American Political Science Association. **Guide to Graduate Study in Political Science.** Washington, D.C., APSA, 1972- . biennial. $15.00(members); $20.00(nonmembers). LC 73-645287. ISSN 0091-9632.

155.   American Political Science Association. **Membership Directory.** Washington, D.C., APSA, 1974- . annual. $15.00(members); $20.00(nonmembers). ISBN 0-915654-64-4 (1985).

These four directories provide a wealth of information about political science as a profession and as an academic discipline. They are the product of extensive questionnaires administered by the principal American professional association of political scientists.

The survey of departments volume provides information on enrollment, salary trends, and similar data on political science departments in American universities. Names and addresses are included in the chairpersons directory. The *Guide to Graduate Study in*

Political Science provides a summary of graduate programs at the doctorate and master's levels. For each university the guide provides information on admission requirements, costs, financial aid, and degree requirements, and gives a description of the program and a list of faculty. The directory of members provides a listing of current political scientists, with their academic training, affiliations, and areas of specialization. In addition to this alphabetical name list, there are classifications by fields of interest, a geographical breakdown by city, and a list of women and minority members.

156. Szabo, Stephen F. **Research Support for Political Scientists: A Guide to Sources of Funds for Research Fellowships, Grants and Contracts.** 2d ed. Washington, D.C., Departmental Services Program, American Political Science Association, 1981. 126p. $6.00. ISBN 0-9156-5443-1.

For identifying and locating financial support for research in political science, this publication is an excellent starting point. The main sections cover four types of funding, both private and governmental: research fellowships, doctoral dissertation research grants, private foundation grants, and government grants. For each funding organization listed, the focus, funding amount, application procedure, contact person, and examples of funded projects are provided. There is also a bibliography of basic sources of information on research support. There is no index that cross-references from research topic to possible funding sources.

GUIDES

157. Englefield, Dermot, and Garvin Drewry, eds. **Information Sources in Politics and Political Science: A Survey Worldwide.** Boston, Butterworths, 1984. 509p. index. (Butterworths Guides to Information Sources). $69.95. LC 84-2819. ISBN 0-408-11470-3.

For the purpose of this literature review the editors have defined "politics" as "the accretion and expression of power in a society" (preface). With this broad framework this book examines reference sources and the literature of politics and political science on a worldwide basis, with the goal of providing a guide for teachers, students, librarians and others, such as journalists and politicians, who need to search for information. This work will be useful for all these users, though the contributors and their emphasis are definitely British and Western. Only English-language publications are included.

The first chapter reviews political science reference sources, including indexing and abstracting services, guides to the literature, and databases. The remaining chapters are bibliographic essays dealing with various approaches to the study of politics (such as comparative politics), or with the literature on various areas or countries. Six chapters deal with British politics, an obvious unique strength of this survey.

The brief index is only to countries and broad topics. There is no author or title access to the items cited in the bibliographic essays.

158. Goehlert, Robert U. **Political Science Research Guide.** Monticello, Ill., Vance Bibliographies, 1982. 168p. $20.00(pbk). LC 82-157151. ISBN 0-88066-152-6.

This guidebook is #P-956 of the Vance bibliographies in the Public Administration series. It identifies the principal reference sources in political science, public administration, and such related areas as international relations, military affairs, peace research, comparative politics, and American and international documentation. Major journals, databases, and general social science reference works are also listed.

This is a very comprehensive listing of current and older titles relevant to political science research. The entries are unannotated and divided into topical lists, some of which are rather lengthy. Other than the detailed table of contents, there is no author, title, or subject index. For a shorter treatment focusing on current works directly relevant to political science, Kalvelage's *Bridges to Knowledge in Political Science: A Handbook for Research* (entry 160) is useful. For another comprehensive coverage of this subject, Holler's *Information Sources of Political Science* (entry 159) has the advantage of having annotations for the entries selected.

159.   Holler, Frederick L. **Information Sources of Political Science.** 4th ed. Santa Barbara, Calif., ABC-Clio, 1986. 417p. index. $65.00. LC 85-11279. ISBN 0-87436-375-6.

With 2,423 citations, this guide provides a comprehensive, authoritative coverage of political science reference sources for researchers, librarians, and students. The fourth edition begins with a revised and expanded political reference theory to provide a systematic framework for accessing information about the political world. The annotated citations cover general sources and the basic reference titles throughout the social sciences before beginning the main section of the bibliography, which contains five sections on political science reference sources: "American Government, Politics, and Public Law;" "International Relations and Organizations;" "Comparative and Area Studies of Politics and Government;" "Political Theory;" and "Public Administration."

The descriptive annotations cover a wide range of material published through the early 1980s, including books, documents, micropublications, and online databases. There are author, title, subject, and typology indexes.

160.   Kalvelage, Carl, Albert P. Melone, and Morley Segal. **Bridges to Knowledge in Political Science: A Handbook for Research.** Pacific Palisades, Calif., Palisades Publishers, 1984. 153p. index. $6.95(pbk). LC 84-61061. ISBN 0-913530-37-9.

For undergraduates and other beginning researchers in political science, this guide can serve as an excellent handy summary of practical information and guidance. The authors, all faculty at American colleges, walk the user through the process of research and term paper preparation. There is advice on selecting and developing topics, using original and secondary sources, constructing footnotes and bibliographies and writing book reports. A major portion of the book is devoted to identifying and discussing appropriate basic reference materials.

This bibliography is a very suitable overview for students, but for a comprehensive treatment, Frederick L. Holler's *Information Sources of Political Science* (entry 159) is recommended. There is no author or title index to the reference works cited.

161.   Stoffle, Carla, Simon Carber, and Samuel Pernacciaro. **Materials and Methods for Political Science Research.** Rev. ed. New York, The Libraryworks, a division of Neal-Schuman Publishers, 1982. bibliog. $9.95(workbook). LC 78-31927. ISBN 0-918212-11-2.

The workbook format was adopted in this volume for the introduction of political science reference materials. It is intended for use in college-level bibliographic instruction situations in libraries. The goal is to allow students to locate information efficiently after their introduction to research through this course of study.

The workbook is organized into 12 chapters around various types of reference sources such as guides, bibliographies, almanacs, and encyclopedias readily found in most medium-sized college libraries. Each chapter includes objectives, a selection from three to five reference titles with annotations, and an assignment. Additional titles for each genre are listed in the appendix. The last chapter focuses on search strategy and methods of research paper preparation. There is an accompanying instructor's manual available. While intended as a tool for bibliographic instruction, the workbook can be used independently as a source of basic reference works and of information on research strategy in political science.

HANDBOOKS

162. **International Handbook of Political Science.** William G. Andrews, ed. Westport, Conn., Greenwood, 1982. 464p. bibliog. index. $55.00. LC 81-6245. ISBN 0-313-22889-2.

As an international survey of political science this handbook provides an overview in 27 of the 34 countries that the author determined had an organized discipline. While the information varies in the essays, coverage in general includes: the state of political science in 1945; the evolution of political science since then; the intellectual structure of the discipline; teaching, research, and associated activities; political science and the world of politics; and the present state and future prospects of the field.

In addition, there are essays on the international development of political science. Each chapter contains a bibliography for the country covered. Five appendixes, on the International Political Science Association and on national associations, and an index conclude this international handbook.

163. Martin, Fenton S. **Political Science Journal Information.** Rev. ed., Washington, D.C., American Political Science Association, 1984. ISBN 0-915-65461-X.

The American Political Science Association has published this guide as a means of encouraging and facilitating scholarly publication. How to prepare research for publication, which publications specialize in various subdisciplines, and what procedures journals use in reviewing and publishing manuscripts are the main points examined.

Information pages for 56 journals constitute this guide. For each title surveyed the usual directory information is provided: name, first year of publication, address, circulation, and subscription rates. Of particular value for prospective authors are the data on the subject areas of interest and the style requirements of the publishers. Authors' failure to consider these matters is the most common reason journal publishers reject manuscripts during initial screening. There are three appendixes: (1) a bibliography on publishing in the social sciences, (2) a series of suggestions for evaluating journals and preparing manuscripts, and (3) a selected list of political science journals.

JOURNALS*

164. **American Journal of Political Science.** Austin, Tex., University of Texas Press, 1957- . quarterly. $40.00/yr. ISSN 0092-5853.

As the official publication of the Midwest Political Science Association, this journal publishes articles by its members. All topics within political science are covered, with some emphasis on American government and politics. There are also articles on international and comparative politics and political philosophy or theory. There is also information on meetings and other Association news. This is a basic title for political science collections.

---

*For more detailed critiques of most of the journals in this section, see *Magazines for Libraries* by Katz (see entry 19).

165. **American Political Science Review.** Washington, D.C., American Political Science Association, 1906- . quarterly. $100.00/yr. ISSN 0003-0554.

An indispensable title for any political science collection, this journal is published by the American Political Science Association, the major professional association of the discipline. The journal represents a cross section of interests of American political scientists and features articles on American politics, international affairs, comparative politics, political theory, and research methodology. About one-third of each issue is devoted to a book review section containing over 100 titles.

166. **American Politics Quarterly.** Newbury Park, Calif., Sage, 1973- . quarterly. $80.00/yr. ISSN 0044-7803.

The scope of this journal is American government and politics, including local, state, and national levels. Political parties, public opinion, legislative behavior, administrative organization, and intergovernmental relations are topics of particular interest. Most of the articles, usually by American academic political scientists, have a marked empirical and theoretical orientation that will largely restrict their audience to professional political scientists.

167. **Annals of the American Academy of Political and Social Science.** Newbury Park, Calif., Sage, 1890- . bimonthly. $60.00/yr. ISSN 0002-7162.

Published by the American Academy of Political and Social Science since 1890, *Annals* devotes each issue to a single theme, which is examined by 8 to 12 authors chosen to provide a variety of viewpoints. Some 400 books are reviewed annually, usually within 6 months of publication. This title, plus *Foreign Affairs* (entry 177) and *American Political Science Review* (entry 165), provide comprehensive coverage of new political science literature. This is a basic title for political science collections.

168. **British Journal of Political Science.** New York, Cambridge University Press, 1971- . quarterly. $106.00/yr. ISSN 0007-1234.

This general British political science journal features articles on all subject matters within the discipline of political science, including political philosophy and political sociology. There is no official orientation or preferred research methodology. The authors are primarily British academic political scientists, though there is a strong representation of American and other English-speaking academics.

169. **Campaigns and Elections: The Journal of Political Action.** Washington, D.C., Campaigns and Elections, 1980- . bimonthly. $48.00/yr. ISSN 0197-0771.

The objective of this journal is to publish a wide range of articles on the contemporary American political scene. The authors, more often practitioners than academics, frequently present firsthand knowledge and observations. The use of television commercials in political campaigns is a typical subject of this journal, whose pragmatic approach and readable style makes it suitable for politicians and the general public as well as for political scientists.

170. **Canadian Journal of Political Science; Revue canadienne de science politique.** Waterloo, Ont., Wilfrid Laurier University Press, 1968- . quarterly. Can.$55.00/yr. ISSN 0008-4239.

The Canadian Political Science Association and the Société Québéçoise de Science Politique jointly publish this bilingual journal. About one or two articles in five are in French in each issue. Although some articles deal with international affairs or political philosophy, the majority in each issue deal with Canadian politics. The extensive book review section emphasizes titles published in Canada.

171. **Cato Journal: An Interdisciplinary Journal of Public Policy Analysis.** Ann Arbor, Mich., Edwards Brothers, 1981- . 3 issues/yr. $15.00/yr. ISSN 0273-3072.

The Cato Institute intends this journal for the general public seriously interested in public policy analysis of domestic or international matters. The United States trade policy, world debt, and the Social Security system are examples of topics recently examined in this periodical. Each issue has a theme around which the articles are planned; this permits the presentation of a variety of approaches by the authors, who are generally professors at leading American universities.

172. **Comparative Political Studies: A Quarterly Journal.** Newbury Park, Calif., Sage, 1968- . quarterly. $78.00/yr. ISSN 0010-4140.

Cross-national comparative political studies are the focus of this journal. Case studies and comparative analyses covering all areas of the world are the main interests of the authors. The articles are based on theoretical models and empirical research, especially quantitative analysis. *Comparative Politics* (entry 173) has a similar focus but places less emphasis on quantitative research, which makes it readable by a wider audience.

173. **Comparative Politics.** New York, Comparative Politics, 1968- . quarterly. $40.00/yr. ISSN 0010-4159.

The Political Science Program of the City University of New York sponsors this publication as a journal of comparative analysis of political behavior and institutions. The scope is international and the approach interdisciplinary, drawing on sociology and economics as well as on political science. The four or five scholarly articles in each issue are generally by American professors.

174. **Comparative Strategy.** New York, Crane, Russak & Co., 1978- . quarterly. $70.00/yr. ISSN 0149-5933.

The grand strategy of the major powers is the focus of this journal, which features studies done from theoretical, empirical, and historical perspectives. Within the overall concentration on strategy, there are frequent articles on nuclear deterrence, arms control, strategic intelligence, geopolitics, alliances, regional security, military organization, and related topics. The authors are government officials, military leaders, research center members, and academics.

175. **Congress and the Presidency.** Washington, D.C., Center for Congressional and Presidential Studies, 1972- . semiannual. $12.00/yr. ISSN 0734-3469.

This journal is jointly published by the Center for Congressional and Presidential Studies of the American University and the United States Capitol Historical Society. The focus here is on the presidency and Congress, the interaction between them, and the making of national policy. Both contemporary and historical topics are studied by the authors, who are generally American political science and history professors.

176. **European Journal of Political Research.** Amsterdam, Elsevier, 1973- . quarterly. $80.00/yr. ISSN 0304-4130.

The European Consortium for Political Research publishes this scholarly journal, which contains articles of a theoretical and comparative nature. The journal's strong emphasis on quantitative research focuses on European politics, such as elections or the political party system in the various nations of Europe. Occasionally there are special issues devoted to one topic.

177.   **Foreign Affairs.** New York, Council on Foreign Relations, 1922- . 5/yr. $28.00/yr. ISSN 0015-7120.

The Council on Foreign Relations, a well-respected nonpartisan organization, publishes this title, which is probably the best known of the many journals of commentary and analysis of international affairs. The particular focus is on American foreign policy. The authors are government officials and journalists as well as academic scholars. This journal provides extensive coverage of new titles on foreign affairs in its book review section and an extensive listing of relevant American and foreign documents. This is a basic title for political science collections.

178.   **Foreign Policy.** Washington, D.C., Carnegie Endowment for International Peace, 1970- . quarterly. $25.00/yr. ISSN 0015-7228.

This quarterly review of American foreign policy and international relations has become an influential factor in molding opinion among government officials, educators, and members of the press. Each issue contains about a dozen articles of commentary and analysis of American foreign policy written by academics, foreign service officers, and members of research institutes dealing with public policy.

179.   **Government and Opposition: A Quarterly Journal of Comparative Politics.** London, Government and Opposition, Ltd., 1965- . quarterly. $80.00/yr. ISSN 0017-257X.

This British journal of comparative political studies is published with the assistance of the highly respected London School of Economics and Political Science. The five or so articles in each issue typically present case studies of political matters in specific countries. These studies contribute to comparative cross-national analysis. Occasionally the entire issue of this periodical is devoted to a single theme.

180.   **History of Political Thought.** Exeter, England, Imprint Academic, 1980- . 3 issues/yr. $49.70/yr. ISSN 0143-781X.

The scope of this fairly new journal is specifically limited to political thought, especially the development of specific political theories and beliefs. This focus includes the classical names of political science, such as Plato, Rousseau, and Thomas More, and contemporary theorists, such as Karl Marx and Hannah Arendt. This British title is of interest to philosophers and historians as well as to political scientists.

181.   **Intergovernmental Perspectives.** Washington, D.C., U.S. Advisory Commission on Intergovernmental Relations, 1975- . quarterly. free. ISSN 0362-8507.

The Advisory Commission on Intergovernmental Relations (ACIR) is a permanent bipartisan body created by Congress in 1959 to monitor the operation of the U.S. federal system and to make recommendations. This responsibility has led to numerous valuable publications, including this journal which features six or seven articles in each issue written by Commission staff members. The articles have a pragmatic rather than scholarly orientation and examine such matters as taxation, mass transit, regulatory provisions, and other activities involving the interface between Washington and state and local governments.

182.   **International Affairs.** Guilford, England, Butterworth Scientific, 1922- . quarterly. $45.00/yr. ISSN 0020-5850.

This review of contemporary international affairs is published by the Royal Institute of International Affairs. It includes a variety of viewpoints, as the Institute is prohibited by its charter from adopting official positions. The authors, however, are generally from British academic and official circles. In addition to the articles, there are about 100 book reviews in each issue. This is a basic title for political science collections.

183. **International Organization.** Cambridge, Mass., MIT Press, 1947- . quarterly. $42.00/yr. ISSN 0020-8183.

The four or five articles in each issue of this journal present scholarly analyses dealing with international organizations and individual nations within the context of the international political and economic system. International relations, international political economy, and regional political and economic integration are all covered by this publication, which is sponsored by the World Peace Foundation.

184. **International Political Science Review; Revue internationale de science politique.** Guilford, England, Butterworth Scientific, 1980- . quarterly. $70.00/yr. ISSN 0192-5121.

"The creation and dissemination of rigorous political inquiry free of any subdisciplinary or other orthodoxy" is the aim of the International Political Science Association, publisher of this journal. Each issue concentrates on a specific theme with a special editor. New or controversial concepts and methodologies are frequently selected for coverage.

185. **International Security.** Cambridge, Mass., MIT Press, 1976- . quarterly. $55.00/yr. ISSN 0162-2889.

The articles in this journal, sponsored by the Harvard Center for Science and International Affairs, typically deal with theory and policy analysis in the fields of international security and strategic studies. Specific topics of interest include strategic resources, military preparedness, terrorism, and comparative politics. The authors are academics, business leaders, scientists, military and government officials, and other subject specialists. This is a basic title for political science collections.

186. **International Studies Quarterly.** Boston, Butterworth, 1957- . quarterly. $65.00/yr. ISSN 0020-8833.

International affairs, particularly matters of current political conflict or controversy, are the focus of this journal, the official publication of the International Studies Association. The articles, scholarly and often interdisciplinary, are written by specialists, academicians, government officials, business executives, and leaders in international organizations from all areas of the world.

187. **Journal of Commonwealth and Comparative Politics.** London, Frank Cass & Co., 1974- . 3 issues/yr. $75.00/yr. ISSN 0306-3631.

Each issue of this British journal contains about five scholarly articles written by American, British, or Commonwealth university professors. Generally the articles present case studies of particular situations or comparative studies examining a number of countries. Topics such as political unity in Canada or African economic integration are representative of the focus of this periodical.

188. **Journal of Conflict Resolution.** Newbury Park, Calif., Sage, 1957- . quarterly. $99.00/yr. ISSN 0022-0027.

The Peace Science Society (International) sponsors this interdisciplinary journal, drawing authors from the various social science fields and other disciplines. Its focus is on conflict within as well as between nations. The articles examine international conflict and intergroup conflict such as conflicts in labor unions or urban ghettos. The articles are theoretical and research-oriented rather than employing historical analysis or commentary on current confrontational situations. Each issue features from six to nine articles with abstracts for each.

189. **Journal of International Affairs.** New York, Columbia University, 1947- . semiannual. $22.00/yr. ISSN 0022-197X.

The School of International and Public Affairs of Columbia University publishes this review of international events. Each issue contains 10 to 15 articles, forming a forum to examine a theme of international importance "from all sides with writers from around the world." The authors are well-known scholars, business leaders, and government officials.

190. **Journal of Policy Analysis and Management.** New York, John Wiley & Sons, 1981- . quarterly. $60.00/yr. ISSN 0276-8739.

The scholarly articles in this journal of the Association for Public Policy Analysis and Management examine and analyze government programs and regulations and their operation. Many articles concentrate on the implementation of social programs or the process by which public policy questions should be decided, with a special interest in the interrelationship between political science and management science.

191. **Journal of Politics.** Gainesville, Fla., Southern Political Science Association, 1939- . quarterly. $30.00/yr. ISSN 0022-3816.

The primary subjects of this official journal of the Southern Political Science Association are American politics and government. It does not have a regional emphasis. The majority of the authors are American professors from well-known universities. There is a marked prevalence of articles based on statistical analysis. Political theory and political thought are at times included, but contemporary political issues, such as voting trends or regulatory policies, receive more attention.

192. **Journal of State Government.** Lexington, Ky., Council of State Governments, 1930- . quarterly. $40.00/yr. ISSN 0039-0097.

The Council of State Governments, an agency created and supported by state governments in the United States, publishes this journal. With a pragmatic rather than a scholarly emphasis, it examines major aspects of state problems, programs, and proposed solutions. The authors are either academics or state government officials or staff. This title would be useful for all interested in state government.

193. **Legislative Studies Quarterly.** Iowa City, Iowa, Comparative Legislative Research Center, University of Iowa, 1976- . quarterly. $48.00/yr. ISSN 0362-9805.

The encouragement of scholarly work on parliaments and legislatures is the purpose of the publisher of this journal, the Comparative Legislative Research Center. The articles concentrate on studies of legislatures throughout the world, especially comparative and cross-national articles. The Legislative Research Reports, with short abstracts of recently published research reports or articles, provide a timely means of keeping aware of current research related to representative assemblies.

194. **National Journal: The Weekly on Politics and Government.** Washington, D.C., National Journal, 1969- . weekly. $364.00/yr. ISSN 0360-4217.

The center of interest of this weekly illustrated review of current events is Capitol Hill, with particular emphasis on such topics as regulatory agencies, foreign trade, and White

House legislative strategy. In addition to 10 or 12 articles by journalists or government officials, each issue has several special report sections which provide updates on major issues and key personalities. While the major intended audience of this not inexpensive title is Washington politicians, lobbyists, congressional staff, and the like, it is suitable for others who seek a source of in-depth reporting on current Washington politics.

195.   **Orbis: A Journal of World Affairs.** Philadelphia, Foreign Policy Research Institute, 1956- . quarterly. $50.00/yr. ISSN 0030-4387.

Each issue of this international affairs journal contains articles written in an objective and pragmatic manner without a particular political orientation. The opening section is generally a forum, with several authors examining from various perspectives a topic of current interest. This journal is published by the Foreign Policy Research Institute, a nonprofit organization devoted to research and analysis of world events affecting the security of the United States.

196.   **PS.** Washington, D.C., American Political Science Association, 1968- . quarterly. $75.00/yr. ISSN 0030-8269.

The American Political Science Association (APSA), the preeminent association of the discipline, distributes *PS* to all its members. An essential source of information on the activities of the APSA and other societies in the field, *PS* contains notices on conferences, meetings, appointments, research support, and calls for papers. There are also short reports on topics of current interest, such as salaries, enrollment in political science courses, and the placement of graduates. Each issue also contains several scholarly articles.

197.   **Parliamentary Affairs: A Journal of Comparative Politics.** Oxford, Oxford University Press, 1947- . quarterly. $64.00/yr. ISSN 0031-2290.

The Hansard Society for Parliamentary Government was founded in 1944 to encourage the spread of information about the British Parliament. The primary focus of its journal is the workings of the British Parliament, with a secondary interest in parliamentary systems throughout the world. There are also some articles on comparative politics, as the subtitle indicates.

198.   **Policy Review.** Washington, D.C., Heritage Foundation, 1977- . quarterly. $15.00/yr. ISSN 0146-5945.

Each issue of this periodical contains a dozen short articles that critique or comment on American public policy, domestic and foreign. The publication is directed to members of the government and their staffs, academics, business leaders, and the general public. This review clearly reveals the political orientation of its publisher, the Heritage Foundation, a conservative think tank.

199.   **Policy Sciences: An International Journal Devoted to the Improvement of Policy Making.** Amsterdam, Elsevier, 1970- . quarterly. $90.00/yr. ISSN 0032-2687.

With a broad and indisciplinary approach, this international journal attempts to improve policymaking through the publication of research articles presenting various case studies or comparative reviews. Political science and management theories and statistical analysis are strongly represented in the articles. The authors are generally American or European academics, members of research institutes, or government officials.

200. **Policy Studies Journal.** Urbana, Ill., Policy Studies Organization, 1972- . quarterly. $45.00/yr. ISSN 0190-292X.

201. **Policy Studies Review.** Urbana, Ill., Policy Studies Organization, 1981- . quarterly. $45.00/yr. ISSN 0278-4416.

These two journals by the same publisher have the same editorial policies and publication practices. The academics, political and social scientists, and public administrators who write in them analyze the public policy of the U.S. federal government on defense, poverty, labor, education, energy, the environment, housing, employment, health, and many other issues of current interest. The issues generally contain several articles and a symposium section with five or six articles examining one topic from various perspectives. These are basic titles for political science collections.

202. **Political Behavior.** New York, Agathon Press, 1979- . $50.00(institutions); $25.00(individuals). ISSN 0190-9320.

The focus of this interdisciplinary journal is on political psychology and political sociology in order to study how political decisions are made. Motivation, attitude formation and change, group and organizational behavior, community psychology, power structures, socialization, and political participation are examples of topics investigated. Most of the authors are American university professors, and most of the articles concern contemporary American politics.

203. **Political Communication and Persuasion: An International Journal.** New York, Crane, Russak & Co., 1980- . quarterly. $66.00/yr. ISSN 0195-7473.

This journal was chosen the Outstanding New Journal of the Year in 1981 by the Association of American Publishers. Its areas of interest are mass media, propaganda, psychological warfare, and political persuasion. The authors, mainly academic political scientists or journalists, often examine governmental and nongovernmental organizations as political communicators.

204. **Political Quarterly.** Oxford, England, Basil Blackwell, 1930- . quarterly. $50.00/yr. ISSN 0032-3179.

The main interests of this British journal are current critical political and economic issues in Great Britain. Domestic matters such as education, unemployment, local government, and foreign policy issues—Britain's military defense, for instance—are examples of topics addressed in recent issues. The editors direct this journal to politicians, public administrators, and informed general readers as well as to scholars.

205. **Political Science Quarterly.** New York, Academy of Political Science, 1886- . quarterly. $35.00/yr. ISSN 0032-3195.

The Academy of Political Science has been publishing this journal since 1886 as a "nonpartisan journal devoted to the study of contemporary and historical aspects of government, politics, and public affairs." Most of the authors are American university professors who reflect a wide variety of political viewpoints. The book review section covers some 30 titles per issue. This is a basic title for political science collections.

206. **Political Studies.** Guildford, England, Butterworth Scientific, 1953- . quarterly. $59.00/yr. ISSN 0032-3217.

This general political science journal is the official publication of the Political Studies Association of the United Kingdom. Members are British university professors. While the periodical covers the entire range of political science, there is a continuing special interest in articles examining British domestic or foreign policy.

207. **Political Theory: An International Journal of Political Philosophy.** Newbury Park, Calif., Sage, 1973- . quarterly. $78.00/yr. ISSN 0090-5917.

As a journal devoted specifically to political philosophy, this title examines the history of political thought, modern political theory, the history of ideas, and normative and analytic philosophy. It is broad in scope, international in coverage, and has no official orientation. Many political viewpoints are expressed by the authors, who are mainly American university professors.

208. **Politics and Society.** Los Altos, Calif., Geron-X, Inc., 1970- . quarterly. $45.00/yr. ISSN 0032-3292.

Political and social criticism of contemporary society, often with a nonestablishment point of view, is the approach of this periodical. Each issue has four or five thought-provoking articles covering political and sociological issues. The authors are mainly American academics. The approach is philosophical analysis and commentary, not empirical research or statistical studies.

209. **Polity.** Amherst, Mass., Northeastern Political Science Association, 1968- . quarterly. $35.00/yr. ISSN 0032-3497.

Polity is the official journal of the Northeastern Political Science Association. It features articles on a wide range of topics dealing with American politics, including contemporary political issues, comparative politics, and political philosophy. In addition to five or six articles, the issues generally include a "Forum" section in which contrasting interpretations or viewpoints are featured.

210. **Presidential Studies Quarterly.** New York, Center for the Study of the Presidency, 1972- . quarterly. $12.00/yr. ISSN 0360-4918.

As the official journal of the Center for the Study of the Presidency, this title examines all aspects of the American presidency. Domestic and foreign policy, decision-making, relations with Congress, and organizational structures are some of the topics covered in the issues, each of which is usually organized around a single theme. The authors represent a broad range of views and not any official position of the Center.

211. **Problems of Communism.** Washington, D.C., U.S. Information Agency, 1952- . bimonthly. $9.00/yr. ISSN 0032-941X.

As a publication of the United States government, this journal provides analysis of contemporary affairs in the Soviet Union and other communist countries. Communist governments and political parties are examined, with considerable attention paid to internal developments, especially dissident movements. Soviet foreign policy is another major topic. The authors are generally American or European academics or government officials, especially diplomats. This periodical makes extensive use of photographs of communist societies and leaders.

212. **Proceedings of the Academy of Political Science.** New York, Academy of Political Science, 1910- . semiannual. $25.00/yr. ISSN 0065-0684.

This journal is published by the highly respected Academy of Political Science, which was founded in 1880. Each issue focuses exclusively on one topic that is considered by as many as 18 articles. The authors are usually professors from leading American universities. The Academy intends through this publication to present objective studies with a range of viewpoints rather than make specific policy recommendations. This is a basic title for political science collections.

213. **Public Administration.** Oxford, England, Basil Blackwell, 1923- . quarterly. $57.00/yr. ISSN 0033-3298.

This British journal, sponsored by the Royal Institute of Public Administration, is a leading periodical in the field. It publishes articles by scholars and practitioners. Most of the articles deal with current British public policymaking and other matters of interest to public administrators, such as privatization and the government's current policies on such policy topics as the environment. In addition to four or five articles, each issue has a book review section.

214. **Public Administration Review.** Washington, D.C., American Society for Public Administration, 1940- . bimonthly. $40.00/yr. ISSN 0033-3352.

As the publication of the American Society for Public Administration, this leading journal in the field attempts to "advance the science, process, and art of public administration." Each issue contains about five articles of a scholarly or professional nature examining current programs and problems or proposing solutions. The authors, generally members of the Society, are government administrators and officials, teachers, or researchers. Each issue has a substantial book review section. This is an essential journal for coverage of American public administration.

215. **Publius: The Journal of Federalism.** Denton, Tex., Center for the Study of Federalism, 1971- . quarterly. $30.00/yr. ISSN 0048-5950.

The Center for the Study of Federalism publishes this journal to encourage increased knowledge about federalism and intergovernmental relations. The Center is an interdisciplinary research and educational institute. Most of the articles deal with American federalism and are written by American academics. The articles in each issue are grouped around a single theme such as the federal role in urban redevelopment. There is an annual Review of the American Federal System issue.

216. **Review of Politics.** Notre Dame, Ind., University of Notre Dame, 1939- . quarterly. $20.00/yr. ISSN 0034-6705.

The articles in *Review of Politics* reflect an interest in American and international politics, political institutions, and political theory. There is a particular emphasis on historical and philosophical analysis of political questions. While some of the articles reflect a Catholic perspective or interest, this is a scholarly political journal with diversified content.

217. **SAIS Review.** Washington, D.C., Johns Hopkins Foreign Policy Institute, 1981- . semiannual. $24.00/yr. ISSN 0036-0775.

The format of this journal, published by the School of Advanced International Studies (SAIS) at Johns Hopkins University, is 15 to 20 articles on foreign policy issues with 5 or 6 focusing on a major theme. As a matter of policy, all points of opinion on the ideological spectrum are included. The authors are government officials, sometimes major figures in current or past administrations, business leaders, and university professors. This is a basic world affairs journal.

218. **State Legislatures.** Denver, Colo., National Conference of State Legislatures, 1975- . 10 issues/yr. $49.00/yr. ISSN 0196-1640.

The National Conference of State Legislatures publishes this journal as part of its objective to improve the quality and effectiveness of state legislatures. To this end, the articles critically examine policy issues among the 50 states. Existing programs are reviewed and new or innovative approaches are tracked. State tax policies and federal-state relations are topics that have been considered in recent issues. Legislative management and state politics are also subjects of regular interest.

219. **Studies in Comparative Communism: An International Interdisciplinary Journal.** Guildford, England, Butterworth Scientific, 1968- . quarterly. $43.00/yr. ISSN 0039-3592.

The School of International Relations at the University of Southern California edits this journal of comparative studies which concentrates on communism. The articles generally focus on analyses of political, economic, social, or military developments in historical or contemporary societies. Comparisons are made among communist states or between segments of divided countries such as Germany or Korea. Marxist ideology is another strong area of interest of this interdisciplinary journal.

220. **Terrorism: An International Journal.** New York, Crane, Russak & Co., 1977- . quarterly. $66.00/yr. ISSN 0149-0389.

This interdisciplinary journal examines all aspects of terrorism from many perspectives—historical, legal, sociological, psychological, philosophical, and political. The scholarly articles deal with the causes, consequences, and control of all forms of terrorist activities. The authors represent many different nationalities and ideological or political orientations.

221. **UN Chronicle.** New York, United Nations, 1964- . quarterly. $14.00/yr. ISSN 0251-7329.

With several previous titles, e.g., *UN Monthly Chronicle* and *United Nations Review*, this periodical has offered a review of current activities of the entire United Nations operation since 1964. Most of the issues focus on political news, but economic and social events are also covered. Agriculture, health, and nuclear disarmament are among other topics regularly discussed. The articles, usually short news reports, are often centered on official statements or agreements. There are numerous photographs. A useful continuing feature lists important future United Nations conferences and events.

222. **The Washington Quarterly: A Review of Strategic and International Issues.** Cambridge, Mass., MIT Press, 1978- . quarterly. $45.00/yr. ISSN 0163-660X.

The Center for Strategic and International Studies at Georgetown University sponsors this review of foreign policy and international relations. The strategic balance between East and West and the superpower rivalry between the United States and the Soviet Union form the framework for the various articles. Each issue has 12 to 15 rather short articles clustered around several related topics.

223. **Western Political Quarterly.** Salt Lake City, University of Utah, 1948- . quarterly. $25.00/yr. ISSN 0043-4078.

Although this title is the official journal of the Western Political Science Association, it is a general political science periodical without a geographical focus or any methodological or ideological restrictions on the articles published. American politics and government are the subject of many articles, but the journal has a strong interest also in international affairs, political policy, and political theory.

224. **Women & Politics.** New York, Haworth Press, 1980- . quarterly. $132.00/yr. ISSN 0195-7732.

Politics is defined very broadly in this new scholarly journal concerning the relationship of women and politics. Some of the articles deal with matters traditionally studied by political scientists, such as gender as a factor in campaigns and elections. Other matters deal with a wide range of women's studies research less directly related to politics. Most of the authors are American women professors, but men are strongly represented as well.

225. **World Affairs: A Quarterly Review of International Problems.** Washington, D.C., Heldref Publications, 1837- . quarterly. $15.00/yr. ISSN 0043-8200.

World Affairs presents articles intended to study issues currently involved in international conflict, in keeping with the objective of its sponsoring organization, the American Peace Society. International relations, foreign policy, diplomatic history, and comparative politics are the subjects most frequently addressed. The articles are written by subject specialists but are suitable for the informed layperson as well as for the scholar.

226. **World Policy Journal.** New York, World Policy Institute, 1983- . quarterly. $26.00/yr. ISSN 0740-2775.

This quarterly on world affairs and international politics can be highly recommended for the serious reading public interested in the existing and future policies of the United States government. Arms negotiations, relations with the Soviet Union, defense spending, and Central America are among the many current issues discussed in recent issues. This journal, of a liberal orientation, seeks to question existing assumptions and policies. It is a basic title for political science collections.

227. **World Politics: A Quarterly Journal of International Relations.** Princeton Pike, N.J., Princeton University Press, 1948- . quarterly. $27.50/yr. ISSN 0043-8871.

The Center for International Studies of Princeton University sponsors this journal of international relations and comparative politics. The authors are generally professors from leading American universities. A typical issue of this periodical contains five or six articles that emphasize historical and political analysis rather than commentary or efforts to influence policy formation. This is a basic title for political science collections.

ORGANIZATIONS

Encyclopedias

228. **Encyclopedia of Associations.** Detroit, Gale, 1961- . 4v. annual. price varies. LC 86-11525. ISSN 0071-0202.

Nearly 25,000 membership organizations are listed and described in this directory of nonprofit organizations, societies, unions, chambers of commerce, fan clubs, etc. Many of these are politically active. The entries are arranged in broad subject categories, including legal and governmental, public affairs, foreign interest, religious, patriotic, and others in all fields. Citations include address, telephone number, membership, chief officials, founding date, purpose, publications, and dates of conventions. Volume 1 contains national organizations of the United States plus name and keyword indexes. Volume 2 contains geographic and executive indexes. Volume 3 provides supplements to update the first volume. Volume 4 covers international organizations.

Scholarly and Professional Associations*

229. **Academy of Political Science.** 2852 Broadway, New York, NY 10025. (212)866-6752.

Founded in 1880, this organization has published the *Political Science Quarterly* (see entry 205) since 1886 and its *Proceedings* (see entry 212) since 1910. These two basic

---

* A number of details in this section are based on information in the *Encyclopedia of Associations* (see entry 228).

political science periodicals promote the Academy's goal of applying political science expertise to the solution of political and social problems.

230. **American Academy of Political and Social Science.** 3937 Chestnut St., Philadelphia, PA 19104. (215)386-4594.

The Academy has published its *Annals* (see entry 167) since 1890 as a leading political science journal devoted to promoting the progress of the discipline and the resolution of political and social problems. It is the policy of the Academy not to take sides or recommend specific policies in matters of controversy, but to present reliable information to the public.

231. **American Political Science Association.** 1527 New Hampshire Ave. NW, Washington, DC 20036. (202)483-2512.

With over 12,000 members, the APSA is the preeminent association of college and university professors of political science and others interested in the discipline. In addition to publishing *American Political Science Review* (see entry 165), a basic journal in the field, the organization serves as a clearinghouse for academics, providing such information as positions open in universities and elsewhere. The APSA holds annual conventions.

232. **American Society for Political and Legal Philosophy.** c/o Prof. Martin P. Golding, Philosophy Department, Duke University, Durham, NC 27708. (919)648-3838.

With over 500 members, this society takes an interdisciplinary approach in promoting the discussion and analysis of political and legal philosophy. Its main fields of interest are political science, the law, and philosophy.

233. **American Society for Public Administration.** 1120 G. St. NW, Ste. 500, Washington, DC 20005. (202)393-7878.

With 16,000 members, this is the major American society for public administration. It includes educators and public officials. The society promotes professional standards, ethics, education, and research in the field through conventions and publications, including the *Public Administration Review* (see entry 214).

234. **Caucus for a New Political Science.** Political Science Department, 420 W. 118th St., Columbia University, New York, NY 10027. (212)280-3644.

The Caucus supports the development of a critical and alternative political science in support of its socialist convictions. Its 800 members are mainly educators, researchers, and students. It publishes the *New Political Science.*

235. **Conference for the Study of Political Thought.** c/o Prof. A. Parel, Department of Political Science, University of Calgary, Calgary, AB, Canada T2N 1N4. (403)220-5920.

This is a professional association of about 400 academics in the disciplines of political philosophy and political theory. Its annual conferences provide a forum for discussion and the presentation of papers.

236. **International Political Science Association.** Institute of Political Science, University of Oslo, Postboks 1097, Blindern, N-0317 Oslo 3, Norway. 2 455169.

Both professional political scientists and institutions, such as libraries and professional associations, are members of this organization, founded in 1949. Its objective is to promote collaboration among political scientists throughout the world by sponsoring publications, workshops, and study groups.

237.   **National Conference of Black Political Scientists.** c/o Michael Combs, Department of Political Science, 240 Stubbs Hall, Louisiana State University, Baton Rouge, LA 70803. (504)388-2141.

In addition to the comprehensive American Political Science Association, there are a number of special interest societies for faculty and related professionals in political science. This one for black political scientists has about 400 members. It promotes research and publication in political science and increased political activity by black Americans.

238.   **Pi Alpha Alpha.** 1120 G. St. NW, Ste. 520, Washington, DC 20005. (202)628-8965.

This honor society recognizes students with superior academic achievement in public affairs and public administration programs in schools that are members of the National Association of Schools of Public Affairs and Administration.

239.   **Pi Sigma Alpha.** 4000 Albemarle St. NW, Ste. 310, Washington, DC 20016. (202)362-5342.

This honor society recognizes academic excellence in the field of political science. Founded in 1920, it now has nearly 100,000 members.

240.   **Policy Studies Organization.** 361 Lincoln Hall, University of Illinois, Urbana, Ill. 61801. (217)359-8541.

As a major organization in the public policy field, this association promotes the application of political and social science research to major policy matters through conferences and two major periodicals: *Policy Studies Journal* (see entry 200) and *Policy Studies Review* (see entry 201).

241.   **Public Choice Society.** 4400 University Dr., George Mason University, Fairfax, VA 22030. (703)951-5944.

This association of professors in the fields of political science and economics encourages the application of economic concepts and methods in political science research.

242.   **Society for Philosophy and Public Affairs.** c/o Diana Meyers, Department of Philosophy/Religion, Montclair State College, Upper Montclair, NJ 07043. (201)893-7406.

This group was founded in 1969 for philosophers, lawyers, and others interested in the relationship between philosophy and public affairs. It encourages the study of political and social matters by philosophers.

243.   **Women's Caucus for Political Science.** c/o Arlene Saxonhouse, Department of Political Science, University of Michigan, Ann Arbor, MI 48109. (313)764-6389.

This association of women political scientists promotes the status and opportunities of women as students in graduate schools and as professionals in universities and other places of employment. It holds its annual convention in conjunction with the American Political Science Association.

Research Centers*

244. **Research Centers Directory.** Detroit, Gale, 1962- . 2v. annual. $355.00/set. LC 60-14807. ISSN 0080-1518.

All major fields of research, including political science and especially government, public affairs, and international affairs, are included in this directory of nonprofit research units that are sponsored by universities or operate independently. The 11th edition (1987) contains approximately 9,200 entries. These research centers are arranged under 17 broad subject fields, with name, acronym, address, telephone number, year founded, chief officer, source of support, fields of research, and publications listed for each. There are indexes by name, acronym, institutional affiliation, subject, and special capabilities.

245. **American Enterprise Institute.** 1150 Seventeenth St. NW, Washington, DC 20036. (202)862-5800.

Since its founding in 1943, this nonpartisan organization has grown to become one of the largest (staff of 150) of the nonprofit research centers. It is an influential publisher of research studies on public policy, especially such matters as economics, government regulations, and foreign affairs.

246. **Brookings Institution.** 1775 Massachusetts Ave. NW, Washington, DC 20036. (202)797-6000.

This is a large nonprofit organization supported by endowment income, foundation gifts, and contracts. The Institution conducts research on economics, government regulations, social policy, and foreign and defense policy. The research supports an extensive educational and publications program. It is one of the best-known think tanks in Washington.

247. **Carnegie Endowment for International Peace.** 11 Dupont Cir. NW, Washington, DC 20036. (202)797-6400.

The Endowment is a nonprofit, independent research center. It is not a fund-granting organization. It sponsors research on international affairs, United States foreign policy, and related topics. Its quarterly periodical, *Foreign Policy* (see entry 178), is an influential journal of commentary and analysis of current international affairs.

248. **Cato Institute.** 224 Second Street SE, Washington, DC 20003. (202)546-0200.

All matters related to public policy, domestic or international, are studied by this independent, nonprofit research organization. It publishes the *Cato Journal* (see entry 171), which contains research articles analyzing current public policy issues.

249. **Center for International Studies.** Princeton University, Corwin Hall, Princeton, NJ 08544.

As a unit of the Woodrow Wilson School of Public and International Affairs at Princeton University, this research institute concentrates on international relations and comparative politics, especially American foreign policy, defense, diplomacy, and world political organization. The Center produces numerous publications, including the journal *World Politics: A Quarterly Journal of International Relations* (see entry 227).

250. **Center for Science and International Affairs.** Harvard University, JFK School of Government, 79 Kennedy St., Cambridge, MA 02138. (617)495-1400.

---

*A number of details in this section are based on information in the *Research Centers Directory* (see entry 244).

A part of the John F. Kennedy School of Government at Harvard University, this nonprofit research organization is active in the fields of international security, arms control, defense strategy, and comparative politics. It publishes the periodical *International Security* (see entry 185).

251. **Center for Strategic and International Studies.** 1800 K St. NW, Washington, DC 20006. (202)887-0200.

This nonprofit research institute is affiliated with Georgetown University. It supports research and publication in a wide range of international affairs, including arms control, strategic studies, political affairs, regional studies, and economics. *The Washington Quarterly: A Review of Strategic and International Issues* (see entry 222) is its periodical publication.

252. **Center for the Study of the Presidency.** 208 E. 75th St., New York, NY 10021. (212)249-1200.

In addition to providing research on all aspects of the presidency, this independent, nonprofit organization serves as a clearinghouse for information on this office. Its publications, including the periodical *Presidential Studies Quarterly* (see entry 210), examines all aspects of the American presidency.

253. **Comparative Legislative Research Center.** University of Iowa. Iowa City, IA 52242. (319)353-5040.

This unit of the Department of Political Science at the University of Iowa publishes the periodical *Legislative Studies Quarterly* (see entry 193), a major source of comparative research on parliaments and legislatures throughout the world.

254. **Council on Foreign Relations.** 58 E. 68th St., New York, NY 10021. (212)743-0400.

Founded in 1921, this is one of the best-known nonprofit research centers in the United States. Unlike most such centers, the Council has members (2,400) who provide some of its financial support. The Council studies foreign policy issues and international events. Its periodical, *Foreign Affairs* (see entry 177), is a major title among the many journals of commentary on international affairs.

255. **European Consortium for Political Research.** University of Essex, Wivenhoe Park, Colchester, Essex, CO4 3SQ, England. 206 872501.

This multinational organization was founded in 1970. Currently 136 European universities and research institutes from 15 countries are members. The Consortium promotes research and teaching in political science by sponsoring exchanges of scholars and conducting workshops. It is the publisher of the *European Journal of Political Research* (see entry 176).

256. **Foreign Policy Institute, Johns Hopkins University.** 1740 Massachusetts Ave. NW, Washington, DC 20036. (202) 785-6800.

Research at this nonpartisan research institute is mainly conducted by professors of the School of Advanced International Studies of Johns Hopkins University. It publishes the *SAIS Review* (see entry 217), which reflects its interest in foreign policy and international events and sponsors a variety of conferences and lectures.

257. **Foreign Policy Research Institute.** 3508 Market St., Science Center, Philadelphia, PA 19104. (215)382-0685.

World affairs, especially political, social, economic, and military matters affecting the security of the United States, are the interest of this independent nonprofit research institute. American foreign policy is a particularly strong focus. It publishes *Orbis: A Journal of World Affairs* (see entry 195).

258. Heritage Foundation. 214 Massachusetts Ave. NE, Washington, DC 20002. (202)546-4400.

Since its founding in 1973, this nonprofit organization has become a leading exponent of conservative thinking on current policy issues, particularly on domestic issues in the United States. It supports research, publications, conferences, seminars, and the like to disseminate its perspective. It publishes *Policy Review* (see entry 198), a quarterly periodical of comment on current policy issues.

259. Hudson Institute. 620 Union Dr., P.O. Box 648, Indianapolis, IN 46206. (317)632-1787.

As most independent nonprofit research centers, this institute is supported by foundation grants and research contracts with corporations and the government. It conducts research on public policy issues, including domestic issues such as urban government, and on international affairs, including matters related to foreign relations and national security.

260. Institute for Defense and Disarmament Studies. 2001 Beacon St., Brookline, MA 02146. (617)734-4216.

This independent nonprofit research organization studies matters related to world military and defense affairs, including armaments, military capabilities, arms control, weapons systems, and military research. In addition to publications dealing with world armaments and arms control, it publishes extensive information about the peace movement, including the *American Peace Directory* and the *Peace Resource Book* (see entry 000 for these titles).

261. Institute for Policy Studies. 1901 Q St. NW, Washington, DC 20009. (202)234-9382.

Foreign policy, military security, disarmament, Third World conditions, and human rights are among the strong interests of this nonprofit research and educational institute. Racial and ethnic minorities in the United States are another focus of research. The institute publishes extensively and supports a wide range of educational efforts ranging from public lectures to doctoral programs. These activities provide a critique of contemporary American politics and society. The institute is a prime example of an influential Washington think tank from the left of the political spectrum.

262. Institute of Public Administration. 55 W. 44th St., New York, NY 10036. (212)730-5480.

Founded in 1906, this institute provides educational and research services related to governmental problems, especially those concerning policy analysis in the fields of administration, regional planning, public finance, personnel management, and government organization. It provides research and technical assistance to local governments on these and other matters related to urban government. The Institute also produces research publications and conducts seminars.

263. Inter-University Consortium for Political and Social Research. University of Michigan, Box 1248, Ann Arbor, MI 48106. (313)764-2570.

The ICPSR is a consortium of 260 institutions that cooperate to collect and distribute social science research data. Many member universities use for research its social, political, and economic data available on machine-readable tapes. Its *Guide to Resources and Services* (see entry 24) lists all available data and services.

264. **Public Administration Service.** 1497 Chain Bridge Rd., McLean, VA 22101. (703)734-8970.

As an independent, nonprofit organization, this research and consulting service endeavors to improve public administration at the local, state, national, and international levels through studies and surveys. Charges for this research provide the support for the service's operations. Resource management, information dissemination, automation systems, and finances are typical of the topics studied by this organization.

265. **Rand Corporation, National Security Research Division.** 1700 Main St., P.O. Box 2138, Santa Monica, CA 90406. (213)393-0411.

This division is one unit of the Rand Corporation, a comprehensive nonprofit research organization. In the public policy field it conducts research in the areas of national security, defense policy, international economics, conflict, and regional studies. Its *Selected Rand Abstracts* (see entry 4) is an index to its wide array of influential research publications.

266. **World Policy Institute.** 777 United Nations Plaza, New York, NY 10017. (212)490-0010.

This institute concentrates its research on efforts to encourage peace and stable international relations. Arms control, defense expenditures, American relations with the Soviet Union, and conflict resolution are topics of particular interest. Its concerns and liberal perspective are communicated through policy recommendations and a variety of publications, including the *World Policy Journal* (see entry 226).

Associations of Government Officials*

267. **Council of State Governments.** P.O. Box 11910, Iron Works Pike, Lexington, KY 40578. (606)252-2291.

This agency serves as a representative and support organization for the 50 American states. The governing board consists of the governor and two legislators from each state. It promotes cooperation among the states and improved management by the state governments. It produces numerous important publications, including the *Book of the States* (see entry 627).

268. **International City Management Association.** 1120 G St. NW, Ste. 300, Washington, DC 20005. (202)626-4600.

The membership of this organization consists mainly of city managers, county managers, and other municipal and local government administrators. It promotes effective administration and collects extensive data on municipal government. The *Municipal Year Book* (see entry 641) is its best-known publication.

269. **National Association of Counties.** 440 First St. NW, Washington, DC 20001. (202)393-6226.

This national organization, composed of county officials grouped in 50 state branches, provides research services to its members. Its various committees study problems facing American county government.

*A number of details in this section are based on information in the *Encyclopedia of Associations* (see entry 228).

270. **National Conference of State Legislatures.** 1050 Seventeenth St., Ste. 2100, Denver, CO 80265. (303)623-7800.

State legislators and state legislative staff constitute the membership of this national organization, whose large staff provides seminars, compiles data, and monitors federal-state relations. The goal is to improve interstate cooperation and the effectiveness of state legislatures. The organization publishes the periodical *State Legislatures* (see entry 218).

271. **National Governors' Association.** Hall of the States, 444 N. Capitol, Washington, DC 20001. (202)624-5300.

The governors of the 50 states and the U.S. dependencies have formed this organization to improve state government and to have a voice in the national political process. It sponsors meetings and conventions to study issues and frequently to adopt official positions on important current issues.

272. **National League of Cities.** 1301 Pennsylvania Ave. NW, Washington, DC 20004. (202)626-3000.

This association represents cities, especially before Congress and federal agencies, develops common policies, and provides training and information to municipal officials. Its goal is to improve the effectiveness of municipal government. It publishes the *Urban Affairs Abstracts* (see entry 134) and directories of local government officials.

273. **United States Conference of Mayors.** 1620 I St. NW, Washington, DC 20006. (202)293-7330.

Membership in this organization is limited to mayors of cities of more than 30,000 population. The goals are to improve municipal government and to promote cooperation among cities and between cities and the federal government. It provides research and technical assistance to cities.

Advocate Organizations*

274. **American Civil Liberties Union.** 132 W. 43rd St., New York, NY 10036. (212)994-9800.

The ACLU has over 200 local chapters and 250,000 members nationally. It supports through publications, protests, court cases, and lobbying the civil liberties guaranteed in the Constitution, specifically freedom of speech, due process of law, and equality before the law. It is well known for defending difficult or unpopular cases.

275. **Americans for Democratic Action.** 815 15th St. NW, Ste. 711, Washington, DC 20005. (202)638-6447.

This organization is composed of citizens from all walks of life interested in promoting liberal political ideas in public policy and foreign policy matters. It attempts to influence public opinion and congressional activity, which it monitors and evaluates. Its ADA rating of congressional votes is a leading indicator of the strength of liberalism in Congress.

---

*A number of details in this section are based on information in the *Encyclopedia of Associations* (see entry 228).

276. **American Peace Society.** 4000 Albemarle St. NW, Washington, DC 20016. (202)362-6195.

Founded in 1828, this peace organization is best known for its publication *World Affairs*, a leading journal of commentary on international events (see entry 225). The society's goal is to promote the peaceful resolution of conflicts among nations.

277. **Amnesty International of the U.S.A.** 322 8th Ave., New York, NY 10001. (212)807-8400.

With over 600 local groups and a quarter of a million members, Amnesty International is a major human rights organization. It works for the release of political prisoners, the abolition of torture, and the end of the death penalty. It publishes *Amnesty International Report* (see entry 722).

278. **Common Cause.** 2030 M St. NW, Washington, DC 20036. (202)833-1200.

This organization is a broadly based national citizens' lobby working for a more open government. It supports such issues as "Sunset" laws and public financing of political campaigns. It opposes the influence of Political Action Committees. It has over a quarter of a million members in state and regional chapters.

279. **Foreign Policy Association.** 205 Lexington Ave., New York, NY 10016. (212)481-8450.

Through radio and television programs, conferences, and publications, including the excellent Headline pamphlet series, this organization attempts to promote a greater interest and understanding of international relations and foreign policy issues. It is nonpartisan in its educational activities.

280. **League of Women Voters of the United States.** 1730 M St. NW, Washington, DC 20036. (202)429-1965.

This association of women (and men) attempts to improve the political process by encouraging registration and voting and by examining public policy issues. It distributes information on issues and candidates, but it does not directly support or oppose candidates or political parties.

281. **Liberty Federation.** 2020 Tate Springs Rd., Lynchburg, VA 24501. (804)528-5000.

Formerly named Moral Majority, this conservative organization was founded by the Reverend Jerry Falwell. Though it does not endorse specific candidates, it encourages the public to register and vote for candidates who support its interpretation of traditional conservative values. Membership exceeds 4 million, with chapters in all states.

282. **National Civic League.** 55 W. 44th St., 6th Fl., New York, NY 10036. (212)730-7930.

Since 1894 this organization has supported the improvement of state and local government by serving as a clearinghouse for information and research. It sponsors the All-American Cities competition.

283. **National Women's Political Caucus.** 1275 K St. NW, Ste. 750, Washington, DC 20005. (202)898-1100.

About 75,000 individuals belong to this organization dedicated to enhancing the role and influence of women in American politics at all levels. It supports women candidates and lobbies for issues such as the Equal Rights Amendment and affirmative action.

284. **Peace Science Society (International).** School of Management, State University of New York, Binghamton, NY 13901. (607)777-4886.

Individuals and institutions throughout the world interested in promoting peace research are members of this society, which publishes the *Journal of Conflict Resolution* (see entry 188).It does not become involved in political activity, but fosters the exchange of ideas and the development of studies related to peace.

285. **People for the American Way.** 1424 Sixteenth St. NW, Ste. 601, Washington, DC 20036. (202)462-4777.

This is a large (250,000 members) organization dedicated to the support of civil liberties in American society. It is involved in educational and media activities fostering the values of pluralism, diversity, freedom of expression, and individualism. It was founded in 1980 by Norman Lear to counteract the use of religion in an antidemocratic and devisive manner for political purposes.

286. **Sane: Committee for a Sane Nuclear Policy.** 711 G St. SE, Washington, DC 20003. (202)546-7100.

Since 1957 this organization has been a leading proponent of arms reduction agreements, the reduction of military expenditures, and the conversion of defense industries into producers of consumer products. It operates through publications, meetings, media programs, and lectures.

287. **United Nations Associations of the United States of America.** 300 E. 42nd St., New York, NY 10017. (212)697-3232.

Founded in 1964, this organization now has 25,000 members in 200 local chapters. It attempts to strengthen the United Nations and its support in the United States. It promotes the annual observance of UN Day.

288. **World Federalist Association.** P.O. Box 15250, Washington, DC 20003. (202)546-3950.

Based on the principles of world federalism, this organization seeks arms control negotiations, the abolition of war, and the establishment of world institutions to handle world problems. It influences public opinion through publications, symposia, lectures, and other educational activities.

289. **World Service Authority of the World Government of World Citizens.** Continental Bldg., Ste. 1101, 1012 Fourteenth St. NW, Washington, DC 20005. (202)638-2662.

The aim of this organization of 250,000 members is the establishment of a world government committed to political, economic, and social justice. It also supports human rights, world peace, and the protection of ethnic and racial minorities.

PUBLISHERS

290. **ABC-Clio Information Services.** Riviera Campus, 2040 Alameda Padre Serra, P.O. Box 4397, Santa Barbara, CA 93140. (805)963-4221.

ABC-Clio publishes important reference books in the social sciences and history fields as well as specifically in the discipline of political science. It publishes *ABC Pol Sci: A Bibliography of Contents: Political Science and Government* (see entry 139), *Historical Abstracts* (see entry 94), and *America: History and Life* (see entry 93), three major periodical indexes. Many of the reference works cited in this volume fall into three of this publisher's major series: ABC-Clio Bibliography series, the War/Peace Bibliography series, and Clio Dictionaries in Political Science. It has also published important monographs such as Frederick L. Holler's *Information Sources of Political Science* (see entry 159) and Richard Dean Burns's *Guide to American Foreign Relations since 1700* (see entry 661).

291. **Congressional Quarterly, Inc.** 1414 Twenty-second St. NW, Washington, DC 20037. (202)887-8500.

Congressional Quarterly has long been a leading publisher of information sources about the U.S. Congress. Its publications range from the *Congressional Quarterly Weekly Report* (see entry 605), which covers each session of Congress, to *Congress and the Nation* (see entry 607), major summary volumes, each covering one administration. Congressional Quarterly also publishes reference titles dealing with other aspects of American politics. Recent titles have covered elections, federal regulations, and the presidency. *Politics in America* (see entry 612) and *Historic Documents* (see entry 543) are two important serials from this publisher.

292. **Europa Publications, Ltd.** 18 Bedford Square, London, WC1B 3JN, England.

Although the efforts of this publishing house are heavily concentrated on one series, this series is the leading example of the yearbook survey of the world's nations, a genre of reference books of central importance to political science. The basic volume of this series is the *Europa Yearbook* (see entry 365), which provides current statistical and directory information on political and economic matters. Europa has over the years supplemented this international volume with yearbooks for each of the major regions of the world. These are noted in the geographical sections of this guide.

293. **Facts on File, Inc.** 460 Park Ave. S., New York, NY 10016. (212)683-2244.

Facts on File, a subsidiary of Commerce Clearing House, is probably best known as the publisher of *Facts on File*, the weekly news digest service. It is also the publisher of numerous atlases, dictionaries, handbooks, and similar reference tools of interest to political science. Its Chronology series has provided many valuable titles, including several recent ones on communist leaders. The *World Encyclopedia of Political Systems & Parties* and the *International Almanac of Electoral History* (see entries 350 and 362) are examples of the substantial research tools now being published by this press.

294. **Gale Research Company.** Book Tower, Detroit, MI 48226. (313)961-2242.

Gale, a major publisher of reference works, is particularly well known for its important directories such as the *Research Centers Directory* (see entry 244), the *Encyclopedia of Associations* (see entry 228), and, specifically related to political science, the *Government Research Directory* (see entry 507) and the *Encyclopedia of Government Advisory Organizations* (see entry 503). Gale also publishes a number of important series, including the American Government and History Information Guide series and the International Relations Information Guide series.

295. **Garland Publishing, Inc.** 136 Madison Ave., New York, NY 10016. (212)686-7492.

Under the series title Garland Reference Library of Social Science, this publisher issues a wide range of materials in political science and related disciplines. Many of these are bibliographies or guides to resources. Several on foreign relations are cited in chapter 5 of this guide. Garland, also a major publisher in the public administration field, recently published numerous important bibliographies in its Public Affairs and Administration series.

296.   **Greenwood Press.** 88 Post Rd. W., Box 5007, Westport, CT 06881. (203)226-3571.
Greenwood is a major publisher of reference titles and monographs in political science and other disciplines. Greenwood has recently published dictionaries, handbooks, biographical directories, and the like in such political science fields as diplomatic history, urban politics, and the American left. It publishes important research compilations such as the *Biographical Dictionary of Internationalists* (see entry 338). Greenwood also publishes the annual *Index to International Public Opinion* (see entry 354) and the series Greenwood Historical Encyclopedia of the World's Political Parties.

297.   **Libraries Unlimited, Inc.** P.O. Box 3988, Englewood, CO 80155-3988. (303)770-1220.
Libraries Unlimited publishes *American Reference Books Annual*, which provides reviews of current books in political science and other fields. It also publishes Reference Sources in the Social Sciences, a series of guides to reference and information sources. It has published a number of bibliographies in recent years on such political science topics as congressional publications and state government documents.

298.   **Scarecrow Press, Inc.** 52 Liberty St., Box 656, Metuchen, NJ 08840. (201)548-8600.
Scarecrow is particularly strong as a publisher of bibliographies. Recent important political science subjects covered include the Ku Klux Klan, campaign communications, Watergate, and Lenin. Scarecrow has also published a number of valuable handbooks and indexes, such as *Unity in Diversity: An Index to Publications of Conservative and Libertarian Institutions* (see entry 535).

299.   **Scholarly Resources, Inc.** 104 Greenhill Ave., Wilmington, DE 19805. (302)654-7713.
Scholarly Resources is a major publisher of material in political science, history, law, and related fields. It has specialized in publishing source materials on microfilm, which serve as a major resource of primary documents for research. Scholarly Resources is also a publisher of important reference books. It has recently published the Guides to European Diplomatic History series and continues to publish the annual *Gallup Poll: Public Opinion* (see entry 542).

300.   **U.S. Government Printing Office.** North Capitol and H St. NW. Washington, DC 20401. (202)783-3238.
The Government Printing Office (GPO) is often called the world's largest publisher, as it produces many of the documents of the U.S. federal government. These constitute primary sources for research in political science and history. The GPO also prints many of the better-known reference sources in those fields, including the *United States Government Manual* (see entry 529), and the *Official Congressional Directory* (see entry 597). Orders for GPO publications should be directed to the Superintendent of Documents, Washington, DC 20402.

COMPUTERIZED SEARCHING

Online

Directories

301. **Computer-Readable Databases: A Directory and Data Sourcebook.** Detroit, Gale, 1976- . irreg. index. $278.00/set. LC 81-64127. ISSN 0271-4477.

This directory of databases had been edited by Professor Martha E. Williams of the University of Illinois since 1976 with various publishers. The fifth edition appeared in 1989 with Kathleen Young Marcaccio as editor. This new edition covers 4,200 databases that are in computer-readable form and publicly available. For each database the basic information includes: name, producer, frequency of update, time span covered, items added per year, corresponding print products, availability, size, language, and processor. Subject matter, indexing, data elements, and user aids are also described. There are separate indexes by subject, producer, and vendor.

302. **Database Directory.** White Plains, N.Y., Knowledge Industries, 1984- . biennial. index. $120.00. LC 85-648717. ISSN 0749-6680.

An alphabetical listing of several thousand bibliographic and factual databases constitute this directory. Such directory information as content, producer, vendor, price, and corresponding print products is included. There are vendor, producer, and subject indexes.

303. **Datapro Directory of Online Services.** Delran, N.J., Datapro, 1982- . 2v. monthly. index. $511.00/yr. LC 82-5102. ISSN 0730-7071.

This service lists and describes databases with the usual array of informational items found in database directories (see other entries in this section). There is a subject index and a glossary of terms related to databases and computerized literature searching. The greatest asset of this title is its monthly update service, since this is a rapidly changing field.

304. **Directory of Online Databases.** New York, Cuadra/Elsevier, 1979- . quarterly. index. $95.00/yr. LC 85-648743. ISSN 0193-6840.

The 1988 issue of this directory contained descriptions of 3,699 databases. The overall growth of the database industry can be understood by noting that the first issue in 1979 covered 400 databases. The alphabetically arranged entries include information on subject, producer, vendor, content, language, coverage, time span, and updating. Five indexes, including a master index of databases, database producers, online services, and vendors, provide access by subject, producer, online service (vendors), and telecommunications (listing networks that can be used to access each vendor).

305. Hall, James L., and Marjorie J. Brown. **Online Bibliographic Databases: A Directory and Sourcebook.** 4th ed. London, Aslib; distr., Detroit, Gale, 1986. 509p. index. $105.00. ISBN 0-935661-11-5.

A British directory produced by Aslib, the library association, the directory contains considerable background information on the nature of databases. There are examples of searching techniques with the various vendors. There is also a bibliography of related readings. This information is in addition to the usual directory information on databases, which forms the core of the publication.

306. **North American Online Directory.** New York, Bowker, 1985- . annual. index. $85.00. LC 85-643536. ISSN 0000-0841.

This reference tool is a directory of the major database producers, with information on their databases, vendors, and support services. There is a brief description of each database under the name of the producing organization. There are alphabetical and subject indexes to the databases. Other sections include listings and descriptions of vendors and telecommunication networks.

Database Vendors

307. **BRS.** Bibliographic Retrieval Services, Inc. 1200 Rte. 7, Latham, NY 12110. (518)783-1161.

Although BRS is a major vendor of databases, its overall catalog is smaller than DIALOG's. It does, however, include some databases not offered by DIALOG. Most of the directories listed in the preceding section list the databases offered by the various vendors. BRS offers an after-hours service known as BRS After Dark.

308. **DIALOG.** DIALOG Information Services, Inc. 3460 Hillview Ave., Palo Alto, CA 94304. (415)858-3785.

As the next section will show, DIALOG is the vendor with the largest number of social sciences databases commonly available in American libraries. For individuals or organizations with limited need, DIALOG offers Knowledge Index, a service that allows access to a selected list of databases at reduced rates.

309. **WILSONLINE.** H. W. Wilson Company, 950 University Ave., Bronx, NY 10452. (800)622-4002.

WILSONLINE, unlike the vendors in the two preceding entries, provides access primarily to databases it has developed based on its familiar print products. These databases, which cover a wide range of topics, include one in the social sciences, *Social Science Index*. For a complete list of vendors and their databases, the directories listed in the preceding section should be consulted.

Databases

310. **ASI (American Statistics Index).** Washington, D.C., Congressional Information Service, 1973- . monthly updates. DIALOG file #102; $90.00/hr.

This database corresponds to the printed *American Statistics Index* (see entry 37). It contains citations, with abstracts, to publications that contain social, economic, and demographic data collected by the United States government. Publications from more than 500 offices, including regional, regulatory, and research agencies, are included.

311. **America: History and Life.** Santa Barbara, Calif., ABC-Clio, 1964- . updates 3 times/yr. DIALOG file #38; $65.00/hr.

This database corresponds to the printed *America: History and Life* (see entry 93). It provides indexing to over 2,000 periodicals in the social sciences and the humanities—specifically history. Citations are also provided to book reviews, dissertations, and monographs.

312. **Biography Master Index.** Detroit, Gale, current edition. irregular updates. DIA-
LOG files #287, #288; $63.00/hr.
File #287 covers surnames beginning with A-L; file #288 covers M-Z. The database
provides access to biographical citations in over 700 source publications for both contem-
porary and historical persons. This database corresponds to Gale's printed *Biography and
Genealogy Master Index* (see entry 7).

313. **CENDATA.** Washington, D.C., Bureau of the Census, 1980- . daily updates. DIA-
LOG file #580; $36.00/hr.
CENDATA contains selected statistical data as well as product information and press
releases from the Census Bureau. Demographic data are available from the 1980 census
and from current reports. Other data cover agriculture, business, trade, and much more.
Though this file does not begin to span the total scope of census data, it is a convenient
method of accessing selected data otherwise scattered through a multitude of printed
sources.

314. **Dissertation Abstracts Online.** Ann Arbor, Mich., University Microfilms Inter-
national, 1861- . monthly updates. DIALOG file #35; $72.00/hr. BRS label: DISS;
$69.00/hr.
This database provides rapid access to the large, comprehensive file of American,
Canadian, and some foreign dissertations in all subject areas. Abstracts are included for
degrees granted after 1980. It includes the contents of four printed indexes: *Dissertation
Abstracts International* (see entry 36), *American Doctoral Dissertations* (see entry 35),
Comprehensive Dissertation Index, and *Masters Abstracts.*

315. **Historical Abstracts.** Santa Barbara, Calif., ABC-Clio, 1973- . updates 3 times/yr.
DIALOG file #39; $65.00/hr.
World history since 1450 is covered in this database, which corresponds to the printed
Historical Abstracts (see entry 94). Political, social, and economic history material is
indexed from over 2,000 periodicals and from dissertations and books. For American history, ABC-Clio provides *America: History and Life* in print and online versions (see entries
93 and 311).

316. **LEGI-SLATE.** Washington, D.C., LEGI-SLATE, Inc., coverage varies. daily
updates. available by annual subscription.
LEGI-SLATE provides complete descriptions and updates of congressional and regulatory activity, including full text of the *Congressional Record* and of bills and resolutions,
updates of committee schedules, reports on congressional votes, full text daily of the *Federal Register*, and profiles and ratings of members of Congress as reported in *The Almanac
of American Politics* (see entry 517). There is also a news service with articles from the
Washington Post, the *National Journal*, and the *Congressional Quarterly Weekly Report*
(see entry 605).

317. **Middle East: Abstracts & Index.** Pittsburgh, Northumberland Press, 1980- . irregular updates. DIALOG file #248; $55.00/hr.
With citations and abstracts to English-language literature drawn from books, dissertations, documents, and over 1,500 journals, this file is a major source of information
about the Middle East, including the Arab-Israeli conflict. It corresponds to the printed
publication of the same name (see entry 422). A second file on this region, *Mideast File*
(DIALOG file #249; $75.00/hr.), coproduced by the Shiloah Centre for Middle Eastern
and African Studies, Tel Aviv, Israel, is also available. It corresponds to the printed publication of the same name (see entry 423).

318. **PAIS International.** New York, Public Affairs Information Service, 1972- . monthly and quarterly updates. DIALOG file #49; $75.00/hr. BRS label: PAIS; $65.00/hr.

For topics related to public policy, business, international relations, political science, and related fields, this database offers citations to material in all formats published worldwide. Approximately 60 percent of the items were originally published in English. The 300,000 citations were drawn from the *PAIS Bulletin* and the *PAIS Foreign Language Index* (see entries 47 and 48).

319. **Social Sciences Index.** New York, H. W. Wilson, 1984- . twice weekly updates. rates vary. WILSONLINE filename: SSI.

This is the online equivalent of the Wilson printed index of the same name (see entry 50). As with all Wilson products, the frequent updating of the online version keeps it more current than the printed title and many other online products. Command and menu formats are available to accommodate both experienced and novice searchers.

320. **Social SciSearch.** Philadelphia, Institute for Scientific Information, 1972- . monthly updates. DIALOG file #7; $63.00/hr.(subscribers). BRS label: SSCI; $62.50/hr.

Like its print equivalent, *Social Science Citation Index* (see entry 000), this multidisciplinary database offers access to more than 1,500 core social science journals, plus some 3,000 others scanned for relevant articles. In addition to retrieval by keywords, authors, journal names, etc., it is possible to search an author's cited references. There are no assigned subject descriptors available for use in searching.

321. **United States Political Science Documents.** Pittsburgh, NASA Industrial Applications Center, University of Pittsburgh, 1975- . quarterly updates. DIALOG file #93; $65.00/hr.

More than 36,000 citations, with abstracts, to articles from 150 journals are included in this index, which parallels the printed index of the same title (see entry 538). Coverage includes foreign policy, international relations, public administration, world politics, political theory and methodology, and related subjects.

322. **Washington Presstext.** Alexandria, Va., Presstext News Service, 1981- . daily updates. DIALOG file #145; $69.00/hr.

With daily updates, this database provides absolutely current, as well as comprehensive, coverage of national and international news and events. It contains over 170 profiles of countries, with discussions of economic conditions, political events, and travel cautions. The file provides the complete text of White House and State Department documents, statements, and news releases. It also includes lists of foreign diplomats in Washington and American diplomats abroad.

323. **World Affairs Report.** Stanford, Calif., California Institute of International Studies, 1970- . monthly updates. DIALOG file #167; $90.00/hr.

This database provides news digests and assessments of the Soviet attitude toward world developments as reported in such Soviet sources as *Pravda, Izvestia,* and Tass. The Soviet view is contrasted with the treatment of events in Western European and American sources. Détente, disarmament, human rights, and a wide range of political, social, and economic issues are covered.

CD-ROMS

Guides

324. Nelson, Nancy Melin. **Library Applications of Optical Disk and CD-Rom Technology.** Westport, Conn., Meckler, 1987. 252p. (Essential Guide to the Library IBM PC, Vol. 8). $19.95. ISBN 0-88736-052-1.

This book is a guide to CD-ROMs, specifically the databases available using this new technology. The information here will have to be supplemented with periodical articles and information from the vendors in order to keep current with this rapidly changing field. This guide lists and describes all CD-ROM bibliographic databases available as of 1987. The contents of each database are outlined. There is also information on the availability of demo disks, equipment requirements, and the producers of the files. In general, the major advantage of CD-ROM databases is that the telephone lines and connect time charges associated with online searching are eliminated. The more time spent searching, the more economical it becomes. CD-ROM databases, however, are usually updated annually or quarterly, while online products are usually provided with monthly or even daily updates.

Databases

325. **Dissertation Abstracts Ondisc.** Ann Arbor, Mich., University Microfilms International, 1861- . annual updates. subscription: $995.00/yr.

This is the CD-ROM version of the online database mentioned in an earlier section (see entry 000). An archival disc covering 1861-1983 is available ($5,495 when introduced in 1987). The current disc, updated annually, covers from 1983 to the present.

326. **General Periodicals Index (GPI).** Foster City, Calif., Information Access, Co., 1985- . updated monthly. subscription: $12,775.00/yr.

Previously this database covered only general and business sources. The current Academic Library (AL) version includes several hundred social science titles as well as references to *Wall Street Journal* and *New York Times* articles and some humanities titles. Now, therefore, it offers basic coverage for social science topics, with coverage limited to the last three years. There is also a Public Library (PL) version, which is limited to general and business titles. This database is often referred to by its former name: *InfoTrac*.

327. **PAIS International Database.** New York, Public Affairs Information Service, 1972- . quarterly updates. subscription: $1,795.00/yr.

The CD-ROM version parallels the online format described above (see entry 318). The producers provide a user's manual and search assistance via a telephone helpline.

328. **WILSONDISC—Social Sciences Index.** New York, H. W. Wilson, 1983- . quarterly updates. subscription: $1,295.00/yr.

This is one of the many titles corresponding to its line of print indexes that the H. W. Wilson Company is now offering on CD-ROM as well as online. WILSONDISC provides various formats for browse, easy menu, and command modes of searching. A valuable feature (where available) allows the user to search WILSONDISC on CD-ROM and then to switch easily online to the same database for the latest citations.

4

Political Science — Geographic Fields

INTERNATIONAL COVERAGE

Atlases

329. Kidron, Michael, and Ronald Segal. **The New State of the World Atlas.** New York, Simon & Schuster, 1984. unpaged maps. $19.95; $10.95(pbk). LC 84-675087. ISBN 0-671-50663-3; 0-671-50664-1(pbk).

A major revision of the author's 1981 *State of the World Atlas*, this new version provides maps to illustrate worldwide political, social, and economic situations. These maps are grouped in 12 broad categories, including natural resources, economy, armaments, environment, and social indicators. The maps are colorful and well designed. There are notes discussing the maps and a list of the data sources used in their construction. Although the information here is readily available elsewhere, the visual impact of the data displayed in map format makes this atlas well worth its modest price.

330. Leonard, Dick, and Richard Natkiel. **World Atlas of Elections: Voting Patterns in 39 Democracies.** London, Economist; distr., Detroit, Gale, 1986. 159p. maps. bibliog. $85.00. ISBN 0-85058-089-7.

The purpose of this atlas is to provide detailed information on the most recent parliamentary and presidential elections in 39 major countries that have democratic systems. This goal is achieved with statistics and, especially, maps and charts that illustrate dramatically those statistics. For each country there is an outline map showing the electoral districts. Different colors and shades are used to indicate winning parties. Additional information is provided with charts.

The sections for the 39 countries all have short introductions highlighting the nation's governmental and electoral systems, the major political parties, and the date of the next election. The atlas format is particularly effective in facilitating comparative and regional political analysis. The maps make instantly apparant such issues as the geographical distribution of support for the Communist Party in India or the areas of Conservative and Labour support in the United Kingdom.

331. Wheatcroft, Andrew. **The World Atlas of Revolutions.** New York, Simon & Schuster, 1983. 208p. $19.95; $10.95(pbk). LC 83-675888. ISBN 0-6714-6286-5; 0-6714-7207-0(pbk).

This atlas, which provides 41 graphic presentations of various revolutions, is organized in 4 sections: (1) "The World Turned Upside Down," including the French Revolution; (2) "Seizure of Power," including the Paris Commune, the Russian Revolution, and other European revolutions; (3) "Freedom Now," (anticolonial revolutions); and (4) "The Revolutionary Mirage," including China, Cuba, South Africa, and revolts by black Americans.

Each of the 41 profiles contains from 3 to 5 pages of text, illustrations, and maps. The maps, which are the most valuable aspect of this volume, pinpoint such matters as the initial areas of revolutionary outbreaks, the locations of massacres or counterattacks, and the locations of major battles. Anyone interested in overviews of major revolutions will find this atlas useful.

Bibliographies

332. Blackey, Robert. **Revolutions and Revolutionists: A Comprehensive Guide to the Literature.** Santa Barbara, Calif., ABC-Clio, 1982. 488p. index. (War/Peace Bibliography Series, No. 17). $55.75. LC 82-6653. ISBN 0-87436-330-6.

"Revolution" is defined by this author as "an upheaval which calls for a fundamental change in the existing order" (introduction). The English, American, French, and Russian revolutions are the best known, but, as this work confirms, there have been a great many others in all times and places. A chronology lists revolutions from 287 B.C. to 1979. The scope is comprehensive, including political, economic, social, and religious movements. Most of the 140 revolutions covered in this work are from the 19th and 20th centuries.

After an introductory essay, "Concepts and Aspects of Revolution," the 6,000 entries cited are divided into geographical and topical chapters, e.g., "Early Modern Europe," "Asia," etc. There is a brief overview for each chapter preceding the bibliographies. Only English-language works are listed. An 18-page section of quotations concludes this comprehensive guide to information and literature on revolutions.

333. Dimitrov, Theodore D. **World Bibliography of International Documentation.** Pleasantville, N.Y., Unifo Publishers, 1981. 2v. $85.00/set. LC 80-5653. ISBN 0-89111-010-0.

This 2-volume bibliography, which covers the period 1919-1980, contains 9,600 entries. The first volume deals with international organizations, especially the United Nations and its specialized agencies. The bibliography lists monographs and periodical articles on the structure and activities of these organizations. International documentation and bibliographic control are additional subjects covered.

The second volume has as its focus politics and world affairs, with three large sections covering world politics, nuclear weapons, and peace. There are also lists of periodicals published by the United Nations and other international organizations and of periodicals that review international problems. While this bibliography certainly gathers many citations for researchers, its unannotated entries, its many excessively long, undivided sections of citations, and the inadequate four-page subject index make it difficult to use efficiently.

334. Echard, William E., comp. and ed. **Foreign Policy of the French Second Empire: A Bibliography.** Westport, Conn., Greenwood, 1988. 416p. index. (Bibliographies and Indexes in World History, No. 12). $75.00. LC 87-37566. ISBN 0-313-23799-9.

The Second Empire in France encompassed the reign of Napoleon III, which lasted from 1852 to 1879, ending with the defeat inflicted on France and Bonapartism by the Franco-Prussian War. The 4,000 citations selected for this bibliography cover all aspects of this period of French history, including the Crimean War and the short reign of the Archduke Maximilian as Emperor of Mexico. This era has recently been of increasing interest to historians and political scientists.

The compiler attempted to include all relevant primary sources, as well as secondary books, periodical articles, and dissertations written in English, French, German, Italian, and Spanish. The unannotated citations are arranged in topical chapters. There is an author index and a detailed subject index.

335. Kenworthy, Leonard S. **Free and Inexpensive Materials on World Affairs.** 7th ed. Kennett Square, Pa., World Affairs Materials, 1983. 92p. bibliog. $5.00(pbk).

Leonard S. Kenworthy, a professor of education, has been responsible for this publication since it first appeared in 1949. This seventh edition lists over 1,600 items selling for $2.00 or less. All the entries deal with world affairs. Some focus on general world problems such as energy or hunger; others deal with the United Nations or specific regions or countries. Addresses and order instructions are included for all items cited. This bibliography is particularly useful for teachers in need of inexpensive supplementary materials and for librarians seeking vertical file material.

336. Knight, David B., and Maureen Davies. **Self-Determination: An Interdisciplinary Annotated Bibliography.** New York, Garland, 1987. 254p. index. (Canadian Review of Studies in Nationalism, Vol. 8; Garland Reference Library of Social Science, Vol. 394). $40.00. ISBN 0-8240-8495-0.

The authors of this bibliography define self-determination as "the right of a group with a distinctive identity to determine its own destiny" (introduction). With this in mind, 535 entries were selected from books, parts of books, and periodical articles published during a 20-year period through 1985. The citations were drawn from many fields besides political science, such as anthropology and geography. Almost all works are in English.

The annotations average about 200 words. There is an author index; the table of contents serves as general topical index. The introduction provides a useful overview of the development of the concept of self-determination.

337. Skidmore, Gail, and Theodore Jurgen Spahn. **From Radical Left to Extreme Right: A Bibliography of Current Periodicals of Protest, Controversy, Advocacy or Dissent, with Dispassionate Content-Summaries to Guide Librarians and Other Educators.** 3d ed., rev. Metuchen, N.J., Scarecrow, 1987. 491p. index. $59.50. LC 86-29735. ISBN 0-8108-1967-8.

The third edition of this title provides annotations for 280 currently published periodicals of protest, advocacy, or dissent. Many others are listed without the content summaries. Some of these have references to annotations in earlier editions. The periodicals are grouped into 21 categories, such as radical left, Marxist-socialist left, civil and human rights, atheism, feminism, gay liberation, conservatism, and race supremacy. There are short introductory commentaries for each category. The most useful feature of this source is the 280 summaries, which offer a dispassionate picture of the content and philosophical orientation of these often controversial periodicals. Each entry also has a full bibliographic description. This bibliography is a useful supplement to William A. Katz's *Magazines for Libraries* (see entry 19), though it certainly does not cover this field comprehensively.

Biographical Sources

338.   Kuehl, Warren F., ed. **Biographical Dictionary of Internationalists.** Westport, Conn., Greenwood, 1983. 934p. index. $75.00. LC 82-15416. ISBN 0313221294.

Biographical information about approximately 600 individuals in internationalism form the content of this work. The subjects are limited to persons alive after 1800 but now deceased. The definition of "internationalist" is broad and somewhat amorphous. It includes persons who have held important positions in international organizations and those who otherwise promoted world organization and cooperation.

The entries average a page and a half in length. They include standard biographical data, but the emphasis is on the subjects' contributions to internationalism. Their ideas, activities, and writings are highlighted. Each entry includes a bibliography of work about the individual and information about the location of personal papers. The appendixes include a chronology on internationalist events and lists of internationalists by career and birthplace.

339.   Lentz, Harris M. **Assassinations and Executions: An Encyclopedia of Political Violence, 1865-1986.** Jefferson, N.C., McFarland, 1988. 275p. bibliog. index. $29.95. LC 87-46838. ISBN 0-89950-312-8.

Assassinations, attempted assassinations, and the executions of public officials, which the author believes are often merely assassinations given legal justification, are presented in chronological order, beginning with Abraham Lincoln's murder in 1865 and ending in 1986. Each entry deals with a world leader who died in a violent manner. The entries range from a sentence to a page about major figures such as Leon Trotsky and Martin Luther King. The entries contain brief factual details about the victim's death or the act of violence and about the fate of the perpetrator if known. There is an index of personal and geographic names but no link to events, movements, or groups of victims or assassins; such information would facilitate research.

Chronologies

340.   Da Graça, John V. **Heads of State and Government.** New York, New York University Press; distr., New York, Columbia University Press, 1985. 265p. $60.00. LC 85-8769. ISBN 0-8147-1778-0.

Da Graça's book presents a chronology of national leaders and heads of state. It does not attempt to be comprehensive. Only states existing today are included, and the starting point for each nation excludes early or legendary figures. The United Kingdom begins with Egbert in 827 and Japan's chronology starts in 1465. Major provinces or states are covered for some of the larger countries. Cabinet ministers and all other officials are excluded. Thirteen major international organizations have been included. In all, over 500 states or regions and 10,000 leaders are covered.

For each country the list of names includes information on dates in office, political party affiliations, and depositions, assassinations, and executions. Family relationships are indicated for dynasties. For a more exhaustive treatment of this subject, see *Regents of Nations* (see entry 341).

341.   Truhart, Peter. **Regents of Nations: Systematic Chronology of States and Their Political Representatives in Past and Present: A Biographical Reference Book.** Munich, New York. Saur, 1984- . 3v. $200.00/set. LC 85-140091. ISBN 3-598-10492-X.

When completed, this title will be the definitive reference source for identifying rulers of the world. Part 1, covering Africa and America, appeared in 1984. Part 2 will cover the remaining continents of the world; Part 3 will be an index to the set. "Thorough" is the only appropriate adjective to describe this work, which covers not only nations but also provinces, colonies, tribes, and some countergovernments. In addition to kings and presidents, tribal chiefs and pretenders are included. In some cases, all cabinet members are listed. The entry for each name includes period in office, title, place and date of birth and death, and a summary of outstanding political events. Coverage extends back to the beginnings of recorded history. The information is arranged under the current name of the nation. The text is in English and German. An earlier attempt to cover this subject definitively was the following title, which was translated from the German: Ross, Martha, and Bertold Spular. *Rulers and Governments of the World*. London, New York, Bowker, 1977/78. 3v. LC 77-70294. ISSN 0859350517.

Directories

342. Current World Leaders. Santa Barbara, Calif., International Academy at Santa Barbara, 1958- . 8 issues/yr. $135.00/yr. LC 79-640995. ISSN 0192-6802.

Published eight times a year in two complementary parts, *Current World Leaders* contains many elements which result in the publication providing a wide range of current information. The *Almanac* section is published three times a year with a listing of key officials for all independent states, international organizations, and alliances. For nations, the chief officials are listed down to the cabinet minister level. The ambassadors to the United States and the representatives to the United Nations are also included.

The Biography & News Speeches and Reports part is published five times a year. The core component is "Country Profiles," five or six pages discussing current political and economic conditions. There are also one-page biographies of world leaders, especially heads of state. Several speeches by political leaders or commentators are included in each issue. This part also serves as an update service between the *Almanac* issues. Since most of the information here is available fairly readily from other sources, the value is in convenience and in currency of information, especially as most other reference sources with similar information are annuals.

343. Ó Maoláin, Ciarán, comp. The Radical Right: A World Directory. Santa Barbara, Calif., ABC-Clio, 1987. 500p. $70.00. LC 88-101188. ISBN 0-87436-514-7.

Some 3,000 radical right organizations are listed in this international directory. While well over half of the entries for American groups appear in the *Encyclopedia of Associations* (see entry 228), listings for the foreign entries would be more difficult to locate in most reference collections. The organizations included fall into three broad categories: ultraconservatives (including libertarian and moralist groups), anticommunist (including émigré groups), and right-wing extremists (including neo-Nazi and racist groups). The organizations are listed by nation, with a short headnote on the recent history of right-wing activity in the country. For each organization, the directory provides name (in the local language and in English), address, names of leaders, membership, publications, international affiliations, and short notes on current political orientation and history.

344. Worldwide Government Directory with Intergovernmental Organizations. Bethesda, Md., National Standards Association, 1981- . annual. $250.00/yr. LC 83-641103. ISSN 0894-1521.

Heads of state, chief agency executives, cabinet ministers, ranking court officers, trade and financial officials, and heads of defense and police forces are listed in this well-organized directory. The information is arranged alphabetically for over 170 countries. Forms of address for the officials are indicated. Over 100 influential intergovernmental organizations are also included, with listings of their principal officials.

The specific feature of particular value in this publication is the inclusion of complete mailing addresses and telephone and fax numbers to facilitate direct communication. The previous title of this annual was *Lambert's Worldwide Government Directory*.

Handbooks

345. Crown's Book of Political Quotations: Over 2500 Lively Quotes from Plato to Reagan. By Michael Jackman. New York, Crown Publishers, 1982. 270p. index. $15.95. LC 82-5015. ISBN 0-517-547376.

Over 2,500 lively and not-so-lively entries constitute this specialized quotations book. The coverage is international, but the emphasis is on the classical political philosophers and current Western political leaders such as U.S. presidents. The quotations are divided into 99 subject categories, including such traditional topics as freedom, justice, and law, and other perhaps less expected ones such as advertising and work. Citations to the sources of the quotations are not given.

The author index includes brief biographical information. The detailed subject index provides a means of quickly locating specific quotations within the subject classification.

346. The Current History Encyclopedia of Developing Nations. Carol L. Thompson, Mary M. Anderberg, and Joan B. Antell, eds. New York, McGraw-Hill, 1982. 395p. illus. maps. index. $45.00. LC 82-21623. ISBN 0-07-064387-3.

Ninety-three developing countries, each with a population of over a million, are profiled in this handbook. The focus is on nations "under pressure of economic development" (preface). A more precise definition of "developing nations" is not provided.

The section for each country begins with an information box, which provides basic statistics on the nation's area, population, and other demographic and economic factors such as ethnic composition, life expectancy, and gross national product. There follows a narrative discussion of the culture, history, and politics of each country. These signed articles provide a convenient source on analysis and interpretation for those who seek a handy introductory overview that goes beyond almanac information.

347. Day, Alan J., and Henry W. Degenhardt, comps. and eds. **Political Parties of the World.** 2d ed. Harlow, England, Longman; distr., Detroit, Gale, 1984. 602p. index. (A Keesing's Reference Publication). $90.00. LC 80-83467. ISBN 0-8103-2034-7.

Arranged by country, this handbook provides concise but comprehensive coverage of over 1,000 political parties of the world. Territories are included as well as nations. Inactive and illegal or underground parties are excluded. For each country there is an introductory statement dealing with the prevailing political situation. For each party, information, as available, is provided on address, date of establishment, leadership, and history. The name is given in English and the local language. The orientation segment for each party clarifies its exact political position. This is especially useful for the varieties of Communist parties.

The appendixes contain tables listing the parties in various international groupings, e.g., Socialist, Christian Democrat, Conservative. There is an index of the parties and of individuals. The *World Encyclopedia of Political Systems & Parties* (see entry 350) is a title with similar content, but its entries, though often lengthier, are limited to major parties.

348. Degenhardt, Henry W., ed. **Revolutionary and Dissent Movements.** Harlow, England, Longman, 1988. 466p. bibliog. index. $140.00. LC 87-29718. ISBN 0-8103-2056-8.

The PLO, the Ku Klux Klan, the Helsinki Group are all in this handbook of over 1,000 illegal and dissident political organizations of all philosophical persuasions. The information is arranged by country, grouped into broad geographical divisions. For each country there is an introductory overview of the current political climate. For each movement described there is information on its history, leadership, orientation, and membership. Specific newsworthy activities are also listed. In some cases, available data permitted only very sketchy entries. There is considerable information on such topics as prominent Soviet dissidents and the various Palestinian factions.

The book concludes with a short bibliography. There are two extensive indexes of party and personal names, which facilitate the use of this source as a directory for locating obscure political movements and their leaders.

349. Degenhardt, Henry W., comp., and Alan J. Day, ed. **Treaties and Alliances of the World.** 4th ed. Detroit, Gale, 1986. 495p. maps. bibliog. index. (Keesing's Reference Publication). $95.00. LC 86-21009. ISBN 0-8103-2347-8.

The new edition of this standard reference source brings its coverage up to 1986. It provides information on various groupings of nations formally brought together by treaties or alliances. Major examples include the United Nations, NATO, the Commonwealth, and the Third World. For each entry there is a narrative section covering the historical background, plus information on membership, institutional organization, and activities. The full text, or excerpts, of the alliance or treaty is provided. Numerous maps, tables, and diagrams supplement the text. There is a subject index.

350. Delury, George E., ed. **World Encyclopedia of Political Systems & Parties.** 2d. ed. New York, Facts on File, 1987. 2v. index. $175.00/set. LC 86-29097. ISBN 0-8160-1539-2.

This political handbook profiles 178 nations and territories. The length of treatment varies from several pages to over 30. For each country the format is similar, though the profiles were written by a variety of contributors. Each opens with an overview of contemporary political and governmental systems. There is then a survey of the executive, legislative, and judicial structures. The primary focus of each chapter is the information on the nation's major political parties. Each party's history, policies, organization, membership, and leadership are reviewed. Only active parties are considered.

Each country's section ends with a discussion of its prospects for stability in the near future and a short bibliography. The contributors to this reference work were especially skillful in concisely summarizing complex matters such as the American political system or the influence of religion on politics in Northern Ireland. Consult *Political Parties of the World* (see entry 347) for a longer list of parties, with shorter entries, for each nation.

351. Gallup, George H. **The International Gallup Polls: Public Opinion 1978.** Wilmington, Del., Scholarly Resources, 1980. 510p. index. $49.50. LC 79-3844. ISSN 0195-8925.

This title supplies an international counterpart to the domestic public opinion information supplied by the Gallup organization. Coverage is limited to social and political questions of general interest, such as crime control, religious preference, and opinions on current political questions and candidates. The opinion surveys are arranged first by the topic covered and then by nation. There is a detailed index by topic and by country surveyed.

As a valuable source of world opinion, this title is comparable to the *Index to International Opinion*, though the Gallup publication has not continued to appear on a regular annual basis since the first two volumes covering 1978 and 1979.

352.   Green, Jonathon, comp. **The Book of Political Quotes.** New York, McGraw-Hill, 1982. 246p. illus. index. $8.95(pbk). LC 82-25908. ISBN 0-07-014354-9.

Over 3,000 political quotations selected from the past 2,000 years constitute the text of this inexpensive volume. The entries are organized into 20 topical chapters bearing titles such as "Hail to the Chief," "Declarations of War," and "Famous Last Words," which indicate the humorous or irreverent approach of the author. This is a very entertaining collection for browsing. It lacks a subject index to facilitate access to specific quotes, but there is a speaker index. *Crown's Book of Political Quotations* (see entry 345), with a detailed subject index, is a better source for reference use.

353.   Grenville, J. A. S. (John Ashley Soames), and Bernard Wasserstein. **The Major International Treaties since 1945: A History and Guide with Texts.** London, New York, Methuen, 1987. 528p. index. $85.00. LC 87-11250. ISBN 0-416-38080-8.

This new compilation, which covers the major international treaties since 1945, continues the coverage began in Grenville's *Major International Treaties 1914-1945*, which was originally published in 1974 and reissued in 1987. In addition to the excerpts from the text of the treaties, essays are included that place these treaties in their political and historical context. There is also a useful chronology of related events. This handbook includes peace treaties, which are omitted from an otherwise similar work by T. B. Millar (*Current International Treaties*. New York, New York University Press, 1984. 558p. $55.00. LC 84-8256. ISBN 081475392). For the treaties that established various major associations of nations, such as the United Nations, NATO, and the Commonwealth, see Degenhardt's *Treaties and Alliances of the World* (entry 349).

354.   **Index to International Public Opinion.** Westport, Conn., Greenwood, 1979- . annual. index. price varies. LC 60-643917. ISSN 0193-905X.

This annual volume has become the essential reference source for conveniently locating information on international public opinion. Included in each volume are opinion surveys from over 100 countries; these surveys cover various issues of importance to social scientists, and contemporary political, social, and economic questions of current interest.

The latest volume is divided into three categories: (1) single nation surveys, (2) multinational surveys, and (3) world surveys. Within these sections each entry lists the date and organization responsible for the survey and the sample size. The question and responses are then presented. There are three indexes: by topic, by country surveyed, and by country referenced in the surveys.

355.   **International Handbook of the Ombudsman. Volume 1: Evolution and Present Function; Volume 2: Country Surveys.** Gerald E. Caiden, ed. Westport, Conn., Greenwood, 1983. $95.00/set. LC 81-20190. ISSN 0313226857.

The institution of the ombudsman, an official designated to protect the public against the abuse of government power by public officials, is thoroughly reviewed in this two-volume set. The first volume contains a collection of essays that comprehensively survey the origins, history, and present status of the ombudsman movement. Some chapters deal with the work of ombudsmen in particular settings, such as schools, prisons, or health-care institutions. This volume also includes a model ombudsman statute and a short selected bibliography.

The second, larger volume contains surveys of over 20 countries, mostly Western democracies. There is extensive coverage of the United States, including information about the ombudsman in various states and certain cities that have strongly developed this function.

356. Janda, Kenneth. **Political Parties: A Cross-National Survey.** New York, Free Press; London, Collier Macmillan, 1980. 1,019p. $120.00. LC 80-15430. ISBN 0-02-916120-7.

The work of the International Comparative Political Parties Project is reported in this hefty volume. The report describes and analyzes 158 political parties operating in 53 countries, over half of which are Third World states. The period covered is 1950-1962, though one chapter traces the histories of the political parties through 1978.

Part 1 discusses the study's coverage, focus, and methodology. The 111 variables studied for each party deal with such concepts as issue orientation, centralization of power, and coherence. Part 2 contains data on the political parties by country. Much of the factual data in Part 2 may be used independently of the first part, though at least some familiarity with the conceptual framework of the study is necessary to understand much of the information presented. This study is particularly valuable for comparative analysis. For ready current information on political parties in a simpler context, see *Political Parties of the World* (entry 347).

357. Kurian, George Thomas. **Encyclopedia of the Third World.** 3d ed. New York, Facts on File, 1987. 3v. $175.00/set. LC 84-10129. ISBN 0816011184.

The Third World is defined in this handbook as the politically nonaligned, economically developing, and less industrialized nations of the world. The third edition contains a wide range of factual information on 126 nations. The country sections all follow the same format, beginning with a basic fact sheet (name, capital, area, head of state, languages, national holidays, etc.), followed by some 35 major categories, including weather, population, ethnic composition, freedom and human rights, foreign policy, political parties, economy, industry, education, legal system, and media. These categories are in turn each subdivided into multiple specific components that provide considerable detailed information that might be difficult to locate elsewhere, especially for the smaller nations. The preface indicates the sources of most of the statistics.

In addition to the impressive array of detailed statistics and facts, the narrative sections provide a useful level of interpretation and analysis not typically found in comparable factbooks or yearbooks. This set also includes a section on acronyms, a listing of international organizations, and a statistical appendix.

358. **Parliaments of the World: A Comparative Reference Compendium.** 2d ed. By the International Centre for Parliamentary Documentation of the Inter-Parliamentary Union. New York, Facts on File, 1986. 2v. index. $95.00/set. LC 84-26008. ISBN 0-8160-1186-9.

The information presented in these two volumes was obtained through a lengthy questionnaire sent to 142 parliaments of sovereign states throughout the world. Eighty-three replied with a mass of data to the International Centre for Parliamentary Documentation, which is a department of the Inter-Parliamentary Union. The aim of the Union is to study and contribute to the strengthening of parliamentary institutions.

This edition is arranged in 15 broad sections, which in turn are divided into 47 chapters. Each chapter deals with a major topic, such as membership, organization, operations, legislative functions, powers, and relationship with the executive authority. Within this framework, material relating to each of the parliaments is presented in tabular form in tables. These tables, with the accompanying text, facilitate comparative analysis. The introductory text for each chapter provides an overview of the subject considered. There is a great deal of specific information for each parliament concerning rules of business, quorum requirements, and other procedural matters.

359. **Political Handbook of the World.** Binghamton, N.Y., CSA Publications, State University of New York, 1989. 921p. index. $89.95. ISBN 0933199058.

This global compendium has a varied publishing history and a long record as a dependable handbook for current political and governmental data. It is now revised annually. The main section in the 1989 edition contains articles on the world's countries arranged alphabetically. Each entry provides encyclopedic information on the country's area, population, urban centers, languages, and monetary units. Included also are narrative sections on the government and political parties and summaries of foreign affairs, international disputes, and domestic issues. Major government officials are listed.

The second major segment of this handbook deals with intergovernmental organizations, from ACCT (Agency for Cultural and Technical Cooperation) to WEU (Western European Union). The purpose, history, function, activities, and leadership of each is outlined. The strength of this title, among the numerous handbooks or yearbooks covering the nations of the world, is its historical and background narratives for each country.

360. Taylor, Charles Lewis, and David A. Jodice. **World Handbook of Political and Social Indicators.** 3d ed. New Haven, Conn., Yale University Press, 1983. 2v. index. $25.00(v.1); $22.50(v.2). LC 82-40447. ISBN 0-300-03027-4(v.1); 0-300-03028-2(v.2).

This statistical compendium presents political, economic, social, and cultural data used to rank the nations of the world. Eight broad topics are covered: (1) size of government and allocation of resources, (2) popular participation and government restraints, (3) wealth and production, (4) inequality and well-being, (5) social mobilization, (6) economic structure, (7) changes within countries, and (8) changing patterns of cross-national distribution. Each topic contains numerous specific rankings, which make comparisons between states dramatic and easy. Australia, for example, appears at the top of the Civil Rights Index and Yemen at the bottom. Sweden has the highest newspaper circulation per thousand population; the United States is in 16th place. Volume 2 concentrates on political protest and government change. Both volumes have detailed subject indexes to the data included.

Sourcebooks

361. **Constitutions of the Countries of the World: A Series of Updated Texts, Constitutional Chronologies and Annotated Bibliographies.** Albert P. Blaustein and Gilbert H. Franz, eds. Dobbs Ferry, N.Y., Oceana, 1971- . 17v. + supplements. looseleaf. $1,000.00/ set. LC 76-14137. (1985 supp.). ISBN 0-379-00467-4.

The once-common difficulty of finding the texts of constitutions, especially of small or newly independent nations, ended with the publication of this set, edited by legal scholars. The constitutions of all independent nations are included. English translations have been provided if official versions in English were not obtainable. The looseleaf binders facilitate the inclusion of supplements to reflect modifications in constitutions or the removal of obsolete texts.

In addition to the constitutional documents, there are, for each country, chronologies and bibliographies that show political and constitutional developments.

362. Mackie, Thomas T., and Richard Rose. **The International Almanac of Electoral History**. 2d. ed. New York, Facts on File, 1982. 422p. $35.00. LC 82-1527. ISBN 0-87196-646-8.

The purpose of this compact sourcebook is to provide "a complete and accurate compilation of election results in Western nations since the beginning of competitive national elections" (preface). Twenty-four nations are included. Coverage for the United States begins with 1828. The sources of the statistical data are identified.

There is a chapter for each country, with a standardized format. First a headnote introduces the nation's political and electoral history. Next is a list of political parties active during the period studied. The total vote for each party and the number of seats won at each election follow. There are appendixes covering European Community elections and a table comparing basic features of election systems in the 24 nations studied.

363. **World Elections on File**. New York, Facts on File, 1987- . 2v. quarterly, with annual cumulations. looseleaf. $195.00/yr. LC 87-172839. ISBN 0-8160-1766-2.

Election statistics and related information are available in summary form in many sources, including the Europa yearbooks and the *Political Handbook of the World* (see entry 359). But for persons requiring more detailed, comprehensive coverage, this new Facts on File serial is the answer. The looseleaf format will ensure current information for the countries of the world. Election statistics, including popular vote and percentages for each candidate and party, form the core of this publication. In addition, the country profile sections contain information on major political officials, major political parties, the schedule of future elections, and an interesting commentary on the validity of recent elections and the overall openness of the political systems. This new title should soon become the standard source for election statistics.

Yearbooks

364. **Countries of the World and Their Leaders Yearbook**. Detroit, Gale, 1974- . 2v. annual. $120.00/set. LC 80-645249. ISSN 0196-2809.

This handy source for quick reference information consists of reproductions of various State Department, CIA, and other government publications. Access to these sources, which are identified in the introduction, would determine if this factbook is worth purchasing. Reprints of *Background Notes on Countries of the World* constitute the core of the work. These reports range from 3 to 15 pages. They cover in almanac format these topics: people, geography, government, economy, history, and foreign relations. Principal officials and key statistics are noted. There are also travel notes on customs, health regulations, and tourist highlights.

This core has been expanded with the addition of the following sections: a directory of officials of foreign governments; a list of American embassies, with the names of major officers; a series of descriptive papers on important international organizations; an article on world climate, with temperature and precipitation statistics for cities throughout the world; and a series of sections for travelers including health regulations and visa requirements.

365. **Europa Yearbook**. London, Europa Publications, 1959- . 2v. annual. $235.00/set. LC 59-2942. ISSN 0071-2302.

As a reliable source of current information with global coverage, the *Europa Yearbook* has built a strong reputation. It contains considerably more directory and statistical information than the two other most similar and long-established yearbooks: the *Statesman's Yearbook* (see entry 369) and the *International Yearbook and Statesmen's Who's Who* (see entry 366).

The opening segment of the *Europa Yearbook* contains information on international organizations. The history, purpose, membership, and activities of major organizations are covered in detail. Many lesser organizations have paragraph entries. The extensive information about the nations of the world is arranged alphabetically. The coverage for each country includes an introductory survey, economic statistics, and information on government, political parties, constitution, religion, press, media, trade and industry, and atomic energy. Leading government officials, cabinet ministers, and diplomatic representatives are listed. In addition to this title with global coverage, specialized Europa yearbooks for various regions of the world are noted in the appropriate chapters of the guide.

366. **International Yearbook and Statesmen's Who's Who.** Eastbrinstead, West Sussex, England, Thomas Skinner, 1953- . annual. $170.00. LC 53-1425. ISSN 0074-9621.

As currently constituted, this standard yearbook contains three sections: (1) information on international organizations, (2) extensive political and economic data arranged in entries for the countries of the world, and (3) biographical sketches. The country sections contain directory and statistical information on government officials, political life, and the economy. There are narrative descriptions of such topics as forestry, railroads, and atomic energy, depending on the nation under consideration. This segment closely resembles the *Statesman's Yearbook* (see entry 369), though this title has a greater array of economic statistics.

The biography segment provides factual paragraph-length sketches of contemporary personalities prominent in government, commerce, education, and religion. Current addresses are included.

367. **Political Risk Yearbook.** New York, Frost & Sullivan, 1987- . annual. $1,000.00. LC 86-1746. ISSN 0889-2725.

368. **Country Facts.** New York, Frost & Sullivan, 1986- . quarterly. $285.00/yr. LC 86-2204. ISSN 0889-5007.

Frost & Sullivan has developed specifically for library use, at reduced rates, the *Political Risk Yearbook*, drawn from their extensive data resources developed for multinational corporations, governmental organizations, and similar customers. The *Yearbook* contains seven regional units: Western Europe, Eastern Europe, Asia and the Pacific, Middle East and North Africa, Sub-Saharan Africa, North and Central America, and South America. The units vary from 400 to 800 pages and sell for about $350.00 individually. Together they cover 85 countries with about 50 pages per country. For each nation there is a fact sheet of political, economic, and demographic data and a list of major officeholders. Since this directory and statistical information are readily available elsewhere, the most noteworthy aspect of this publication is the series of 18-month and 5-year forecasts on economic matters (economic performance, trade policies, fiscal and monetary policies) and political matters (regime stability, opposition groups, potential turmoil).

For many users of directory and handbook data, other sources, such as the Europa yearbooks, are quite sufficient. For those requiring greater detail, and especially in-depth analyses of future political and economic conditions, the *Political Risk Yearbook* is a useful, if expensive, alternative.

For greater currency, Frost & Sullivan also offers *Country Facts*, a quarterly update of the "Fact Sheet" sections of the *Yearbook*. All of the Frost & Sullivan data are also available in various machine-readable formats.

369. **Statesman's Yearbook.** New York, St. Martin's Press, 1864- . annual. $60.00. LC 04-3776. ISSN 0081-4601.

This venerable British title continues to serve as a comprehensive compendium of current information about the nations of the world. The major section covers the countries in alphabetic arrangement. For each nation there is material on area, population, constitution, defense, economy, energy, trade, communications, justice, education, religion, and welfare. Major governmental officials are noted. The entries tend to emphasize narrative background information over statistics, in contrast to the generally similar *International Yearbook and Statesmen's Who's Who* (see entry 366). The *Statesman's Yearbook* is the only title in the yearbook genre to provide directory and statistical information for the provinces and states of major nations such as India, Germany, and the United States. This is by far the least expensive title in the international handbook category.

There is also a segment that describes the history, structure, purpose, membership, and activities of international organizations. A short bibliography follows both sections.

370. **The World Factbook.** Central Intelligence Agency. Washington, D.C., GPO, 1981-. annual. $10.00(pbk). LC 81-641760. ISSN 0277-1527. S/N 041-015-00153-1.

The Central Intelligence Agency annually produces this handbook of the world based on data provided by the CIA and other federal agencies. For each country there are one or two pages of data on that nation's geography, people, government, economy, communications, and defense forces. These main headings are subdivided into over 50 elements, such as ethnic groups, political leaders, exports, major industries, and military budget. Principal officeholders and key statistics are noted. The statistics are detailed and current. There are also 13 colored maps.

As a straightforward factbook this title compares very favorably with many much more expensive, commercially published handbooks and yearbooks. It is softbound and contains no narrative commentary or analysis. Gale has reprinted this title as: *Handbook of the Nations: A Brief Guide to the Economy, Government, Land, Demographics, Communications, and National Defense Establishment of Each of 223 Nations and Other Political Entities.* 7th ed. Compiled by Directorate of Intelligence, U.S. Central Intelligence Agency. Detroit, Gale, 1987. 290p. maps. $80.00.ISBN 0-8103-1593-9; ISSN 0194-3790.

371. **A Yearbook of the Commonwealth.** London, HMSO, 1969- . annual. £16.95. LC 85-19420. ISSN 0084-4047.

This yearbook provides a wide variety of standard handbook and directory information for the many members of the worldwide Commonwealth of Nations. For each member country there are lists of major government officials and diplomatic representatives. There are also digests of constitutions and notes on current constitutional developments. Each year features a review of historical, social, and political events. This title, while providing some additional detail, largely duplicates the information available in commercially produced yearbooks such as the *Europa Yearbook* (see entry 365).

AFRICA

Bibliographies

372. **Africa Bibliography.** Manchester, England, Manchester University Press, 1984- . annual. index. price varies. LC 86-656067. ISSN 0266-6731.

The International African Institute sponsors this annual bibliography, which covers books, periodical articles, essays, and chapters from edited volumes. An extensive list of periodicals is scanned. The unannotated entries are arranged into two main sections. The first contains general articles for the continent as a whole. The second section is arranged first by country and then by topic. There are author and subject indexes. Politics and public administration, government, and law are the topics directly related to political science, with many others pertaining to other social sciences and to history.

373. **Bibliographies on South African Political History.** O. Geyser, P. W. Coetzer, and J. H. Roux, eds. Boston, G. K. Hall, 1979-1982. 3v. (Bibliographies and Guides in African Studies). price varies. LC 78-11842. ISBN 0-8161-82442-2 (v.1); 0-8161-8245-0 (v.2); 0-8161-8518-2 (v.3).

Together the three volumes of this set provide an essential element in the bibliography on the Republic of South Africa and its role in southern Africa. The first volume is a register of the more important collections of primary sources. For each collection there is a brief description of the collection and collector, with an inventory of the major materials and a note on accessibility.

Volume 2 constitutes a bibliography of secondary materials. The monographs are arranged in 20 subject chapters. Volume 3 uses the same classified arrangement for periodical articles, with an emphasis on South African periodicals. The entries in these volumes are not annotated.

374. **A Bibliography for the Study of African Politics.** Waltham, Mass., Waltham Press, 1973-1983. 3v. $15.00(v.1&2); $18.00(v.3). ISBN 0-918456-10-X (v.1); 0-910456-11-8 (v.2); 0-918456-17-9 (v.3).

The first volume of this bibliography, published in 1973, was prepared by Robert B. Shaw and Richard L. Sklar. Volume 2, by Alan C. Soloman, extended coverage of the bibliography to include the period 1971-1975. Each of these volumes contained about 3,950 entries.

The latest volume, prepared by Eric R. Siegel, adds 5,720 entries, bringing coverage up to 1980. All aspects of political science have been included. Politically relevant material in related social science fields was selectively added. Newspaper articles, government documents, and unpublished material were excluded. Most of the items cited are in English, though there are many works in other European languages, especially French. In terms of organization, all three volumes have the material divided into two sections, one covering general works for all of Africa and the other dealing with works on particular countries. There is an author index but no subject classification or index. This is an unfortunate omission because the country bibliographies, some as long as 30 pages, are simply undivided alphabetical lists.

375. **A Current Bibliography on African Affairs.** Washington, D.C., African Bibliographic Center, 1962-1967; Westport, Conn., Greenwood, 1968-1972; Farmingdale, N.Y., Baywood Publishing, 1973- . quarterly. $75.00/yr. LC 78-123. ISSN 0011-3255.

This quarterly publication, which combines features associated with a periodical index and a bibliography of books, provides a key source for African studies. Journal articles, books, and government documents are included in this annotated listing of current materials covering all aspects of African political, economic, social, and cultural life.

The source material is international and African in scope, though mainly English-language. The citations are grouped under broad subject headings or by country. There is an author but no subject index. In addition to the bibliography, each issue generally contains a brief book review section and one or two bibliographic essays.

376. Scheven, Yvette. **Bibliographies for African Studies 1970-1986.** London, Hans Zell, 1988. 550p. index. $125.00. LC 88-44704. ISBN 0905450337.

The 1988 volume cumulates 3 previous volumes, providing convenient coverage for 16 years, 1970-1986. This guide to bibliographies is limited to the fields of the social sciences and humanities. All African states, except the Arab countries of North Africa, are included. English and French are the primary languages. Afrikaans and Arabic were omitted. Bibliographies appearing as books, parts of edited volumes, or periodical articles are included.

The entries contain full bibliographic information and short content annotations. They are arranged in two main sections: topical and geographical by country. Author, title, and detailed subject indexes complete this excellent guide to bibliographies on Africa.

377. Schoeman, Elna. **The Namibian Issue, 1920-1980: A Select and Annotated Bibliography.** Boston, G. K. Hall, 1982. 247p. map. index. $40.00. LC 81-20311. ISBN 0-8161-8437-2.

The controversy and conflict over Namibia, or South West Africa, has generated a considerable literature in the 60 years covered in this bibliography. The 1,489 entries have brief but informative content annotations. All viewpoints are included, though this bibliography was based mainly on material publicly available in the Republic of South Africa. The various aspects of the Namibian question are covered in 16 subject chapters. In addition to the bibliography, there is a useful map and a comprehensive chronology of the conflict. Author and subject indexes provide good access to all citations.

Biographical Sources

378. Gastrow, Shelagh. **Who's Who in South African Politics.** Johannesburg, Ravan Press; distr., New York, Harper & Row, 1987. 365p. $19.95. LC 88-154398. ISBN 0869753363.

This collection of biographical sketches attempts to cover the major personalities who were "setting the political pace" (preface) in South Africa. A few other persons with a long history of political involvement are also included. Although the coverage is not comprehensive or beyond debate, this directory does provide biographical information on individuals not otherwise readily found in most reference collections. Of the 112 individuals portrayed, about half are white and half black, colored, or Indian.

Each of the profiles, which vary from one to five pages, includes a photograph and contains personal and career information gathered from books, periodicals, newspapers, and, in some cases, interviews. The sources are cited at the end of each entry. The introduction provides an overview of South Africa's political system and major political parties. There are also lists of relevant acronyms, government officials, and leaders of major political parties. This title has been updated frequently in recent years.

379. Kirk-Greene, Anthony H. M. **A Biographical Dictionary of the British Colonial Governor,** Volume 1: **Africa.** Stanford, Calif., Hoover Institution Press, 1980. (Hoover Press Bibliographical Series). 320p. $31.95. LC 80-8194. ISBN 0-8179-2611-9.

Biographical information for nearly 200 "men who built, ruled, and developed" (foreword) the British colonies in Africa is offered in this first volume of a projected series on British colonial governors. Although the colonial era is past, the author points out that these individuals played a major role in laying down the foundations of postcolonial Africa. The book covers 20 African former colonies from 1875 to 1968.

The brief biographical data includes family background, birth and death dates, marriage and children, education, career, governorships, honors, publications, clubs, recreations, and retirement dates. There is also a list of selected sources of biographical information. The introduction discusses each of these elements and includes observations such as the prevalence of public school education and membership in certain clubs. There are also several tables whose tabulations also contribute to providing a composite picture of the British colonial governor. An appendix contains a chronological list of the governors by country.

Dictionaries and Encyclopedias

380. Phillips, Claude S. **The African Political Dictionary.** Santa Barbara, Calif., ABC-Clio, 1984. 245p. maps. bibliog. index. (Clio Dictionaries in Political Science, No. 6). $30.00; $10.75(pbk). LC 82-24353. ISBN 0-87436-036-6; 0-87436-040-4(pbk).

As with the other titles in the Clio Dictionaries in Political Science series, this dictionary is intended to supplement a college course. The entries have been grouped in 10 subject chapters paralleling topics in a course on African political systems. Examples of these chapters are: "Land and People," "Colonial Perspective," "Government Institutions and Processes," and "Africa and the World." Within these categories, terms dealing with major events, political theories, and governmental structures—the "language of African political systems" (preface)—are defined. The definitions are followed by a "Significance" paragraph of interpretation. Each statement ranges in length from a few sentences to a page or more.

There is a general subject index for using this dictionary as a reference source without relation to its classroom function. In addition to the definitions, there are several maps, a short bibliography, and a series of charts and tables in the appendixes.

Handbooks

381. **Africa Guide 1984.** 8th ed. Saffron Walden, England, World of Information; distr., New York, Ballantine Books/Random House, 1984. 382p. illus. maps. $24.95(pbk). LC 77-642758. ISBN 0-345-31300-3.

Although not as well known in the United States as other similar handbooks, this title offers a narrative overview with a British perspective, in addition to generally available directory and statistical information. This eighth edition, which contains 14 articles by specialists, deals with Africa in general and with certain specific countries such as South Africa and Nigeria. Economic conditions receive major attention along with political events.

The major segment of this handbook consists of country-by-country chapters providing key economic statistics and basic information on the government. There is also travel information. Each chapter ends with a narrative description of the country's current economic and political situation. This is a good choice, especially for the price, for basic handbook information and an overview of Africa and its nations.

382. Cook, Chris, and David Killingray. **African Political Facts since 1945.** New York, Facts on File, 1983. 263p. bibliog. index. $19.95. LC 81-17514. ISBN 0-87196-381-7.

As a compilation of information, this handbook covers the political history of modern Africa from 1945 to 1980. The first section, a chronology of major events, is followed by listings of governors and heads of state for all African countries and sections identifying and describing parliaments and constitutions, political parties, and trade unions. Conflicts and foreign affairs are similarly reviewed. After these narrative sections, two statistical chapters cover demographic and economic data. The final segment features paragraph-length biographies of about 150 leading politicians.

The index, which resembles a table of contents, does not facilitate the use of this volume as a fact-finding source. The assembled facts, however, are presented in well-organized chapters for a handy overview of African politics.

383. Davies, Robert H. **The Struggle for South Africa: A Reference Guide to Movements, Organizations, and Institutions.** London, Zed Books; distr., Totowa, N.J., Biblio Distribution Center, 1985. 2v. illus. map. index. $29.50. LC 85-119546. ISBN 0862322243 (v.1), 0862322251(pbk); 0862322561 (v.2), 086232257X(pbk).

This handbook was written at the Centre of African Studies at Eduardo Mondlane University, Mozambique, for Mozambican officials and others on the frontline of the struggle against South Africa and its policy of apartheid. It is written from an anti-South African and Marxist perspective, which is evident in the overview of South African history and the introductory notes to the chapters.

The main section of this reference source is a guide to organizations, movements, institutions, and groups in South Africa supporting or attacking the existing apartheid structures. The analysis of the purpose and activities of the entries is followed by a bibliography for further reading. This is a useful handbook for the study of the South African liberation movement.

384. Omond, Roger. **The Apartheid Handbook.** 2d ed. New York, Penguin, 1986. 232p. $5.95(pbk). LC 86-19830. ISBN 0-14-022749-0.

This inexpensive volume is a useful guide to the racial policies known as apartheid in the Republic of South Africa. It was written by a South African journalist using a question-and-answer format. The entries are grouped around various subject categories such as pass laws, housing, sex, censorship, and the homelands. The questions are used to address these issues, with historical information, current status reports and statistics, and individual examples provided. Though somewhat unusual, and at times even contrived, the format is an effective vehicle for making readily available considerable information on the harsh impact of apartheid in daily life.

Sourcebooks

385. Marshall, H. H. **From Dependence to Statehood in Commonwealth Africa: Selected Documents, World War I to Independence.** Dobbs Ferry, N.Y. Oceana, 1980- . 4v. $40.00/vol. LC 80-10407. ISBN 0379203480(v.1).

To date, two volumes, Southern Africa (volume 1) and Central Africa (volume 2), have been published in this set, which will have four volumes to include all of the former British colonies in Africa. The documents reproduced all date from World War I up to, but not including, independence. The documents, reproduced in full or in part, are arranged by country.

A nearly 100-page introduction provides a historical overview. This is a convenient source of primary documents dealing with the important period leading up to independence for Commonwealth Africa.

Yearbooks

386. **Africa Contemporary Record: Annual Survey and Documents.** New York, Africana Publishing, 1968/69- . annual. $249.50. LC 70-7957. ISSN 0065-3845.

This annual volume contains three distinct parts. The first is a series of some 20 essays on current issues, especially international political relations regarding Africa, but also including economic and environmental matters. The second part is a country-by-country review of events of the year. The narratives here run to about 10 pages per country, covering political, economic, and social events. The third part contains the text of selected documents by such organizations as the Organization of African Unity. This source is an excellent, albeit not inexpensive, means of reviewing current events in Africa. The index facilitates looking up specific information.

387. **Africa South of the Sahara.** London, Europa Publications, 1981- . annual. $145.00. LC 78-112271. ISSN 0065-3896.

Now in its 17th edition, this annual handbook, one in the Europa regional handbook series, is a leading source of current directory and statistical information as well as narrative background commentary. The volume begins with 20 5- to 10-page essays of general information for the continent south of the Sahara, including history, economic trends, social conditions, and religions. There is also a bibliography of current periodical articles concerning Africa. The second part of this handbook is a directory of regional organizations such as the African Development Bank and the Franc Zone.

Part 3, the core of this publication, consists of the country surveys, with one section for each sub-Saharan nation. The country chapters contain short narrative sections on such topics as physical features, population, recent history, and the economy. There then follows a very detailed statistical section with demographic and economic data. The final section is a directory of government, financial, and media institutions with their major personnel. Each country section ends with a select bibliography.

AMERICAS

Bibliographies

388. **Bibliographic Guide to Latin American Studies.** Boston, G. K. Hall, 1978- . annual. Price varies. LC 79-643128. ISSN 0162-5314.

This major research tool is a series of annual bibliographies based on two of the largest Latin American collections in the U.S.: the University of Texas at Austin and the Library of Congress. Each annual bibliography includes books, serials, and nonbook materials cataloged (regardless of publication date) during the previous year. All subjects for all countries of Latin America are covered, with many languages represented. The entries, which are not annotated, are arranged in one alphabetical sequence that provides access by main entry, title, series title, and subject. The *Catalog of the Latin American Collection of the University of Texas at Austin* (G. K. Hall, 1969, plus supplements) provides coverage for earlier periods.

389. Delorme, Robert L. **Latin America 1979-1983: A Social Science Bibliography.** Santa Barbara, Calif., ABC-Clio, 1984. 225p. index. $45.00. LC 84-11133. ISBN 0-87436-394-2.

This volume extends coverage to 1983 for the author's earlier work, *Latin America: Social Science Information Sources, 1967-1979*, published in 1981. This bibliography contains a total of 3,728 citations for books, book chapters, and periodical articles. Most of these are in English, though some are in Spanish or Portuguese.

The unannotated entries are listed under the names of the countries covered, with "Bibliographies and Reference Sources" the only topical division. Within these broad categories the entries are divided into books and articles, then listed alphabetically. Detailed author and subject indexes provide access to specific citations or topics.

390.   Gutierrez, Margo, Milton Jamail, and Chandler Stolp, comps. **Sourcebook on Central American Refugee Policy: A Bibliography with Subject and Country Index.** Austin, Tex., Central American Refugee Policy Research Project, Lyndon B. Johnson School of Public Affairs, and the Central American Resource Center, 1985. 69p. (Special Project Report). $7.50(pbk). LC 85-168403. ISBN 0-89940-851-6.

This bibliography is a product of a research seminar at the Lyndon B. Johnson School of Public Affairs at the University of Texas. It is concerned with the Central American refugee policy, including the policies of the United States and Central American governments, the sanctuary movement, and the issue of political asylum.

The 800 unannotated entries cover books; newspaper, journal, and magazine articles; government documents; reports; bulletins; and unpublished papers. Much of this material reflects a Texas focus, with many citations to Texas newspapers. There are also many newspaper articles in Spanish cited from Mexican dailies.

The entries are grouped by publication format into four alphabetical lists. Access is by a subject and country index, which in many cases has long lists of references.

391.   **Latin American Politics: A Historical Bibliography.** Santa Barbara, Calif., ABC-Clio, 1984. 290p. index. (Clio Bibliography Series, No. 16). $60.50. LC 83-27156. ISBN 0-87436-377-2.

As with many other bibliographies produced in the Clio Bibliography series, this title draws on the publisher's existing history database, *America: History and Life* (see entry 311), to provide a specialized listing. This one includes over 3,000 citations drawn from 2,000 periodical titles. The journal articles, which appeared from 1973 through 1982, cover all aspects of Latin American and Caribbean political history and politics. No books are cited.

The entries are arranged by country, with chronological subdivisions for the larger nations. Each citation has a paragraph-length signed abstract of the article's content. There is an author index and a detailed subject index.

392.   Nordquist, Joan, comp. **Current Central America-U.S. Relations.** Santa Cruz, Calif., Reference and Research Services Press, 1987. 68p. (Contemporary Social Issues, No. 5). $15.00(pbk). ISBN 0-937855-09-X.

Current Central American-United States relations are the subject of this bibliography, which is part of the publisher's Contemporary Social Issues series. A more topical subject could hardly be found at this time, since Honduras, Nicaragua, and El Salvador have all been center stage recently. The bibliography covers publications for the period 1982-1986, with the items arranged by country.

The books, periodical articles, and government documents that are included in the selection reflect a balanced spectrum of opinion and sources on controversial matters such as the Contras. In addition to the citations, this book includes a list of organizations and periodicals involved in the study and coverage of current events in Central America.

393a. Reid, Darrel R. **Bibliography of Canadian and Comparative Federalism, 1980-1985.** Kingston, Ont., Institute of Intergovernmental Relations, Queen's University, 1988. 492p. index. $39.00(pbk). ISBN 0-88911-451-X.

393b. Reid, Darrel R. **Bibliography of Canadian and Comparative Federalism, 1986.** Kingston, Ont., Institute of Intergovernmental Relations, Queen's University, 1988. index. $49.95. LC 89-93063. ISSN 0-88911-458-7.

These bibliographies, sponsored by the Institute of Intergovernmental Relations of Queen's University, focus on "items that relate to the interaction of the various levels of government" (introduction) within Canada. Other references deal with the theory of federal government or comparative federalism, so that these works can be useful to others than those interested strictly in Canada.

The 1980-1985 bibliography contains 3,418 citations from books, parts of books, periodical articles, and government documents. Both English- and French-language titles are included. These works conclude with author, title, and subject indexes.

394. Weinrich, Peter. **Social Protest from the Left in Canada, 1870-1970.** Toronto, University of Toronto Press, 1982. 627p. $65.00. C82-094366-5. ISBN 0-8020-5567-2.

This massive bibliography of over 6,000 selected citations concentrates on materials published in English or French on social and political protest from the left in all areas of Canada except Quebec, for which other bibliographies already exist. The author has included communist, socialist, labor, pacifist, native rights, feminist, and other movements that advocated social or political reform which, "by the standard of the time ... seemed revolutionary, drastic, or far-reaching" (preface). The entries are arranged alphabetically within sections arranged by the year of publication. Very brief annotations and location codes for Canadian libraries are included. There are detailed author and title indexes but no subject index.

Biographical Sources

395. **Biographical Dictionary of Latin American and Caribbean Political Leaders.** Robert J. Alexander, ed. New York, Greenwood, 1988. 509p. index. $75.00. LC 87-17805. ISBN 0-313-24353-0.

This convenient information source contains 450 biographical sketches of political leaders from Latin America and the Caribbean. The signed entries, by well-known scholars, range from a paragraph to over a page and end with bibliographies. Many of the 19th- and 20th-century political figures are well known, but the inclusion of others who are less well known or from less-studied Caribbean and Central American states adds greatly to the worth of this book. There is a subject/name index and a listing of names by country.

396. Camp, Roderic A. **Mexican Political Biographies, 1935-1981.** 2d ed., rev. and expanded. Tucson, University of Arizona Press, 1982. 447p. bibliog. $35.00. LC 82-2768. ISBN 0-8165-0743-0.

The second edition of this title provides biographies of over 1,300 Mexican public figures, living or deceased, who were prominent in Mexican political life from 1935 to mid-1980. The biographical sketches, arranged alphabetically by surname, contain the following elements: date and place of birth; education; elective, party, and governmental positions; interest group activities; personal and family data; and military experience. Sources of additional information are listed.

The appendixes contain lists of high government officeholders and political party leaders from the 1930s. Though the biographies are brief, this is a good source of biographical information on individuals not generally included in other reference works.

397. **Who Is Who in Government and Politics in Latin America; Quién es Quién en la Política y los Gobiernos de América Latina.** Bettina Corke, ed. New York, Decade Media Books, 1984. 509p. index. $65.00. LC 84-070526. ISBN 0-91365-02-4.

This title is a bilingual edition, really two books in one, with the information presented in both English and Spanish. More than 1,000 entries are included, drawn from the Spanish-speaking countries of Latin America plus Brazil and Haiti. The small non-Spanish-speaking Caribbean islands were omitted. Argentina, Mexico, and Brazil have the most entries.

The biographical entries are arranged by country, then alphabetically. There is a useful list of the biographees at the beginning of each chapter. For each subject there is information on occupation, career, education, publications, honors, memberships, and hobbies as well as name, address, and date of birth. No effort was made to go beyond these facts. Most of the information was obtained through questionnaires filled out by the subjects. While there is much useful information about individuals who might be difficult to locate readily in other sources, this edition is by no means comprehensive or definitive. Many prominent politicians and other influential persons are absent or have very abbreviated coverage.

Dictionaries and Encyclopedias

398. Rossi, Ernest E., and Jack C. Plano. **The Latin American Political Dictionary.** Santa Barbara, Calif., ABC-Clio, 1980. 261p. index. $25.25. LC 79-27128. ISBN 0-87436-302-0.

This dictionary is arranged topically to facilitate its use as a supplement to a course in Latin American politics. The chapters can also provide an overview of each topic for the more casual reader. The detailed index also permits use of this dictionary as a reference guide to the specialized language of Latin American politics.

The 10 subject chapters include "Geographic, Population, and Social Structure"; "Political Parties, Pressure Groups, and Elections"; and "United States-Latin American Relations." These and others cover comprehensively Latin American politics. Each term has a definition plus a "Significance" statement of interpretation. Most terms are in English, but Spanish and Portuguese are used when there is no English equivalent.

Handbooks

399. **The Atlas of Central America and the Caribbean.** The Diagram Group. New York, Macmillan, 1985. $50.00. LC 85-676696. ISSN 0-02-908020-7.

Although there are maps throughout this volume, it is best considered a handbook of general information because the maps are not detailed or a major source of information.

The volume begins with a series of one- or two-page overviews of the geography, climate, and animal life of the area, followed by several pages of historical information. There are similar short profiles of the population, economy, and current political situation in the region.

The main section consists of a series of country-by-country profiles for each nation. These range from two pages for the smaller Caribbean islands to five pages for a major state like Honduras. Each unit features a narrative summary of the history, culture, and economy of the country, plus tables and charts to provide statistical and directory information. This title provides useful overviews of the countries of the region for those who want the basic facts and statistics outlined in a concise manner with brief narrative commentaries.

400. **Latin American Political Movements.** Ciarán Ó Maoláin, ed. New York, Facts on File, 1985. 287p. index. $24.95. ISBN 0-582-90275-4.

The aim of this political handbook is to provide in a compact form basic information on political parties, guerrilla movements, pressure groups, and other organizations, legal and illegal, involved in the 20 Latin American republics and Puerto Rico.

The alphabetical arrangement of the volume is by country name. Each of the 21 sections begins with a brief background section of 1 or 2 pages outlining the country's political history, constitutional background, and the results of recent elections. The parties and movements are then listed alphabetically by name. Information on the group's leaders, orientation, history, politics, membership, and publications is then provided. The volume ends with a name index.

401. **Political Parties of the Americas: Canada, Latin America, and the West Indies.** Robert J. Alexander, ed. Westport, Conn., Greenwood, 1982. 2v. index. (Greenwood Historical Encyclopedia of the World's Political Parties). $65.00/set. LC 81-6952. ISSN 0-313-21474-3.

The chapters of this handbook consider the political parties of the nearly four dozen countries and territories of the Americas, specifically Canada, Latin America, and the Caribbean. The United States (but not its territories) is omitted, as it has been covered in *Political Parties and Civic Action Groups* by Edward L. Schapsmeier (see entry 528).

Each country-by-country section begins with a historical overview of the political history of the nation and ends with a short bibliography. The sketches of the political parties, which vary in length from a paragraph to several pages, include information on founding date, political orientation, electoral history, and leadership. Active and inactive parties are included. The descriptions are listed under the English names of the parties, with cross-references from local languages. The appendixes contain a chronology of major political events for each country and a genealogy showing party splits and mergers. There is also a table arranging the parties from the various nations into ideological or interest groups.

Indexes

402. **Hispanic American Periodicals Index.** Los Angeles, University of California, Latin American Center, 1978- . annual. $235.00. LC 86-644301. ISSN 0361-5502.

Hispanic American Periodicals Index, or *HAPI* as it is sometimes called, is an annual index of nearly 250 journals published throughout the world that regularly contain articles on Latin America. Leading journals treating Hispanics in the United States are also indexed. Journals published in Latin America are indexed in full. Items from other journals are included only if they concern Latin America or Hispanics in the United States. A key to periodicals lists all titles indexed. All disciplines of the social sciences and humanities are included.

The index is divided into three sections: subject, author, and book reviews. Most subject headings are in English except for terms for which there is no commonly accepted translation. Although annual publication eliminates this title as a source for very recent material, it is the standard source for comprehensive coverage of the retrospective periodical literature.

Yearbooks

403. Canadian Annual Review of Politics and Public Affairs. Toronto, University of Toronto Press, 1960- . annual. index. $50.00. LC 72-96452. ISSN 0315-1433.

Since 1960 this publication has featured a series of essays that reviews the year's political and economic developments in Canada. The signed essays are for the most part written by Canadian academics. In recent years the essays have been grouped under four topics: parliament and politics, the provinces, external affairs and defense, and the national economy.

In addition to the essays, each volume contains a chronology of major Canadian events, obituary notes, and subject and name indexes. This review may be read for a narrative introduction or overview of current Canadian political affairs or used as a reference source for specific information.

404. Latin America and Caribbean Contemporary Record. New York, Holmes & Meier, 1983- . annual. index. $255.00. LC 83-646058. ISSN 0736-9700.

Beginning with the volume for 1981/82, this series provides a well-organized review of current events in Latin America. The first part provides authoritative essays on important political, economic, and social questions. The second segment consists of a series of country-by-country reviews of recent events in narrative format. The third part consists of the texts of documents and treaties. The fourth part is an extensive set of historical and current statistics of demographic and economic data. The final section provides an annotated bibliography of recent books on Latin America. There are name and subject indexes. This annual is an excellent, albeit not inexpensive, source for reviewing current events in Latin America or for searching for specific information.

405. South America, Central America, and the Caribbean. London, Europa Publications, 1986- . annual. $90.00. LC 87-643803. ISSN 0268-0661.

With this first edition, this title joins the other Europa regional handbooks as excellent sources of current directory and statistical information. Following the series format, this volume begins with a group of essays on major background matters for the entire region, such as economic conditions or the struggle between dictatorship and democracy. The first part also contains a select bibliography and a list of research institutes studying Latin America and the Caribbean. The second part is a directory of regional organizations such as the Organization of American States.

The main section consists of a country-by-country series of articles on each nation of the region. Each section begins with several short essays on history and the economy. These are followed by a statistical section with detailed demographic, economic, and social data. Finally, there is a directory of major governmental, business, and media organizations with their key personnel. Each country survey ends with a brief bibliography.

ASIA AND THE MIDDLE EAST

Atlases

406.   Dempsey, M. W., comp. **Atlas of the Arab World.** New York, Facts on File, 1983. illus. maps. $16.95. LC 83-1725. ISBN 0-87196-138-5.

This slim atlas gathers together in 2 sections a wide variety of current information on 21 Arab countries. The first part consists of 38 double-page maps that portray graphically basic geographic, political, historical, and social information on the Arab world. Weather patterns, health conditions, literacy, the rise and fall of empires, and the prevalence of television sets are examples of the topics profiled. The maps are colorful and easy to interpret. Each has a legend specifying the symbols or color combinations used. These maps provide a strong visual interpretation of many dimensions of the region.

Following the maps there is a narrative section with one- to two-page descriptions of each Arab nation. There are information boxes and factual and statistical facts on the geography, population, government, history, and economy for each of the 21 states.

Bibliographies

407.   Chen, Gilbert F. **Nationalism in East Asia: An Annotated Bibliography of Selected Works.** New York, Garland, 1981. 170p. index. (Canadian Review of Studies in Nationalism, Vol. 1; Garland Reference Library of Social Science, Vol. 70). $22.00. LC 80-8490. ISBN 0-8240-9497-2.

Nationalism in East Asia (China, Japan, Korea) is the subject of this bibliography. The author believes that nationalism has been "the principal motivating force behind most revolutions and modernizing experiments in East Asia" (introduction). The volume does not attempt to be a comprehensive listing of titles, but is rather a carefully selected group of 288 works fully annotated by the author, who is a distinguished Sinologist, or by other specialist.

The citations are grouped into six chapters, dealing with (1) Chinese nationalism, (2) communist nationalism in China, (3) nationalism in China in Chinese and Japanese sources, (4) nationalism in Japan, (5) nationalism in prewar Japan, and (6) Korean nationalism. About half the works cited are in English and about half in Asian languages, which makes this bibliography appropriate for undergraduate students and advanced researchers alike. The bibliographies are introduced by essays that provide historical orientation. There is a subject index.

408.   Kuniholm, Bruce R. **The Palestine Problem and United States Policy: A Guide to Issues and References.** Claremont, Calif., Regina Books, 1986. 157p. map. bibliog. index. (Guides to Contemporary Issues, No. 5). $18.95; $11.95(pbk). LC 85-25687. ISBN 0-941690-18-0; 0-941690-19-9(pbk).

With two very distinct components, this title usefully and objectively deals with two complex issues: the Palestinian problem and American policy in the Middle East. The first part provides in essay form an overview of the Israeli-Palestinian conflict and American involvement. The second segment is a bibliography of some 564 citations to books, documents, and periodical articles published in the last decade. The entries are grouped under topical categories which have brief introductory notes. Only English-language works are included. There is an author index but no title index.

409. Mahler, Gregory S. **Bibliography of Israeli Politics.** Boulder, Colo., Westview Press, 1985. 133p. index. (Westview Special Studies on the Middle East). $18.00. LC 85-3229. ISBN 0-8133-7042-6.

The author, a scholar of Israeli politics, has attempted in this bibliography to provide students and researchers with a listing of current resources to support the study of Israeli politics. The volume contains 1,419 citations from English-language documents, articles, and books published in the United States, Europe, and Israel. Though obviously not comprehensive, this bibliography is a good starting point and certainly covers the material most students would want on the modern state of Israel.

As the compiler notes in his introduction, some of the political topics he includes in this bibliography are common to all nations. Political structures, political behavior, parties, voting patterns, and pressure groups fall in this category. Other topics are uniquely Israeli or at least characteristic of the political system of that nation. Religion, Zionism, military security, immigration, and social tension are examples of those topics selected by the author. The unannotated entries are arranged alphabetically by author, with a detailed keyword subject index.

410. **The Middle East in Conflict: A Historical Bibliography.** Santa Barbara, Calif., ABC-Clio, 1985. 302p. index. (Clio Bibliography Series, No. 19). $60.50. LC 83-27530. ISBN 0974363810.

For the purpose of this bibliography the term "the Middle East" is defined to include the Fertile Crescent (including Turkey, Cyprus, and Lebanon), the Arabian Peninsula, North Africa, and the Northern Tier (Iran, Afghanistan, and Pakistan). The first five chapters cover general (multinational) articles and such topics as international relations, trade, the world wars, and intraregional conflicts. This last chapter provides coverage of the Arab-Israeli conflict and the Gulf War between Iran and Iraq. The remaining chapters are arranged by region and then by individual nation. Despite the title, all aspects of political, historical, and economic studies are included. The 3,258 entries represent articles published between 1973 and 1982. Each citation has a short abstract of contents. These entries were culled from the ABC-Clio database covering 2,000 journals published in 90 countries and 40 languages. There are comprehensive author and title indexes.

Biographical Sources

411. Shavit, David. **The United States in the Middle East: A Historical Dictionary.** Westport, Conn., Greenwood, 1988. 441p. bibliog. index. $65.00. LC 87-24965. ISBN 0-313-25341-2.

This reference source attempts to provide, in several components, an overview of United States involvement in the Middle East. The principal section constitutes a biographical dictionary of Americans involved in the Middle East, with data on places of service, occupation, and education. Where available, sources of additional information and writings are identified.

Other features include a chronology of American involvement in the Middle East and an annotated list of institutions or organizations in the region founded or supported mainly by Americans.

Dictionaries and Encyclopedias

412. Bilancia, Philip R. **Dictionary of Chinese Law and Government.** Stanford, Calif., Stanford University Press, 1981. 822p. index. $45.00. LC 73-80618. ISBN 0-8047-0864-9.

Political and legal terms used by Chinese writers are difficult for Western students. In these fields, flucuations in revolutionary policy add to difficulties caused by changing forms of romanization and the basic ideographic nature of the Chinese language.

This dictionary provides 25,000 words and phrases in use from 1933 to 1977 in the fields of political science, government, and law. Each of these Chinese terms, arranged by the Wade-Giles romanization, has the Chinese character, the English translation, and the definition. There are numerous examples and cross-references. This is an essential tool for anyone approaching the study of political science in Chinese.

413. Rolef, Susan Hattis, ed. **Political Dictionary of the State of Israel.** New York, Macmillan, 1987. 351p. maps. $45.00. LC 87-14161. ISBN 0-02-916421-4.

The signed entries in this dictionary vary in length from one-paragraph definitions to essays approaching 10,000 words. The authors, all Israelis, include scholars, politicians, and journalists. The Israeli perspective is visible but the approach is temperate. The entries cover major issues, events, institutions, and individuals associated with Israeli history and the Arab-Israeli conflict. This is a well-written source for brief but informative considerations of terms such as "the Law of Returns," "the Six-Day War," and "the Occupied Territories," which are so frequently found now in the news or in political writings.

414. Shimoni, Yaacov, ed. **Political Dictionary of the Arab World.** New York, Macmillan, 1988. 520p. $50.00. LC 87-12392. ISBN 0-02-916422-2.

As a concise political compendium on the Arab World (the Middle East and Arab Africa), this dictionary or handbook offers concise information on the present and recent past. It is a revised and updated edition of the *Political Dictionary of the Middle East in the 20th Century* published in 1972. This book, however, excludes coverage of Israel, which has been treated in the *Political Dictionary of the State of Israel* (see entry 413).

The 550 alphabeticlly arranged entries cover such topics as nations, peoples, political movements, leaders, ideologies, wars, alliances, and treaties. The unsigned articles vary in length from a paragraph to several pages. This dictionary was compiled under the auspices of the University of Tel Aviv; all the contributors are Israeli. The editor has striven, generally successfully, to present "as accurate and objective picture as possible" (foreword), while realizing that complete objectivity is not possible.

415. Ziring, Lawrence, and C. I. Eugene Kim. **The Asian Political Dictionary.** Santa Barbara, Calif., ABC-Clio, 1985. 438p. maps. index. (Clio Dictionaries in Political Science, No. 10). $37.50; $15.00(pbk). LC 85-5994. ISBN 0-87436-386-3; 0-874360369-1(pbk).

416. Ziring, Lawrence. **The Middle East Political Dictionary.** Santa Barbara, Calif., ABC-Clio, 1984. 452p. illus. maps. bibliog. index. (Clio Dictionaries in Political Science, No. 5). $37.50. LC 82-22673. ISBN 0-87436-044-7.

Both these dictionaries, like all titles in the Clio Dictionaries in Political Science series, are designed to supplement college courses. The definitions are therefore not in one alphabet but divided into topical chapters that would parallel a course. The Middle East dictionary includes chapters on Islam and on Israelis and Palestinians. The Asian title has more general chapters, such as "Militarism and the Armed Forces," and "Modernization and Development." Both have chapters on political geography and international relations and diplomacy.

The approximately 300 definitions in each dictionary cover events, movements, conflicts, ethnic groups, institutions, and terms drawn from theoretical political science as well as the language of the political processes in the various nations covered. Each definition also has a "Significance" paragraph of interpretive information. Each volume includes a detailed index, which permits ignoring the topical arrangement and using the dictionaries as direct sources of reference information.

Directories

417. Fenton, Thomas P., and Mary J. Heffron, comps. and eds. **Middle East: A Directory of Resources.** Maryknoll, N.Y., Orbis, 1988. 144p. illus. index. $9.95(pbk). LC 88-1603. ISBN 0-88344-533-6.

The Middle East is defined in this work to include five Arabic nations of Africa north of the Sahara: Egypt, Libya, Tunisia, Algeria, and Morocco. The compilers have sought out resources on this Middle East that would provide alternatives to traditional American or Western conceptions or that reflect an interest in fundamental changes in existing political and cultural policies and practices in the area.

The resources are grouped in five chapters, covering organizations, books, periodicals, pamphlets and articles, and audiovisuals. In each case the major annotated entries are supplemented by unannotated lists. There is also a list of university centers with Middle East outreach programs and a list of religious organizations interested in the area. This tool concludes with separate indexes by organization, individual, title, area, and subject.

Handbooks

418. Bacharach, Jere L. **A Middle East Studies Handbook.** Seattle, University of Washington Press, 1984. 160p. $20.00; $9.95(pbk). LC 84-2225. ISBN 0295961384; 0295961449(pbk).

This very useful handbook covers the period from A.D. 570, the birth of Muhammad, to the early 1980s. The 10 chapters constitute an excellent ready reference companion for students and scholars of the Middle East. The guide begins with a section on the transliteration of Islamic names. The Islamic calendar and regional dynastic genealogical tables follow. There is a chronology of historical events and a 50-page historical atlas with black-and-white maps. There is also a gazetteer and glossary. In short, probably most of the background information a beginning or advanced scholar would need to assist in the study of the Middle East has been conveniently gathered into this one volume.

419. Benvenisti, Meron. **The West Bank Handbook: A Political Lexicon.** Boulder, Colo., Westview Press, 1987 (c1986). 228p. maps. $28.00. LC 86-50979. ISBN 0-9133-0473-3.

The intention of this handbook is to acquaint Israelis and Arabs with "the facts as well as the institutions and agencies affecting their daily lives" (foreword). This has been achieved, in an apparently even-handed manner, in this glossary of social, economic, institutional, legal, cultural and political terms related to the West Bank.

Political parties, refugee camps, Israeli settlements, demographic patterns, terrorism, and land seizure are some of the topics covered in entries, which vary from a paragraph to a page long. The entries provide historical and statistical information. A detailed alphabetic table of contents and cross-references serves as an index. Fifteen black-and-white line maps follow the text.

420. **The Middle East: Political and Economic Survey.** Peter Mansfield, ed. 5th ed. Oxford, New York, Oxford University Press, 1980. 579p. index. $35.00. LC 79-23699. ISBN 0-19-21851-1.

The term "Middle East," which admits various interpretations, has been defined in this source to include Saudi Arabia and the smaller Arabian countries, Egypt, Sudan, Iraq, Jordan, Syria, Lebanon, Iran, and Israel. There is a lengthy introductory chapter discussing the land, people, history, politics, and economic conditions of the region. Another chapter deals with the oil industry in the Middle East.

The core of this handbook is the series of 10 chapters on the individual countries covered. The information is presented in textual analysis rather than in reference book format. There is a statistical appendix which covers population, a few basic economic indicators, and statistics on oil. This work is valuable for background reading; for ready reference use for facts, names, and statistics, Europa's *The Middle East and North Africa* is preferable (see entry 424).

421. **Political Parties of Asia and the Pacific.** Haruhiro, Fukui, editor-in-chief. Westport, Conn., Greenwood, 1985. 2v. index. (Greenwood Historical Encyclopedia of the World's Political Parties). $165.00. LC 84-19252. ISBN 031321350X(set).

This third guide to political parties in the Greenwood series covers Asia and the Pacific in separate chapters for the 41 nations or territories of the region. The chapters vary in length from 2 pages to 185 (for Japan). Some 70 academic political scientists, about half from the region, contributed to this work.

Each nation's chapter begins with a brief summary of political history and a selective bibliography. The sketches of the parties include information on founding date, political orientation, electoral history, and leadership. The appendixes contain a chronology of major political events for each country and a genealogy showing party splits and mergers. There is also a table that arranged the parties from the various nations by ideological or interest types. The detailed index includes people, organizations, and events.

Indexes

422. **The Middle East: Abstracts and Index.** Pittsburgh: Northumberland Press, 1978- . annual. index. $200.00. LC 78-645468. ISSN 0162-766X.

All fields of interest and disciplines, with the sole exceptions of science and medicine, are covered in this comprehensive index. Politics and related fields, such as history and economics, form a major emphasis. In addition to some 1,500 journals scanned for entries, this index also includes books, dissertations, government documents, research reports, speeches, statements, and interviews. Primarily English-language material is included. All entries except brief news articles have detailed content abstracts.

The entries, grouped in 21 sections, cover general considerations, the Arab-Israeli conflict, the Arab World, OPEC, Islam, and the nations of the Middle East. Within each chapter the citations are arranged by format with journal articles first. There is an author and detailed subject index. The only drawback to this well-prepared index to current Middle East literature is the lag in publication: the 1982 volume appeared in 1986. This index is also available online through the DIALOG database service (see entry 317).

423. **Mideast File.** Shiloah Center for Middle Eastern and African Studies, Tel-Aviv University. Oxford, England; Medford, N.J., Learned Information, 1982- . quarterly. $450.00/yr. OC 82-64511. ISSN 0262-818X.

This bibliography identifies and indexes current political, economic, military, historical, and social material published about Middle Eastern countries. Books, journal articles, selected newspaper articles, government publications, research reports and speeches are included. The books and book reviews are simply cited; the other material is abstracted.

While the majority of the publications cited are in English, a significant minority are in Arabic or Hebrew, with English abstracts, which provides a range and diversity of coverage not found in other indexing or abstracting services covering the Middle East. The arrangement is by country and major subject, with the author and permuted subject index providing access to specific citations. This index is also available online through the DIALOG database service (see entry 000).

Yearbooks

424. **The Middle East and North Africa.** London, Europa Publications, 1948- . annual. $135.00. LC 79-3102. ISSN 0076-8502.

425. **The Far East and Australasia.** London, Europa Publications, 1969- . annual. $155.00. LC 74-47170. ISSN 0071-3791.

As with the other Europa regional handbooks, these titles are an excellent source of current directory, statistical, and background information. Following the series format, these titles begin with a group of essays on major background matters for the entire region, such as economic conditions or efforts toward regional cooperation. Key issues – for example, the Israeli-Arab conflict – are given continuous coverage over the years. This first section also contains a list of research institutes and a bibliography of periodical articles. The second part is a directory of regional organizations, including ANZUS, OPEC, and the Arab League.

The main section of these handbooks is a country-by-country series of articles on each nation of the region. Each survey begins with several short essays on history and the economy. These are followed by a statistical section with detailed demographic, economic, and social data. Finally, there is a directory of major governmental, business, and media organizations with their key personnel. Each country survey ends with a brief bibliography. A condensed version of the regional handbooks, containing the statistical and directory information, can be found in the publisher's basic handbook, the *Europa Yearbook* (see entry 365).

426. **Middle East Contemporary Survey.** New York, Holmes & Meier, 1977- . annual. $198.00. LC 78-64825. ISSN 0163-5476.

Beginning with 1976/77, this series has provided a well-organized review of events in the Middle East. The first part of each year's volume contains authoritative essays on important current political, economic, and social questions. The Arab-Israeli conflict has been a prime topic over the years.

The second major segment consists of country-by-country reviews of recent events in all the nations of the region. These surveys of current developments include detailed economic and demographic statistics and much directory information. This annual provides a well-documented review, although in some controversial matters its relationship to Israel (it is published in cooperation with the Shiloah Center of Tel Aviv University) is evident.

BRITAIN

Atlases

427. Kinnear, Michael. **The British Voter: An Atlas and Survey since 1885.** New York, St. Martin's Press, 1981(c1968). 172p. maps. bibliog. index. $40.00. LC 81-40533. ISBN 0-312-10563-0.

The social, economic, and organizational background of British politics is examined in this volume, which covers the peroid 1885 to 1979. The format consists of a series of maps showing the boundaries of the parliamentary constituencies. Each of the 26 general elections held in Britain since 1885, and certain other elections such as the 1975 Common Market Referendum, is depicted. The maps illustrate the changing strengths of the major political parties and the voting patterns of constituencies. There are also maps illustrating social variables such as the voting patterns of occupational and religious groups. The volume also includes a bibliography, an index of constituencies, and a general index.

428. Waller, Robert. **The Atlas of British Politics.** Dover, N.H., Longwood, 1985. 205p. maps. bibliog. $29.00. $13.95(pbk). LC 84-675366. ISBN 0-7099-3608-7; 0-7099-3609-5(pbk).

This atlas is intended to serve as a complementary volume to the author's handbook, *Almanac of British Politics* (see entry 438) or to be used independently as a graphic interpretation of the political geography of the United Kingdom. The statistical bases for this atlas are the 1981 census and the 1983 general elections. There are 13 sections of maps, beginning with a national section and continuing with 12 sections covering the regions of England plus Scotland, Wales, and Northern Ireland. Each section is accompanied by a short narrative description of the information displayed on the maps.

All the clear and easy-to-read maps use the parliamentary constituencies as the basic units for each region. The maps deal first with the support for each major political party in the elections. Social variables, such as the percentages of middle class workers, owner-occupied homes, and car ownership, follow. Educational qualifications and, for Northern Ireland, religious affiliation are also portrayed. This atlas graphically presents the geographic and social divisions in British political life.

Bibliographies

429. Bryan, Gordon, comp. **Scottish Nationalism and Cultural Identity in the Twentieth Century: An Annotated Bibliography of Secondary Sources.** Westport, Conn., Greenwood, 1984. 180p. index. (Bibliographies and Indexes in Law and Political Science, No. 1). $35.00. LC 84-4667. ISBN 0-3132-3998-3; ISSN 0742-6909.

Although Scotland's ancient sovereignty ended in 1707 with the union with England, the sense of separateness has continued and inspired a considerable literature. This bibliography covers both the political and cultural aspects of Scottish nationalism.

The 894 citations were all selected from twentieth-century writings appearing in Great Britain or the United States. They include books, book chapters, articles, and pamphlets. Most of the entries, especially for the journals, are from Scottish publications. The bibliography is divided into 10 chapters, which provide a survey of general publications and bibliographies and then various chronological periods and specific topics such as the language question. Each item is accompanied by a short annotation. The appendixes offer lists of leading Scottish nationalist journals and of cultural and political organizations.

430. Goehlert, Robert U., and Fenton S. Martin. **The Parliament of Great Britain: A Bibliography.** Lexington, Mass., Lexington Books/D. C. Heath, 1983. 209p. index. (The Lexington Books Special Series in Libraries and Librarianship). $29.95. LC 82-47920. ISBN 0-669-05700-2.

The compilers have attempted to produce a comprehensive bibliography on "the history, development, and legislative process of Parliament" (introduction). All other peripheral or related matters concerning politics and government in general have been excluded. The day-to-day proceedings of Parliament have also been omitted. Within this framework, citations have been limited to English-language material published in the last 100 years. The bibliography attempts to include all scholarly research in books, journals, dissertations, and essays, and selected documents.

The nearly 3,000 unannotated entries are arranged in topical chapters: "Origins and Development," "Legislative Process," "House of Commons," "House of Lords," "Organization," "Pressures on Parliament," "Reforms," "Parliament and the Electorate," "Members," and "Support and Housing of Parliament." In addition, there is a chapter on reference works, an author index, and a detailed subject index.

431. Rees, Philip. **Fascism in Britain.** Atlantic Highland, N.J., Humanities, 1980 (c1979). 243p. index. $27.50. LC 79-307471. ISBN 0-391-00908-7.

Sir Oswald Mosley and the other lesser-known figures of British fascism are all covered in this bibliography, intended to cover the history of fascism in the United Kingdom from its beginnings in 1923 to 1977. The citations are arranged in 20 topical chapters covering comprehensively all aspects and time periods in this subject.

The author has selectively included material from books, journal articles, and editorials, and much ephemeral material, including the actual publications of fascist groups. The annotations are informative, interesting to read, and especially useful for difficult-to-obtain items, for which library locations in Britain are provided.

Biographical Sources

432. **Biographical Dictionary of British Radicals in the Seventeenth Century.** Richard L. Greaves and Robert Zaller, eds. Brighton, England, Harvester Press, 1982/83. 3v. $180.00/set. ISBN 0-85527-133-7(v.1), 0-7108-0430-X(v.2), 0-7108-0486-5(v.3).

For the purpose of this biographical directory, radicals are defined as "those who sought fundamental change by striking at the very root of contemporary assumptions and institutions" (introduction). Many of these individuals were political or social reformers; others were literary figures or theologians with radical inclinations. Approximately 1,000 names appear in this 3-volume set.

Each biographical entry is signed. The authors are mainly affiliated with British and American universities. The sketches, which vary in length from half a page to several pages, contain personal and family details. Information is also provided on the career and ideological principles of each biographical subject. A brief bibliography of sources accompanies each biography.

433. **Biographical Dictionary of Modern British Radicals.** Joseph O. Baylen and Norbert J. Gossman, eds. Hassocks, England, Harvester Press; Atlantic Highland, N.J., Humanities, 1979-1988. 3v. index. LC 81-484609. ISBN 0710813198.

The introduction of this set concludes that for its purposes a radical is anyone who has advocated substantial change in British political, economic, or social institutions. Each volume includes over 200 subjects, with biographies that vary in length from half a page to seven pages. Each entry identifies the individual and the political and social movements of the times, and relates the major factual details. All the biographies are signed and include bibliographies. As the introduction notes, this set supplements the *Dictionary of National Biography* by covering lesser known radicals and also by sometimes "correcting" some of the *DNB* entries.

Chronologies

434. Pickrill, D. A. **Minister of the Crown.** Boston, Routledge & Kegan Paul, 1981. 135p. bibliog. index. $18.95. ISBN 0-7100-0916-X.

Pickrill lists in chronological order all the ministers of the crown, that is, holders of offices of ministerial level in the United Kingdom, from the date the positions first became known to 1980. Before the chronological list, there is a brief historical introduction for each office including changes in name. For the individuals listed, there is information on the period of time served, changes in name or title, and other offices held. There is a short bibliography of sources used in compiling the lists.

Handbooks

435. Butler, David, and Gareth Butler. **British Political Facts 1900-1985.** 6th ed. New York, St. Martin's Press, 1986. 536p. index. $45.00. LC 85-18479. ISBN 0-312-10467-7.

This handbook is the most complete and up-to-date reference work on 20th-century British politics. The sixth edition extends coverage from 1979 to 1985. The densely packed pages of lists and tables can be divided into two sections: (1) political information about the British government and (2) social and economic information, which serves as a background to the political activities. The former category includes information on ministries and officers of Parliament, political party leaders and membership, and general election statistics. The second part contains demographic and economic statistics, plus information on such matters as the press, broadcasting, and church membership. The handbook concludes with a bibliographic note on the major sources for research on British politics. A general alphabetical index is supplemented by an in-depth separate index of ministries.

436. Craig, Frederick, W. S. **British Electoral Facts, 1832-1980.** 4th ed. Chichester, England, Parliamentary Research Services, 1981. 203p. $14.00. LC 81-217225. ISSN 0-900178-20-5(pbk).

Now in its fourth edition, this useful collection of election statistics covers from 1832 through 1980. The tables provide a convenient basis for studies of elections and voting behavior. The statistical summaries cover first the general elections and by-elections for England, Scotland, Wales, and Northern Ireland, and then provide a total for the United Kingdom.

There are also a variety of tables with data on such topics as campaign expenses, size of electorate, turnout, public opinion, women candidates and recent elections for the European Parliament. The appendixes contain listings of reasons for general elections, principal changes in the electoral system since 1832, and Acts of Parliament relevant to elections. There is a bibliography on British elections and a very helpful list of the abbreviations of party names.

437. Flackes, William D. **Northern Ireland: A Political Directory, 1968-83.** London, British Broadcasting Corp., 1982. 323p. map. $10.00. LC 84-170703. ISBN 0563202092(pbk).

This handbook is a guide to the turbulent politics of Northern Ireland from 1968-1983. The main section is an alphabetical dictionary that includes people, organizations, political parties, religious groups, and key events and places in the province. Additional sections include a chronology of events since 1921, a summary of recent election statistics, and descriptions of governments, parliaments, and security systems, including the police and the army. There is much other related information, such as a tabulation of deaths from sectarian violence over the years. This is the most comprehensive current guide to politics in Ulster.

438. Waller, Robert. **Almanac of British Politics.** 3d ed. London, New York, Croom Helm, 1987. $40.00; $25.00(pbk). LC 87-6691. ISBN 0-7099-2798-3; 0-7099-2784-4(pbk).

By means of profiles of individual parliamentary constituencies, this handbook attempts to describe the political geography of Great Britain and Northern Ireland. Each of the constituencies has a one-page profile that begins with a narrative description of the political history of the electoral district. Boundary modifications and changes in the social character of the electorate are noted. These short essays try to point out "the individuality of each locality" (introduction) and the variable indicators influencing elections. Statistics for each district include such social data as the percentage of owner-occupied housing, of racial minorities, and of middle-class inhabitants. Recent election results and a list of recent MPs are also included for each constituency. This book, comparable to the *Almanac of American Politics* (see entry 517), is a basic sourcebook for understanding British elections. It is a companion to the author's *Atlas of British Politics* (see entry 428).

EUROPE

Atlases

439. Freeman, Michael. **An Atlas of Nazi Germany.** New York, Macmillan, 1987. 205p. $55.99. index. LC 87-12261. ISBN 0-02-910681-8.

Unlike most historical atlases, which provide detailed maps, this atlas offers a graphic approach, with visual representations in the form of outline maps, charts, diagrams, tables, and photographs. These are used to illustrate the salient themes in the political, economic, and military history of the Third Reich. The book is divided into six parts, covering the rise of the Nazi party, its administrative and political structures, German society, population, and the war. Each part contains several sections featuring short essays accompanied by the integrated visual material. This coordinated combination of visual and written information has provided useful clarifications, especially for such aspects as the overlapping of political and military jurisdictions and the rapidly changing geographical boundaries. There is also a list of references, a bibliography, a glossary, and an index. The outline maps may not provide sufficient detail for some scholarly uses.

440. Sallnow, John, and Anna John. **An Electoral Atlas of Europe, 1968-1981: A Political Geographic Compendium Including 76 Maps.** Cartography by Sarah K. Webber. London, Boston, Butterworth, 1982. 149p. index. $59.95. LC 82-171318. ISBN 0-4081-0800-2.

The maps in this atlas provide graphic displays of political party strength in Western Europe. The maps for each country portray the outcome of national elections from the late

1960s to the early 1980s. For each of the 18 countries surveyed there is, in addition to the maps, a brief narrative survey of political trends, electoral systems, and the political parties involved. Tabulations of election statistics are also provided. Each chapter concludes with a short list of references. There are indexes to personal names and to political parties.

Bibliographies

441. Buse, Dieter, and J. Doerr. **German Nationalism: A Bibliographic Approach.** New York, Garland, 1985. 230p. (Canadian Review of Studies in Nationalism, Vol. 5; Garland Reference Library of Social Science, Vol. 161). index. $35.00. LC 82-49159. ISBN 0-8240-9160-4(pbk).

This bibliography, one of the series of Garland studies on nationalism in various countries, has as its focus nationalism in Germany during the 19th and 20th centuries. The compilers have included books, articles, and research studies, including a great many in German.

The bibliography is divided into a series of chapters. After the first general section, each chapter covers chronological divisions of approximately 30 to 50 years. All of the entries in this selective bibliography are annotated. The careful selection of materials for inclusion and the introductory essays to each chapter, which review the history and literature of the period surveyed, have made this bibliography a valuable guide to the literature of German nationalism. There are author and subject indexes.

442. **Church and State in Postwar Eastern Europe: A Bibliographical Survey.** Paul Mojzes, comp.; G. E. Gorman, advisory ed. Westport, Conn., Greenwood, 1987. 109p. (Bibliographies and Indexes in Religious Studies, No. 11). bibliog. index. $35.00. LC 87-8358. ISBN 0-313-24002-7.

Mojzes's bibliography covers English-language material on a topic of considerable current interest for religious studies and political science: church-state relations in Eastern Europe. He deals with all the countries of Eastern Europe, including the Soviet Union. There are annotations for most entries. Generous cross-references and the author and subject indexes provide effective access to the material, which includes a balanced selection with various publications by East European governments. An opening essay offers an overview of the predominate church in each nation and of the historical and current status of church-state relations.

443. Egan, David R., and Melinda A. Egan. **Russian Autocrats from Ivan the Great to the Fall of the Romanov Dynasty: An Annotated Bibliography of English Language Sources to 1985.** Metuchen, N.J., Scarecrow, 1987. 512p. index. $49.50. LC 86-28003. ISBN 0-8108-1958-9.

The lives and policies of 26 Russian rulers, from Ivan the Great to Nicholas II (1462-1917), are covered in this bibliography. Coverage is comprehensive, with popular as well as scholarly works, including monographs, essays, periodical articles, memoirs, letters, and dissertations. While all of the sources are in English, many are translations from German, French, and, especially, Russian. Each citation has an informative descriptive annotation that clearly indicates the scope and focus of the work. Arrangement is chronological by ruler, with larger sections divided into general studies, domestic policy, and foreign and military affairs. There are author and subject indexes.

444. Hopkins, Michael. **Policy Formation in the European Communities: A Bibliographical Guide to Community Documentation, 1958-1978.** London, Mansell; distr., New York, H. W. Wilson, 1981. 339p. index. $42.00. ISBN 0-7201-1597-3.

The objective of this guide is to provide bibliographic control and greater use of the wealth of key policy documents that have been prepared by or for the Commission of the European Communities during the period 1958 to 1978. The commission is the chief policymaking body of the European Communities, now known as the European Community (EC).

The 600 citations to key documents include reports, communications, and memoranda, the primary sources produced by the commission in the conduct of its business. The first chapter describes the process for proposals as they become official policy. Most of the subsequent chapters deal with individual policy matters such as agriculture, monetary affairs, and science and research. For each chapter there is a short essay outlining policy and citations to major documents. The entries are all annotated in considerable detail with references to related documents. There are three indexes in this valuable guide to EC publications: author/title, subject, and document by numerical order.

445. Kehr, Helen. **The Nazi Era, 1919-1945: A Select Bibliography of Published Works from the Early Roots to 1980.** Helen Kehr and Janet Langmaid, comps. London, Mansell; distr. H. W. Wilson, 1982. 612p. index. $48.00. LC 83-216788. ISBN 0-7201-1618-X.

In dealing with the vast literature concerning National Socialism and the Third Reich, this excellent bibliography, necessarily selective, has focused on the "German outlook of the time" (introduction). Some 20 languages are represented among the approximately 6,500 citations, with a majority in English or German. The bibliography is based on the Wiener Library of the Institute of Contemporary History in London.

The unannotated entries are arranged in nine topical chapters, which cover either various chronological periods or subject aspects of the Nazi era. The extent of coverage is certainly impressive. It begins with the roots of Nazism, goes on to discuss Nazi ideology and the struggle for power, and then covers the Third Reich in all aspects—administration, economy, religion, and culture. It concludes with the war, war crimes, and the fall of the Third Reich. There is a full index of authors, names, and subjects. For a shorter bibliography concentrating on English-language titles, note Louis Snyder's *The Third Reich* (entry 450).

446. Lodge, Juliet, ed. **The European Community: Bibliographical Excursions.** Phoenix, Ariz., Oryx Press, 1983. 259p. $36.00. LC 83-2213. ISBN 0-89774-099-8.

The editor intended this book to be an introduction to the European Community (EC) for students and general readers. It is divided into three parts, covering integration theory, decisionmaking and institutions, and internal policies and external relations. These parts are in turn divided into various chapters which focus on such specific topics as the European Parliament, agricultural policy, and relations with Eastern European states. Each chapter begins with a short descriptive essay followed by an unannotated bibliography.

This bibliographic essay can be used as a handbook by those looking not for citations but for concise descriptions of the organization and activities of the EC. The section on EC official publications and the list of common abbreviations should also be valuable for reference use. There are no author, title, or subject indexes.

447. Low, Alfred D. **The Anschluss Movement, 1918-1938: Background and Aftermath: An Annotated Bibliography of German and Austrian Nationalism.** New York, Garland, 1984. 186p. (Canadian Review of Studies in Nationalism, Vol. 4; Garland Reference Library of Social Science, Vol. 151). index. $35.00. LC 82-49174. ISBN 0-8240-9177-9.

The Anschluss movement, the effort to unite Austria with Germany, was an important European force from the end of World War I to Hitler's annexation of Austria in 1938. This bibliography covers the movement comprehensively, including its historical roots and its aftereffects in contemporary Europe.

The 500 entries include many works in German, French, and other languages as well as in English. Foreign-language titles are translated, and all entries are annotated. The citations are organized into five sections based on chronological units or type of material (books, chapters, articles). The entries are arranged alphabetically with in each chapter with an overall author index.

448. **Nationalism in the Balkans: An Annotated Bibliography.** Gale Stokes, ed. New York, Garland, 1984. 243p. (Canadian Review of Studies in Nationalism, Vol. 3; Garland Reference Library of Social Science, Vol. 160). $48.00. LC 82-49160. ISBN 0-8240-9161-2.

Though many may consider Balkan nationalism a "notorious" subject (introduction), Gale Stokes designed this bibliography to aid the serious study of this topic. The nearly 600 citations are organized into four chapters dealing with nationalism in Greece, Romania, Bulgaria, and Yugoslavia. Each chapter is written by a scholar of the nation covered. There is also a chapter on general or theoretical studies on the region and an introductory essay on Balkan nationalism by the editor. The citations include books and journal articles in major European languages as well as in English. All entries have content annotations. Both specialists and students will find this title useful in beginning research on Balkan nationalism.

449. Rees, Philip. **Fascism and Pre-Fascism in Europe, 1890-1945: A Bibliography of the Extreme Right.** Totowa, N.J., Barnes & Noble, 1984. 330p. index. $29.95. LC 84-433. ISBN 0-389-20472-2.

The vast literature concerning the extreme right in Europe from 1890 to 1945 is covered in this bibliography. It is, of necessity, a selective listing, concentrating on the most significant writings on the ideology and practice of the extreme right. Great Britain was omitted, as it was covered in the author's *Fascism in Britain: An Annotated Bibliography* (see entry 431). Other topics, such as the Holocaust, were covered only briefly due to the existence of other bibliographies. Fascism in this work includes all varieties of extreme right political behavior.

The citations include books, periodical articles, and dissertations, most written after 1945. The first chapter covers fascism as a general phenomenon. The remaining chapters are arranged by country, with subdivisions covering history, economics, sociology, parties, and prominent individuals. Additional subject access is provided by the name index, which includes subjects as well as authors.

450. Snyder, Louis L., ed. **The Third Reich, 1933-1945: A Bibliographical Guide to German National Socialism.** New York, Garland, 1987. 284p. index. (Canadian Review of Studies in Nationalism, Vol. 7). $42.00. LC 87-7608. ISBN 0-8240-8463-2.

Though the Third Reich lasted only 12 years, National Socialism has remained a topic of enormous interest for historians, political scientists, and the general public alike. This bibliography presents 850 titles of books, journal articles, and documents chosen to give a representative sample from the enormous literature on this topic. Most of the sources selected are in English. The citations are divided into 13 chapters, some on such general topics as politics, economics, and religion, and other dealing with more specific aspects, such as the Resistance and the Holocaust.

The annotations vary from a sentence to a paragraph in length and are limited to a description of the contents and theme of the items cited. The author felt that the literature was so controversial that readers should make their own judgments as to value. The author has, however, indicated with asterisks the citations he considers especially outstanding. The introduction discusses briefly various historiographical controversies prominent in the literature of National Socialism. For a more comprehensive bibliography for advanced research, note Helen Kehr's *The Nazi Era* (entry 445), which has 6,500 citations in many languages.

Biographical Sources

451. Biographical Dictionary of Dissidents in the Soviet Union, 1956-1975. S. P. de Boer, E. J. Driessen, and H. L. Verhaar, comps. and eds. Boston, Martinus Nijhoff, 1982. 679p. bibliog. $165.00. LC 81-22433. ISBN 90-247-2538-0.

This biographical dictionary was compiled under the auspices of the Institute of Eastern European Studies of the University of Amsterdam. The 3,400 entries represent dissidents—persons who opposed in some manner the Soviet regime. The entries vary from a few lines to several pages, depending on the material available. Unverified information is indicated with a question mark. Personal data, dissident activities, and nationality are given whenever possible. The texts of major criminal codes dealing with political offenses are cited. There is also a glossary of terms and a selected bibliography.

452. Biographical Dictionary of Modern European Radicals and Socialists, Volume 1: 1780-1815. David Nicholls and Peter Marsh, eds. Brighton, England, Harvester Press; New York, St. Martin's Press, 1988. 291p. index. $30.00. LC 87-36961. ISBN 0312019688.

Forty-eight British, American, and European scholars contributed to this biographical dictionary, which provides short, 1- to 4-page biographies of 187 radicals, 86 of whom were French. The first volume of this multivolume project covers 1780-1815. The introduction describes the forces influencing society in this period as "complex and diverse," which made it difficult to formulate a precise definition of the category of persons suitable for inclusion. The definition adopted specified individuals who had wished to make political, economic, or social changes that could not be incorporated into the existing structures. Each of the signed portraits begins with a brief identification of the subject, followed by biographical information, an assessment of the subject's radical beliefs and activities, and a short bibliography for further reading. English radicals were omitted, as they are covered in the *Biographical Dictionary of Modern British Radicals* (see entry 433).

453. Directory of European Political Scientists. 4th ed., rev. Compiled and edited by the Central Services, European Consortium for Political Research, University of Exeter. Munich, New York, K. G. Saur, 1985. 627p. index. $75.00. ISBN 3-598-10317-0.

This directory of European political scientists includes 2,153 individuals. For each entry the following elements of information are provided: birth date, nationality, address, degrees, doctoral thesis, appointments, selected publications, and areas of research and fields of interest. The entries are arranged alphabetically and numbered. The extensive index lists individuals by number according to broad subject fields and areas of specialization. This feature makes it possible to readily identify, for example, all political scientists studying Eurocommunism or specializing in policy analysis.

454. Grant, Michael. **The Roman Emperors: A Biographical Guide to the Rulers of Imperial Rome, 31 BC-AD 476.** New York, Scribners 1985. 367p. index. $25.00. LC 85-8391. ISBN 0-684-18380-9.

As a convenient source of the basic facts about the Roman emperors, this title serves much the same information functions as the various biographical directories of American presidents or contemporary rulers. In all, 92 emperors are included, with individual biographies that vary in length from 2 to 8 pages. Another 100 individuals who reigned briefly or were unsuccessful claimants are mentioned in passing. In addition to political and military information on their reigns, the author has tried to include personal matters that could disclose "what sort of men they were" (foreword). There are also 11 maps, 7 genealogical tables, a list of Latin technical terms, and an index of Latin and Greek authors. The essays, unfortunately, have no references to the specific sources used.

455. Wistrich, Robert S. **Who's Who in Nazi Germany.** New York, Macmillan, 1982. 359p. bibliog. $17.75. LC 82-4704. ISBN 0-02-630600-X.

In this biographical directory Wistrich has provided biographies of nearly 350 prominent Nazis. These figures are drawn from all walks of life: politics, government, the military, literature and the arts, and entertainment. Opponents as well as the leaders of the Third Reich are included, providing a collective portrait of Nazism as it functioned in all aspects of German society and culture.

The biographical entries vary in length from a page for minor individuals to over seven pages for Hitler. Personal data and career highlights are covered. In addition to the biographies, there is a bibliography of source materials and a glossary of terms.

Dictionaries and Encyclopedias

456. McCrea, Barbara P., Jack C. Plano, and George Klein. **The Soviet and East European Political Dictionary.** Santa Barbara, Calif., ABC-Clio, 1984. 367p. index. (Clio Dictionaries in Political Science, No. 4). $30.00; $10.75(pbk). LC 83-6418. ISBN 0-87436-333-0; 0-87436-347-0(pbk).

Like all the titles in the Clio Dictionaries in Political Science series, this dictionary is not arranged in a single alphabetical sequence. The entries are grouped within subject chapters. This format has been adopted so that the book can be used as a supplement in an academic course on the Soviet Union or Eastern Europe.

The approximately 300 terms are in 8 chapters, covering historical perspectives, ideology and theory, Communist party structures and processes, governmental structures and processes, the economic system, the legal system, citizen and state, and foreign policy. For each term there is a one-paragraph definition plus a "Significance" statement of interpretative comment. There is a detailed subject index for those wishing to look up terms directly without regard to the topical arrangement. This dictionary is more useful as a ready reference for students and others than as a source of in-depth information or analysis.

457. Parker, Geoffrey, and Brenda Parker. **A Dictionary of the European Communities.** London, Boston, Butterworth, 1981. 84p. $14.95. LC 82-123132. ISBN 0-4081-0732-4(pbk).

458. Paxton, John. **A Dictionary of the European Communities.** 2d ed. New York, St. Martin's Press, 1982. 282p. $27.50. LC 82-10375. ISBN 0-3122-0099-4.

These two dictionaries are very similar in content, format, and currency. Both offer a series of entries on the background and current politics, policies, and operations of the

European Communities. Organizational units, conventions, treaties, councils, and court cases are all included, as are prominent individuals. These dictionaries are most useful for scholars or persons who, having official or business relations with the European Communities, require detailed information. Summary descriptions in general handbooks, such as the *Europa Yearbook* (see entry 365) or the *Statesman's Yearbook* (see entry 369), will suffice for most other needs.

459. Rossi, Ernest E., and Barbara P. McCrea. **The European Political Dictionary.** Santa Barbara, Calif., ABC-Clio, 1985. 408p. maps. index. (Clio Dictionaries in Political Science, No. 7). $42.50; $15.00(pbk). LC 84-24389. ISBN 0-87436-046-3; 0-87436-367-5(pbk).

This title in the Clio Dictionaries in Political Science series deals with Europe, or more accurately, with Great Britain, France, the Federal Republic of Germany, and the Soviet Union. Each country has a chapter of definitions covering the major structures of government, political parties, election results, and prominent individuals. Historical and theoretical terms have also been included. In addition to these sections devoted to the four major powers, there is a chapter on regionalism in Western Europe, especially the European Communities.

As with the other titles in this series, each of the 325 main entries has 2 paragraphs: the first provides the definition and the second, labeled "Significance," provides interpretation and analysis. The "Guide to Countries" lists all references to all of the European nations. There is also a very detailed index, which permits the searcher to directly access terms without having to refer to the topical arrangement of the entries.

Handbooks

460. Cook, Chris, and Geoff Pugh. **Sources in European Political History. Volume I: The European Left.** New York, Facts on File, 1987. 237p. bibliog. (Sources in European Political History). $35.00. LC 82-7365. ISBN 0-8160-1016-1.

The personal papers of prominent individuals active in socialist, communist, anarchist, labor, and other radical or revolutionary movements in Europe from 1848 to 1945 are covered in this guide. Papers on the British and Irish left are excluded, as they have been included in previous volumes by Cook. Eastern European collections have also been excluded unless they have been deposited in the West.

The approximately 1,000 individuals in this compilation are arranged alphabetically. Each of the entries, which range from a paragraph to a page, has a brief note of identification and background information, followed by a listing and concise description (including location) of the collections of papers. This is an important resource for political research that involves the use of primary historical records.

461. Cook, Chris, and John Paxton. **European Political Facts, 1789-1848.** New York, Facts on File, 1981. 195p. index. $19.95. LC 80-21495. ISBN 0-8719-6377-9.

462. Babuscio, Jack, and Richard Minta Dunn. **European Political Facts, 1648-1789.** New York, Facts on File, 1984. 387p. index. $24.95. LC 83-25390. ISBN 0-87196-992-0.

With these two volumes, the European Political Facts series now covers from 1648 to 1973. The other two volumes are by Cook and Paxton and cover 1848-1918 and 1918-1973 (both published in 1978). Although the content and arrangement vary slightly among the four volumes, this series generally contains a broad selection of handbook information for the study of European politics. Generally included for each period are chronologies of major political events, rosters of heads of state and other key officeholders, lists of treaties, lists of colonies and dependencies, descriptions of parliamentary systems and political parties, and compilations of statistics on population, economics, elections, social trends, etc. Some of the topics are arranged in subject chapters, others by country. There is in each of these very useful compendiums a table of contents and subject index to help searchers locate specific information.

463. Dwyer, Joseph D., ed. **Russia, the Soviet Union, and Eastern Europe: A Survey of Holdings at the Hoover Institution on War, Revolution and Peace.** Stanford, Calif., Hoover Institution Press, 1980. 233p. (Hoover Press Library Survey, No. 6). $18.95. LC 78-70888. ISBN 0-8179-5011-7.

This handbook is a survey of the holdings, published and unpublished, of the Russian and East European collection at the Hoover Institution. In addition to books, this well-known collection has strong holdings of periodicals and newspapers. The holdings focus on history, politics, and international relations.

The survey covers 11 European countries: the Soviet Union, the previous Soviet satellites, Albania, Greece, and Yugoslavia. For each country the handbook provides an overview of the collection, a review of reference works, and a descriptive breakdown of the various types of materials or historical periods included. Reseachers interested in Eastern Europe will find this an excellent guide to the resources of this renown library.

464. **Historical Dictionary of Fascist Italy.** Philip V. Cannistraro, ed. Westport, Conn., Greenwood, 1982. 657p. maps. index. $49.95. LC 81-4493. ISBN 0-313-21327-8.

The *Dictionary* "represents the most comprehensive reference source on Italian Fascism published to date" (preface). It is a response to the growing scholarly interest in Italian fascism and the resulting quantity of published material. Its aim is to serve as a handbook with all the basic definitions and factual data needed by students and scholars. The editor, who was assisted by a wide range of experts, has attempted to avoid any political or historiographical preconceptions or prejudices.

The entries in this historical dictionary cover important political events and individuals, as well as related matters in the fields of economics, the military, the arts, and entertainment. There is a thorough subject index, plus a series of valuable appendixes; these include a chronology, lists of major officeholders and military officers, and a list of place names changed by the fascists.

465. McHale, Vincent E., ed. **Political Parties of Europe.** Sharon Skowronski, assistant ed., Westport, Conn., Greenwood, 1983. 2v. index. (The Greenwood Historical Encyclopedia of the World's Political Parties). $95.00/set; $65.00/vol. LC 83-15408. ISBN 0-313-21405-0/set; 0-313-23804-9(v.1); 0-313-23805-8(v.2).

The first volume of this handbook covers Albania through Norway, with Poland through Yugoslavia contained in the second volume. For each country there is a chapter that begins with a substantial introductory essay surveying the history and major political events of the country. The current political and social climate is also analyzed. The introduction is followed by an alphabetical listing of the political parties, existing and defunct. Some of these entries are only a paragraph or two in length, while others range up to five pages. The entry for each party includes a brief history, founding date, key leaders, political objectives, and an assessment of the party's current status. The syntheses provided for long-established parties, such as the Tories/Conservatives in England, are very useful. Bibliographies follow both the introductions and the entries for the political parties. There are three appendixes: a chronology of major political events for each country, a genealogy of parties noting splits and mergers, and a classification of the parties by type of political orientation.

466.   Mayne, Richard, ed. **Western Europe.** New York, Facts on File, 1986. 699p. maps. index. (Handbooks to the Modern World). $40.00. LC 85-29242. ISBN 0-8160-1251-X.

With a number of varied parts, this handbook provides a comprehensive overview of Europe, specifically of the continent's 27 noncommunist countries (including Turkey). The first part consists of country-by-country chapters that contain almanac-type information on the geography, population, government, and economy of each nation. Education, social security, and mass media are also covered. Principal officials and key statistics are provided.

The most valuable parts of this title are the second and third, which contain signed articles on European political, economic, and social affairs and on Western European integration. Most of the contributors are British scholars. For the most recent statistic or name, the annually revised handbooks and almanacs are preferable, but for background information and analysis, this title is an excellent source.

467.   O'Clery, Conor. **The Dictionary of Political Quotations on Ireland 1886-1987: Phrases Make History Here.** Boston, G. K. Hall, 1987. 232p. index. $25.00. LC 87-2886. ISBN 0-8161-8939-0.

As the subtitle of this book indicates, words and phrases have often been important in Irish history. This dictionary provides a selection of quotations for the hundred years beginning in 1886, with an emphasis on the long struggle with Great Britain. Unionist reaction to nationalist aspirations, the civil war in the south after partition in 1921, the later civil rights movement and IRA activity in Ulster, and the political role of the Catholic church in the Republic are topics that are covered in depth.

Each quotation is placed in context with a brief note, and the source is identified. Since the quotations are arranged in chronological order, they may be read through as an oral commentary on the events of Irish history. Author and subject indexes make this a handy book.

468.   Overton, David. **Common Market Digest: An Information Guide to the European Communities.** New York, Facts on File, 1983. 387p. index. $45.00. LC 83-14172. ISBN 0-87196-854-1.

The European Communities, or the European Economic Community (EEC), as The Common Market is sometimes called, came into existence in 1957. It is now the major expression of regionalism in Western Europe. This handbook presents a comprehensive guide to the Community, its programs and activities.

The topics are arranged in subject chapters which include considerations of economics, agriculture, industry, energy, technology, social developments, external affairs, etc. In each chapter the work of the various commissions and committees of the EEC is outlined. Relevant publications are noted throughout the text. In addition to these entries in the subject chapters, there is a chronology of the history of the European Communities and a list of related abbreviations. There is a comprehensive subject, title, and name (individual, organizational, and country) index.

469.   Schöpfin, George, ed. **The Soviet Union and Eastern Europe.** 2d ed. New York, Facts on File, 1986. 637p. maps. index. (Handbooks to the Modern World). $40.00. LC 85-25403. ISBN 0-8160-1260-1.

The second edition of this handbook provides concise information on political history and on economic, social, and cultural conditions for the Soviet Union and the countries of Eastern Europe—the Soviet "satellites." The information reflects conditions in the early 1980s, before the great changes occurring at the end of the decade. The various political units within the Soviet Union, ranging from the Ukraine to Estonia, are not covered systematically or in detail.

The format used consists of a series of essays written by a variety of specialists. Nationalism, political dissent, and economic conditions are topics generally given considerable attention. There is a detailed index plus an abundant number of maps and charts.

470. Stammen, Theo. **Political Parties in Europe.** Westport, Conn., Meckler, a division of Microform Review, 1981. 321p. illus. maps. bibliog. $42.50. LC 80-26948. ISBN 0-930466-28-4.

Unlike Vincent E. McHale's book, *Political Parties of Europe* (see entry 465), which provides descriptive sketches of the various political parties of Europe, this book examines the historical development of political parties in Western Europe in the context of "the present policy of European unification" (preface). This treatment does not follow the typical format of a reference book, but the author intended it as such, and it does include a great deal of information arranged for easy access.

The first of the handbook's five parts is a historical evaluation of European political integration. The second part, of greatest reference value, is an analysis of national party systems in 17 major countries of Western Europe. For each nation there is introductory information on politics and the party system, with profiles of major parties. Other parts offer a comparison of the national party systems in Europe and an analysis of transnational party relationships. The final parts contain the text of key documents, such as the treaty creating the European Economic Community. This book was written as an examination of the likelihood of the emergence of an all-European transnational party system, but it may be used as a reference source for information on political parties regardless of the searcher's specific interests.

Statistics Sources

471. Shoup, Paul S. **The East European and Soviet Data Handbook: Political, Social, and Developmental Indicators, 1945-1975.** New York, Columbia University Press, 1981. 482p. bibliog. $40.00. LC 80-25682. ISBN 0-231-04252-3.

This handbook makes readily available to researchers and students basic social science statistical data for the Eastern European countries and the Soviet Union. Generally, the time frame covered is 1945 to 1975. These data are intended to facilitate comparative and historical analysis, especially regarding social change.

The 219 statistical tables fall into eight sections: population, party membership, national and religious affiliation, educational attainment, class, party leaders, occupations and standard of living. There is an introductory essay discussing the reliability and interpretation of the data. There is also an extensive bibliography citing the sources of the data.

Yearbooks

472. **European Yearbook.** Council of Europe. The Hague, Nijhoff, 1956- . annual. price varies. LC 55-3837. ISSN 0071-3139.

The *European Yearbook*, or *Annuaire européen*, has been published since 1956 by the Council of Europe, founded in 1949 to promote European unity. The specific aim of this publication is to encourage the study of European organizations and their activities. The Benelux Economic Union, the European Community, the Council of Europe itself, and other international and cooperative European organizations are covered. These sections typically include a chronology of key events, a discussion of major policies or agreements, and background historical information on the organizations.

In addition to this reporting on European organizations, the *Yearbook* has featured a bibliography on European integration, articles, and the text of relevant documents. This yearbook is too slow in appearing to be particularly useful for current information, but it remains an excellent source for historical coverage.

473. **Yearbook of the European Communities.** Brussels, Editions Delta, 1977- . index. $62.00. LC 78-645793. ISSN 0771-7962.

This annual, which also bears the title in French and German, began publishing in 1977. It is designed to be a comprehensive handbook or guide to the structure, personnel, activities, and policies of the European Community, much as *The United States Government Manual* covers the American government.

The manual begins with such practical information as addresses and phone numbers for embassies and information offices and lists of official publications and national holidays for the European Community member states. There follow sections discussing the treaties creating the Community, its institutions, and its policies on such matters as agriculture, energy, taxation, and customs union. The European Parliament, the Council, the Commission, and other related agencies are outlined. There is also a brief consideration of other European organizations, such as the European Space Agency. There are detailed indexes of abbreviations, of subjects, of names, and of publications. All information is presented in French, English, and German.

UNITED STATES—GENERAL

Bibliographies

474. **Bibliography of Original Meaning of the United States Constitution.** Washington, D.C., U.S. Department of Justice, Federal Justice Research Program, 1988. 287p. $9.00. ISBN 027-000-0131309. J1.20/2:C76/2.

Prepared by the faculty and students at the University of San Diego School of Law, this bibliography on the U.S. Constitution is limited to material dealing specifically with the meanings of its provisions as understood by those who framed those provisions. It provides unannotated citations to the meanings of the framers of the original Constitution and subsequent amendments as found in: (1) the debates of the framing bodies; (2) the debates of the ratifying bodies and related commentaries; (3) the scholarly works of the early commentators; (4) the United States Supreme Court cases; and (5) the scholarly works of modern commentators.

This bibliography will be especially useful for those involved in litigation or historical scholarship that elicits questions on the original meaning of the Constitution. For a bibliography with a broader orientation, see *The Constitution of the United States: A Guide to Current Scholarly Research* by Bernard D. Reams (entry 486).

475. Bowman, James S., and Ronald L. Monet. **Gubernatorial and Presidential Transitions: An Annotated Bibliography and Resource Guide.** New York, Garland, 1988. 113p. index. $37.00. LC 87-25152. ISBN 0-8240-7218-9.

This short bibliography provides 211 citations, including books, periodical articles, and dissertations drawn from the last 25 years. Only two of the six chapters deal specifically with gubernatorial and presidential transitions. The others cover executive management and functions. All of the citations have short descriptive annotations. The introduction provides an overview of the subject, with mention of particularly useful works. Important journals, professional associations, and institutions are pointed out as aids to further research. There is an author index and a series of 16 appendixes dealing mainly with specifics of gubernatorial transition.

476. **Church and State in America: A Bibliographical Guide.** John F. Wilson, ed. New York, Greenwood, 1986. 2v. $49.95(v.1); $55.95(v.2). LC 85-31698. ISBN 031325236X(v.1); 0313259143(v.2).

The first volume of this bibliography is entitled *The Colonial and Early National Period*, the second *The Civil War to the Present*. Each volume follows the same format: a series of signed lengthy bibliographic essays followed by extensive listings of periodical articles and books. Some of the critical essays deal with chronological periods; others focus on particular themes such as new religions, women, or religion and education. The editor, who is the head of the Princeton Project on Church and State, chose a broad scope for this bibliography, which contains many works on the cultural interpretations of church-state relations, including titles dealing with the increasingly politicized aspects of many of these relationships in recent years in the United States.

477. Coleman, Patrick K., and Charles R. Lamb, comps. **The Nonpartisan League, 1915-22: An Annotated Bibliography.** St. Paul, Minn., Minnesota Historical Society Press, 1985. 86p. illus. index. $12.95(pbk). LC 85-21480. ISBN 0-87351-189-1.

The Nonpartisan League (NPL) enjoyed a short prominence for about a decade after its organization in North Dakota in 1915. The authors of this bibliography note in their introduction the intense struggle for economic justice carried out by the farmers in the NPL and the continuing interest of historians in this agrarian protest movement.

This bibliography contains 1,010 citations. Short descriptive annotations are provided for most entries. Books, periodical articles, pamphlets, government documents, and archival and manuscript collections are included. There are detailed author and subject indexes.

478. Davis, Lenwood G., and Janet L. Sims-Wood, comps. **The Ku Klux Klan: A Bibliography.** Westport, Conn., Greenwood, 1984. 643p. index. $49.95. LC 83-1709. ISBN 0-313-22949-X.

Access to materials about the Ku Klux Klan has been significantly improved by this bibliography of nearly 10,000 items. The compilation is divided into eight sections by format, including major works, books, pamphlets, dissertations, documents, speeches, and KKK publications. A large portion of the entries are newspaper citations, primarily to the *New York Times*.

The lack of a subject index is particularly unfortunate because the entries in each section are arranged alphabetically by title. There are useful lists of archival and manuscript collections and of Klan publications.

479. Doenecke, Justus D. **Anti-intervention: A Bibliographical Introduction to Isolationism and Pacifism from World War I to the Early Cold War.** New York, Garland, 1987. 421p. index. (Garland Reference Library of Social Science, Vol. 396). $60.00. LC 87-8635. ISBN 0-8260-8482-9.

Opposition to American involvement in overseas affairs, particularly conflicts, was an important political theme during the time covered by this bibliography. Over 1,600 citations are provided, with arrangement by topic and time period. The opening chapter is on general writings that characterize the background and nature of anti-interventionist and pacifist sentiments. The entries were selected from books, periodicals, and dissertations. Unpublished sources, popular magazine articles, and government publications were excluded. Some primary sources are included. The entries have brief annotations. There is an author index and two subject indexes—by topic and by personal name.

480. The Dynamic Constitution: A Historical Bibliography. Suzanne Robitalle Ontiveros, ed. Santa Barbara, Calif., ABC-Clio, 1986. 343p. index. $32.50. LC 86-20618. ISBN 0874364701.

"To honor the upcoming bicentennial of the Constitution" (preface), this bibliography of 1,370 citations was compiled. The chronological limits of coverage are 1777 to 1985; the equally broad subject coverage includes works from the fields of history and political science. Most of the citations refer to journal articles, but books and dissertations are also included. The citations were culled from an ABC-Clio history database, *America: History and Life* (see entry 93), with the abstracts retained for the articles. The entries are arranged in five long, basically chronological divisions.

There is an author index and a thorough subject index. The text of the Constitution is also included. For another effort on this topic see Russell Wheeler's *Writing and Ratification of the U.S. Constitution: A Bibliography.*

481. Fisher, William H. The Invisible Empire: A Bibliography of the Ku Klux Klan. Metuchen, N.J., Scarecrow, 1980. 202p. index. $10.00. LC 80-10133. ISBN 0-8108-1288-6.

Fisher's bibliography of over 1,000 items is divided into two parts, for the 19th and the 20th centuries. In both sections there are three categories: (1) dissertations, manuscripts/archives, (2) monographs, and (3) periodical articles. Eye-witness accounts, government documents, popular commentaries, and many manuscript collections are included in these categories. Most entries have short annotations. There are author and subject indexes.

For another bibliography on this topic, see Davis and Sims-Wood's *The Ku Klux Klan: A Bibliography* (entry 478). That work provides over 10,000 citations, but the majority are to newspaper articles.

482. Hall, Kermit L. A Comprehensive Bibliography of American Constitutional and Legal History, 1896-1979. Millwood, N.Y., Kraus International, 1984. 5v. index. $650.00/set. LC 82-48983. ISBN 0-527-37408-3.

Five volumes containing 18,000 citations provide a "comprehensive, not complete" (introduction) bibliography of the history of American law and constitutionalism. These publications, which cover 1896-1979, are limited to generally available books, journal articles, and doctoral dissertations published in English in the United States. The articles cited are from 750 journals, an indication of the widespread dispersion of the literature on constitutional law in the United States.

The numbered, unannotated entries are arranged in seven topical chapters, covering general surveys and texts, institutions (federal, state, and local), constitutional doctrine, legal doctrine, and titles with biographical, chronological, and geographical emphases. Many entries are listed in several categories, making a total of over 68,000 citations. Volume 5 contains the indexes: an author index for authors, editors, compilers, or translators; a subject index for persons, concepts, terms, and places.

483. Kaid, Lynda Lee, and Anne Johnston Wadsworth. Political Campaign Communication: A Bibliography and Guide to the Literature 1973-1982. Metuchen, N.J., Scarecrow, 1985. 217p. index. $16.50. LC 84-23508. ISBN 0-8108-1764-0.

This volume covering 1973-1982 is a continuation of an earlier one with the same title published in 1974, which covered 1950-1972. That earlier volume contained 1,500 entries, while the newer one, covering half as many years, contains 2,461 entries. Political campaign communication is obviously a topic of growing interest and research.

This bibliography includes books, journal articles, pamphlets, dissertations and theses. Government documents and popular magazine articles are excluded. Only English-language material is cited. All citations are in one list, alphabetized by main entry. There is a subject index to provide access, though many of the entries have long lists of references. The appendix contains a "Guide to the Literature," which lists professional and scholarly journals, indexing and abstracting services, databases, and other sources of information on political campaign communications.

484. McCarrick, Earlean M. **U.S. Constitution: A Guide to Information Sources.** Detroit, Gale, 1980. 390p. index. (American Government and History Information Guide Series, Vol. 4; Gale Information Guide Library). $28.00. LC 74-15403. ISBN 0-8103-1203-4.

In this bibliography 1,600 primary (documents, court cases) and secondary (books, journal articles) items are cited. While not comprehensive, the bibliography provides a wide selection of historical and contemporary titles, both scholarly and more popular works suitable for the general public and students. Each citation has a short descriptive annotation.

The opening chapters list reference sources, general interpretative works, and studies on the background and formative years of the Constitution. The middle section of the bibliography deals with the Constitution itself and covers the executive, legislative, and judicial branches of government. The remaining chapters deal with the amendments to the Constitution. The entries are arranged in each chapter alphabetically by author; they are not grouped by topic. The detailed subject index provides access.

485. Nelson, Barbara J. **American Women and Politics: A Selected Bibliography and Resource Guide.** New York, Garland, 1984. 255p. index. (Garland Reference Library of Social Science, Vol. 174). $42.00. LC 82-49142. ISBN 0-8242-9139-6.

The author, a professor at Princeton, has compiled this bibliography as an outgrowth of her teaching. Its format follows teaching practice by beginning with a very broad view of the topic of American women and politics. Opening chapters cover the history of feminism and women's rights in the United States, the nature versus nurture debate, women in the family, women at work, and women and education. These topics are "profoundly political in implication" (introduction). The remaining chapters deal with specifically political subjects such as voting, campaign work, and political leadership.

There are 1,611 unannotated citations for books and journal articles. Popular magazines and newspapers are included on a topic only when there was otherwise a lack of material. The last chapter on reference sources deals with all aspects of women's studies and feminism. There are subject and author indexes.

486. Reams, Bernard D., and Stuart D. Yoak. **The Constitution of the United States: A Guide and Bibliography to Current Scholarly Research.** Dobbs Ferry, N.Y., Oceana, 1987. 545p. index. LC 87-11244. ISBN 0-379-20888-1.

The materials in this bibliography are arranged according to each section of the Constitution and its amendments. Author, title, and subject indexes provide traditional access points. There are also additional chapters for bibliographies, general texts, and government publications. The primary and secondary sources cited include legal treatises, periodical articles (including law review articles), and government publications printed from 1970 to 1986. This bibliography, prepared for the bicentennial of the Constitution, is suitable for general and undergraduate researchers seeking commentaries on and analyses of the Constitution.

487.   Rockwood, D. Stephen, Cecelia Brown, Kenneth Eshleman, and Deborah Shaffer. **American Third Parties since the Civil War: An Annotated Bibliography.** New York, Garland, 1985. 177p. index. (Garland Reference Library of Social Science, Vol. 227). $25.00. LC 83-49298. ISBN 0-8240-8970-7.

This selective bibliography is intended as a starting point for scholars and students studying third parties in the United States. As such it has not attempted to be comprehensive or to duplicate material in earlier bibliographies. The emphasis is on material published during the last half of this century. This limited focus will assist those who seek easy access to the major recent writings on American third parties.

The first chapter is on the theory and practice of third parties. Subsequent chapters deal with specific parties and cite primary and secondary sources. There are 1- or 2-sentence annotations for each of the 619 entries. At the beginning of each bibliography there is a short introductory essay tracing the history and development of the party considered. There are author and title indexes but no subject index.

488.   Smith, Myron J., Jr. **Watergate: An Annotated Bibliography of Sources in English, 1972-1982.** Metuchen, N.J., Scarecrow, 1983. 329p. index. $27.50. LC 83-4408. ISBN 0-8108-1623-7.

More than 2,500 English-language items are listed in this bibliography of the Watergate episode. Comprehensive and inclusive, this bibliography encompasses congressional documents, court decisions, memoirs, and video and sound recordings, as well as books, periodical and journal articles, and dissertations. The chronological limits were 1972 to June 1982. A list of basic reference works precedes the main bibliography.

The entries have brief but informative annotations. They are listed in one alphabetical sequence without topical subdivisions. Access is provided by the subject index. There are a number of additional features: a chronology of Watergate events, an edited version of the House Judiciary Committee report on the impeachment investigation of President Nixon, and a selection of short biographies of key individuals.

489.   Stephenson, D. Grier, Jr. **The Supreme Court and the American Republic: An Annotated Bibliography.** New York, Garland, 1981. 281p. (Garland Reference Library of Social Science, Vol. 85). $25.00. LC 80-8978. ISBN 0824093569.

Keeping in mind Alexis de Tocqueville's observation that almost every political question in America becomes a legal question, the author has provided a bibliography of 1,300 entries on the chief court, the Supreme Court of the United States. This bibliography does not attempt to be comprehensive, but concentrates on standard and readily available works. The citations have brief descriptive annotations.

The first chapters cover briefly the essentials of legal research sources. Six topical chapters focus on the history and development of the court and its role in constitutional interpretation. For matters dealing with the institutional development of the court, the powers of the three branches of government, and with civil rights, individual sections include relevant Supreme Court decisions with brief notes on their import. These are followed by citations to commentaries and analyses.

The final chapter covers biographical and autobiographical materials on individual Supreme Court judges. The two appendixes list the members of the court by chronological periods and by order of confirmation.

Biographical Sources

490. **American Leaders 1789-1987: A Biographical Summary.** Washington, D.C., Congressional Quarterly, 1987. 427p. index. $19.95. LC 86-30937. ISBN 0-87187-413-X.

Brief biographies of from two to six lines are provided for "American leaders" from the federal (presidents, vice presidents, justices of the Supreme Court, members of Congress) and state (governors only) levels of American government. For these individuals this is a convenient quick reference compilation for birth and death dates, party affiliation, and dates of service.

The volume also has a number of interesting tabulations drawn from Congressional Quarterly's data, such as black members of Congress or women members of Congress. Much of this information is readily available elsewhere, including in Congressional Quarterly's *Members of Congress* (see entry 610), which has the same information as in this volume for all senators and members of Congress to 1985.

491. Johnpoll, Bernard K., and Harvey Klehr, eds. **Biographical Dictionary of the American Left.** Westport, Conn., Greenwood, 1986. 493p. index. $65.00. LC 85-27252. ISBN 0-313-24200-3.

The leadership of the American left is represented in this biographical dictionary by some 275 entries written by 45 contributors. The subjects represent the various branches of the American left, including anarchists, syndicalists, socialists, and communists; all oppose the capitalist system. While none of these movements has ever come to power, the authors point out that their influence and membership have been considerable at various times in the history of the United States.

The portraits vary from one to seven pages in length. In addition to the usual biographical details, the sketches attempt broad subjects to highlight their major contributions to the American left and their place in the broader context of American political and social history. The appendixes break down the individuals by radical party affiliation, birthplace, birth date, and ethnic origin.

492. Stineman, Esther. **American Political Women: Contemporary and Historical Profiles.** Littleton, Colo., Libraries Unlimited, 1980. 228p. bibliog. index. $19.50. LC 80-24478. ISBN 0-87287-238-6.

Sixty portraits of American political women are presented in this biographical volume. The subjects are congresswomen, ambassadors, presidential assistants, governors, lieutenant governors, mayors, and many "firsts" who served during the 1970s and early 1980s. In most cases correspondence or interviews were used to compose the two- to three-page biographies. A list of selected speeches and works by and about the subject follows each biographical portrait.

There is also a 20-page annotated bibliography on all aspects of women in politics. Several valuable appendixes list: women in Congress, 1917-1980; women ambassadors, 1980; women chiefs of mission, 1933-1980; women federal judges, 1980; and women serving in key departmental, agency, and White House positions, 1980.

493. **Who's Who in American Politics 1987-1988.** 11th ed. New York, R. R. Bowker, 1987. 1,811p. index. $149.95. ISBN 0-8352-2219-5; ISSN 0000-0205.

Who's Who in American Politics, first published in 1967 and now in its 11th edition, has become the standard biographical directory of Americans currently active in local, state, or national politics. Of the 23,566 subjects included in this edition, 2,657 are appearing for the first time. The biographical entries are arranged by state, including territories. There is a name index.

Data in each sketch may include, as available: party affiliation; date and place of birth; names of parents, spouse and children; education; current and past political, governmental and business positions; military service; honors and awards; publications; memberships; religion; legal residence; and current mailing address. It might be well to remember that the information here is basically what the subjects wished to provide. At the beginning of the directory there are lists of cabinet members, members of Congress, state governors, and state political party chairs.

Dictionaries and Encyclopedias

494. Elliot, Jeffrey M., and Sheikh R. Ali. **The Presidential-Congressional Political Dictionary.** Santa Barbara, Calif., ABC-Clio, 1984. 365p. index. (Clio Dictionaries in Political Science, Vol. 9). $28.00; $15.00(pbk). LC 84-6326. ISBN 0874363578; 0874363587(pbk).

More than 750 terms linking the presidency and Congress are defined in this dictionary. The terms are arranged alphabetically in 12 chapters, including 6 on the president and the executive agencies and 6 on Congress and its committees and staff. These topical chapters parallel the arrangement commonly found in introductory texts on American government. Each definition is followed by a "Significance" paragraph, which interprets the historical and contemporary importance of the term.

The detailed index provides direct access to the main entries and other subjects, events, and individuals noted in the dictionary. The appendix has 10 sections, including organizational charts and tables of popular and electoral votes for president.

495. **Encyclopedia of the American Constitution.** Leonard W. Levy, Kenneth L. Karst, and Dennis J. Mahoney, eds. New York, Macmillan, 1986. 4v. index. $320.00/set. LC 86-3038. ISBN 0-02-918610-2.

With more than 2,000 articles, this impressive publication appeared in time for the 1987 bicentennial of the United States Constitution. The four volumes cover the major political, legal, and historical aspects of the Constitution. The signed articles vary in length from several paragraphs to eight or nine pages and range from biographical entries to considerations of constitutional doctrines and historical periods. Important court decisions and public acts are also covered.

The appendixes contain chronologies on the birth of the Constitution and on important events in the development of American constitutional law. There are also a four-page glossary of legal terms and a case index that includes a headnote explaining how to read legal citations. The set concludes with a name index and a detailed subject index.

This definitive work on the American Constitution is as suitable in content and writing style for students and the general public as for legal experts. Many of the articles on topics such as the Sacco and Vanzetti case, euthanasia, flag desecration, and equal protection under the law will appeal to a wide audience with diverse informational needs.

496. Filler, Louis. **Dictionary of American Conservatism.** New York, Philosophical Library, 1987. 380p. $29.95. LC 86-22665. ISBN 0-8022-2506-3.

Louis Filler offers this interesting compilation as the first dictionary of conservatism to be published in America. He has attempted to include selected "representative figures, visible personalities, and symbolic slogans and ideas" (foreword). Specific issues and events and influential writings are also covered. Most definitions are about one paragraph long, with some running to a page.

Filler's vague writing style and proconservative preferences are noticeable throughout this dictionary. Many readers will not appreciate his partisanship and the lack of clarity and context in his definitions. Nonetheless, this work is a useful reference source, since its contents range from identifications of personalities in the public eye, such as Richard Viguerie and William Buckley, to a succinct listing of the basic tenets of American conservatism.

497. Greene, Jack P., ed. **Encyclopedia of American Political History: Studies of the Principal Movements and Ideas.** New York, Scribner, 1984. 3v. index. $180.00/set. LC 84-1355. ISBN 0-684-17003-5.

For the general reader or student, this encyclopedia provides readable and authoritative articles prepared by American scholars who were selected to represent a broad range of ideological positions and historical viewpoints.

The format focuses on 90 articles covering important political events such as the American Revolution and the New Deal, selected documents such as the Constitution and *The Federalist*, and, in particular, the issues, themes, institutions, processes, and developments that have been significant through American history. Church and state, civil disobedience, machine politics, immigration, socialism, and state government are examples of these topics. The entries are narrative accounts averaging 10 pages in length. A substantial annotated bibliography follows each article. A detailed subject index provides access to specific terms. A 25-page introduction entitled "Historiography of American Political History," precedes the essays.

498. Plano, Jack C., and Milton Greenberg. **The American Political Dictionary.** 7th ed. New York, Holt, Rinehart & Winston, 1985. 606p. index. $24.95. LC 84-12822. ISBN 0-03-002844-2.

Rather than the usual alphabetical dictionary arrangement, this standard political dictionary, now in its 7th edition, divides the entries into 14 topical chapters, treating such subjects as the U.S. Constitution; civil liberties; the legislative, executive, and judicial branches; foreign policy; and national defense.

There are concise, clear definitions for over 1,200 terms. Numerous cross-references to other entries are provided. Important court cases and statutes are cited. All definitions include a short paragraph labeled "Significance," which provides useful analysis, especially for terms such as "Watergate," "advise and consent," and "Third World," where historical or political context is valuable. The detailed index provides for direct access to the terms defined.

499. Shafritz, Jay M. **The Dorsey Dictionary of American Government and Politics.** Chicago, Dorsey Press, 1988. 661p. illus. $34.95; $18.95(pbk). LC 87-72401. ISBN 0-256-05639-0; 0-256-05589-0(pbk).

With more than 4,000 entries, this dictionary attempts to provide all commonly used terms and concepts related to American government and politics, including the three major branches of government and such topics as foreign policy and public administration. According to the preface, "it captures and codifies the living language of American government and politics." It also includes short biographies of key persons, descriptions of landmark laws and Supreme Court decisions, and chronologies of major events.

This useful tool is clearly more than a dictionary of definitions, despite its title. It also contains over 100 fact boxes and, in general, attempts to assemble for the reader the necessary facts to understand the topics covered. The author has not failed to include newer terms and very current information. Photographs, cartoons, and charts add interest to the text. There are, in addition, five appendixes, which include an annotated copy of the Constitution, a guide to federal documents, a guide to statistical information on the American government, a review of relevant online databases, and a list of the key concepts used throughout the book.

500. Whisker, James B. **A Dictionary of Concepts on American Politics.** New York, John Wiley & Sons, 1980. 285p. index. $12.95(pbk). LC 80-15591. ISBN 0-471-07716-X.

The author, a professor of American government, attempts in this dictionary to provide students with concise definitions of the major ideas, concepts, events, and institutions that have shaped the American political tradition. These definitions are categorized into 12 topical chapters reflecting the organizational framework of a study of American politics. Headings include "The Founding of the Republic"; "Civil Liberties"; "International and Military Affairs"; and "The Presidency, Congress, and the Court System." Each chapter closes with a short selection of relevant court cases. Jack C. Plano and Milton Greenberg's *The American Political Dictionary* (see entry 498) is similarly arranged by topic, but with a more extensive coverage on the meaning and significance of the terms.

501. Young, Michael L. **The American Dictionary of Campaigns and Elections.** Lanham, Md., Hamilton Press, 1987. 246p. bibliog. index. $24.95. LC 87-14828. ISBN 0-8191-5446-6.

The specialized vocabulary of campaigns and elections is defined in this dictionary. The entries are arranged alphabetically within seven topical divisions, covering campaign processes, media and politics, polling and public opinion, electoral strategies and tactics, parties and PACs, voting and political behavior, and money and politics. There is an index covering all terms, plus numerous cross-references. The definitions are concise yet sufficient to provide a clear understanding of each term's basic meaning; additional background information clarifies the context of the term's usage in contemporary American politics.

Directories

502. **Black Elected Officials: A National Roster 1984.** Joint Center for Political Studies. New York, UNIPUB, 1984. 428p. $27.50(pbk). LC 84-051421. ISBN 0-89059-033-8.

This roster, which has been published since 1971, is a directory of national, state, and local black elected officials. The state-by-state listing identifies federal, state, county, and municipal officeholders, including judicial officials, police chiefs, and school superintendents. Titles and addresses are provided for all entries.

In addition to the directory information, there are also various charts, graphs, and statistical tables identifying the percentage of blacks in various political jurisdictions and the percentage of black government officials. These annual statistical analyses can be used for historical or comparative studies of black participation in American politics.

503. **Encyclopedia of Governmental Advisory Organizations 1986-87: A Reference Guide to Approximately 5,000 Permanent, Continuing, and Ad Hoc U.S. Presidential Advisory Committees, Congressional Advisory Committees, Public Advisory Committees, Interagency Committees, and Other Government-Related Boards, Panels, Task Forces, Commissions, Conferences, and Other Similar Bodies Serving in a Consultative Coordinating, Advisory, Research, or Investigative Capacity.** 5th ed. Denise M. Allard and Donna Batten, eds. Detroit, Gale, 1985. 1,133p. index. $425.00. ISBN 0-8103-0255-1; ISSN 0092-8380.

This comprehensive directory covers 5,422 existing or defunct governmental advisory organizations. These include presidential advisory committees, public advisory committees, and interagency committees ranging from the Interagency Integrated Pest Management Coordinating Committee to the Upper Mississippi River Basin Commission. These entries are arranged in 10 subject sections from agriculture to transportation.

For each organization, up to 13 points of information are provided, including name, address, key personnel, history and authority, program, membership and staff, publications and reports, and meetings. The text of the Federal Advisory Committee Act appears in an appendix. Five indexes provide multiple access points to the organizations: by key personnel, by presidential administration, by federal department, by keyword of name, and by publications and reports.

504. **Federal Executive Directory.** Washington, D.C., Carroll Publishing, 1980- . bimonthly. index. $140.00/yr. LC 80-664147. ISSN 0270-563X.

505. **Federal Regional Executive Directory.** Washington, D.C., Carroll Publishing, 1984- . semiannual. index. $125.00/yr. LC 84-644216. ISSN 0742-1729.

These two directories by Carroll Publishing offer extensive listings of federal government officials in Washington and in regional offices throughout the United States. The first section of the *Federal Executive Directory* lists officeholders alphabetically and includes telephone numbers and reference numbers to their organizational or congressional listings in the directory. These main sections list all the agencies of the executive branch and all the committees of Congress. For all units the key officials are listed with title, office number, and telephone number(s). There is a keyword index to the organizational and congressional listings.

The *Federal Regional Executive Directory* provides similar information for field offices of federal agencies. In addition to the alphabetical and organizational listings of executives, there are keyword subject and geographic indexes. There are also maps delineating the jurisdictions of the regional offices of the federal agencies. For less expensive, but less comprehensive and less up-to-date listings of federal officeholders, see the standard *United States Government Manual* (entry 529) and other commercially produced directories noted in this guide.

506. **Government Programs and Projects Directory.** Detroit, Gale, 1983- . irreg. $135.00/yr. LC 83-645478. ISSN 0737-5255.

Currently issued in three sections a year, this directory lists, identifies, and describes 1,574 programs and projects administered by the United States federal government. This source conveniently assembles much information derived directly from government agencies, from those agencies' annual reports and other publications, and heavily from the *Catalog of Federal Domestic Assistance*, a government publication. The Gale publication's coverage extends beyond that catalog to cover regulation, enforcement, and research activities as well as domestic assistance.

The entries are arranged alphabetically by agency. For each program the following may be provided: name, acronym, address, authorization, current funding, and a description of purpose and activities. Indexing by name and keyword facilitates access to the entries.

507. **Government Research Directory.** Detroit, Gale, 1980- . irreg. index. $335.00. LC 85-647549. ISSN 0882-3776.

The fourth edition (1987) of this directory has entries for approximately 3,000 United States government research and development centers, institutes, laboratories, test facilities, experiment centers, and data collection and analysis centers. These agencies conduct research in the fields of agriculture, business, defense, education, energy, engineering, the humanities, medicine, and basic and applied sciences. The entries are arranged by the parent agencies, which are drawn from the legislative and judicial branches and independent agencies as well as from the many executive branch agencies.

For each entry there is a paragraph containing the following: name, address, and telephone number; date of establishment; name of head of unit; size and composition of staff; and information on organization, research activities, publications, and services. There is a combined name, keyword, and parent agency index as well as separate geographic and subject indexes.

508.   National Directory of Women Elected Officials, 1987. Washington, D.C., National Women's Political Caucus, 1987. free.

Nearly 2,000 women serving in major political offices are identified in the 1987 edition of this directory. It is arranged by state with short biographical sketches outlining political activities. Date and place of birth, education, years of service, and local and Washington addresses and phone numbers are provided.

Women in the 100th Congress form the largest section. Other sections include listings with addresses of women holding statewide elective offices, women mayors of cities with population above 30,000, women officials of counties with populations over 100,000, and women serving on the Republican and Democratic national committees.

There are two interesting statistical tables that show the dramatic growth of women elected officials in the last decade and the percentage of women legislators in the 50 states. There is no master name index to the various sections.

509.   Roeder, Edward. PACs Americana: A Directory of Political Action Committees (PACs) and Their Interests. Washington, D.C., Sunshine Services, 1982. 859p. $200.00(pbk). LC 81-85581. ISBN 0-942236-00-9.

Political Action Committees (PACs), which have become an increasingly prominent component of contemporary American elections, are required by law to register and report on their activities and funding. The files of the Federal Election Commission have provided much of the information in this directory, which covers PACs registered to May 1982.

The first of three sections lists alphabetically the names of the sponsors of PACs and identifies their committees. The second section lists the PACs alphabetically by name with brief information on expenditures. The third section provides an outline of various political or economic interests with a list of PAC sponsors attached to each interest group.

The appendixes contain a list of 100 major PACs ranked by size of contributions, and data on PAC contributions arranged by state. For a source with a similar focus but a distinct approach, see Weinberger and Greevy's *The PAC Directory* (see entry 513).

510.   Taylor's Encyclopedia of Government Officials, Federal and State. Dallas, Political Research, 1967- . biennial. index. $375.00. LC 67-22269. ISSN 0082-2183.

This "encyclopedia" is basically a directory of government officeholders, both federal and state. Its major components are (1) listings of federal officials, including the president, vice president, and selected staffs; the cabinet, with about 25 top officials for each department; members of congress and senators listed by committee; chief judges of the federal judiciary; U.S. ambassadors; and the heads of independent agencies; (2) state entries with listings for governors and other major officials, United States senators and representatives, and all state senators and representatives; (3) photos of most of these officeholders; (4) state maps showing federal and state legislative districts, color-coded to show party control; and (5) names of delegates to the latest presidential convention.

There is no biographical information supplied on these officials. There is much miscellaneous information throughout the volume, such as a history of states' admission to the Union, a chronology of the Constitution, and a glossary. These features are noted only in the table of contents. There is an index of names. The subscription price includes quarterly updates.

511.   **The Washington Lobbyists & Lawyers Directory.** Paul Donovan, ed. 6th ed. 403p. Washington, D.C., Communications Services, 1984. $36.00. ISBN 0916459004.

The former title of this directory, the *Washington Influence Directory*, pointed to the organized efforts by lobbyists to influence the policies of the federal government. As a directory of lobbyists and lobbying organizations, this source contains several main sections, including an alphabetical listing of lobbyists and the organizations they represent; an alphabetical listing of lobbying and similar organizations and the individuals affiliated with them; and a list of political action groups and their sponsors.

For additional information on political action groups, consult *PACs Americana* (see entry 509), or *The PAC Directory* (see entry 513). *Washington Representatives* (entry 512) is another directory of lobbyists.

512.   **Washington Representatives.** Washington, D.C., Columbia Books, 1977- . annual. index. $50.00(pbk). LC 76-21152. ISBN 0-910416-49-4.

More than 10,000 individuals are included in this directory of lobbyists, legal advisers, consultants, and foreign agents. Most are officers of trade and professional associations; others represent labor unions, individual corporations, or special interest causes ranging from ERA to handgun control. An introductory essay outlines their general activities and their role in the American political process.

The material is arranged in four sections: (1) an alphabetical list of individuals, with addresses, phone numbers, notes on background, and lists of clients; (2) an alphabetical list of organizations, with addresses, phone numbers, and the names of persons who represent them; (3) an index of these organizations by their industry group or the principal subject of their legislative concern; and (4) a country-by-country index of foreign governments and organizations with special representation in Washington. For another directory of lobbyists, see *The Washington Lobbyists and Lawyers Directory* (entry 511).

513.   Weinberger, Marvin, and David U. Greevy, comps. **The PAC Directory: A Complete Guide to Political Action Committees.** Cambridge, Mass., Ballinger, 1982. 1v. (various paging). $185.00. LC 82-11480. ISBN 0-88410-856-2; ISSN 0733-0936.

Like Edward Roeder's *PACs Americana* (see entry 509), this directory provides comprehensive coverage of PACs, political action committees. The Federal Election Campaign Act of 1971, which requires that PACs register and disclose information on their sponsors, activities, and finances, has largely made possible these directories. While Roeder's work concentrates on identifying the sponsors of PACs, this directory focuses on the activities and, especially, the finances of the PACs themselves.

There are seven sections in this extremely well-organized and informative compilation. Section 2 is a PAC directory, providing name, address, contact persons, phone number, and sponsoring organization for each entry. Section 3 lists all corporate PACs by the Standard Industrial Classification categories. The other sections cover finances, with summaries of financial contributions and expenditures for elections in the 1977-1980 period. Details are provided of candidates who received more than $1,500. There are also lists of the top PAC contributors and the top House and Senate recipients.

514. Wilcox, Laird, comp. **Guide to the American Left: Directory and Bibliography.** Kansas City, Mo., Editorial Research Service, 1986. 86p. $14.95(spiralbound). ISBN 0-933592-40-X.

515. Wilcox, Laird, comp. **Guide to the American Right: Directory and Bibliography.** Kansas City, Mo., Editorial Research Service, 1986. 80p. $14.95(spiralbound). ISBN 0-933592-41-8.

These two directories list organizations at both ends of the American political spectrum. The first title covers liberal, socialist, communist, protest, and other left-wing organizations. The companion volume lists conservative, nationalistic, patriotic, anticommunist, and other right-wing groups. Both volumes have the same format. The entries all contain addresses and a brief indication of the interests and activities of the organizations. Both directories also contain bibliographies of the publications of the organizations and lists of major "alternative" collections in libraries.

Handbooks

516. Austin, Erik W. **Political Facts of the United States since 1789.** New York, Columbia University Press, 1986. 518p. $30.00. LC 86-2605. ISBN 0-231-06094-7.

The efforts of the compilers to assemble the basic facts necessary to understand the American political system and political events have resulted in this hefty volume of names, facts, and statistics. Coverage extends from the founding of the nations to 1985, with a distinct emphasis on national politics.

The data are organized in seven chapters, dealing with the executive, judicial, and legislative branches of the national leadership; state politics; parties and elections; foreign affairs; the armed forces; revenue and public expenditure; and demographic information. Election results and lists of officeholders constitute the core of the book. There is also information on such diverse matters as voter turnout, active military personnel, and black population by state. Most of the data were taken from standard works, such as indicated in the list of sources. The merging of information from varying sources for unified historical tables, however, will make this a convenient reference tool for many.

517. Barone, Michael, and Grant Ujifusa. **The Almanac of American Politics 1986: The President, the Senators, the Representatives, the Governors: Their Records and Election Results, Their States and Districts.** Washington, D.C., National Journal, 1985. 1,593p. illus. index. $34.95; $28.95(pbk). ISBN 0-89234-032-0; 0-89234-033-9(pbk).

State overviews of the contemporary political situation are the major focus of this very useful and readable compilation of facts and statistics. For each state profile there are segments on the governor, the senators, and all representatives. In addition to personal and career information and a photograph, the material on the members of Congress includes committee assignments, votes on key bills, and ratings by about a dozen interest groups with a wide spectrum of political orientations. Campaign contributions and expenditures are also noted, as well as recent election results. The state profiles include data on the share of the federal tax burden and share of federal expenditures. For each state and congressional district, there is a demographic profile focusing on income, racial, and ethnic data.

Preceding the main section is a series of short essays on the presidency and Congress. These, as well as the narrative descriptions preceding each state summary, are an outstanding feature of this handbook. While some readers may not agree with the opinions expressed, they provide colorful insight into the personalities and careers of the politicians and a vivid snapshot of the realities of their districts and constituents. The almanac ends with a section on campaign finances and a list of congressional committee assignments. This publications, which began in 1975, is now revised biennially.

518. Blake, Fay M., and H. Morton Newman. **Verbis Non Factis: Words Meant to Influence Political Choices in the United States, 1800-1980.** Metuchen, N.J., Scarecrow, 1984. 143p. index. $13.50. LC 84-1325. ISBN 0-8108-1688-1.

This reference source contains 1,062 American political slogans used between 1800 and 1980. Slogans here are "short sentences or jingles which arose in the course of a political campaign" (introduction). They are used on banners, buttons, bumper stickers, and now, of course, in television commercials. "Tippecanoe and Tyler, Too" (1840), "Moral Majority" (1980), and "A Vote for Al Smith Is a Vote for the Pope" (1928) are three examples from a book made for browsing.

The slogans are listed chronologically, with the year, the candidate, and the political party that used the slogan identified. At least one citation to a publication in which the slogan appeared is provided. There are three indexes of the slogans: by political party, by name of individual, and by keyword.

519. **The Capital Source: The Who's Who, What, Where in Washington.** Washington, D.C., National Journal, 1985- . semiannual. $20.00/issue. LC 86-642431.

As the subtitle proclaims, this is another handbook or guide to all the information on all the people and organizations that anyone would presumably need to effectively deal with the Washington scene. The listings are grouped into four large categories: (1) government, including the White House, the cabinet, the Senate and House (including all committees), federal courts, and foreign embassies; (2) corporate, including financial institutions, unions, interest groups, and think tanks; (3) professional, including associations, law firms, advertising companies, public relations firms, and private clubs; and (4) media, including television, columnists, newspapers, foreign press, and publishing companies.

The entries are brief: name, title, address, and phone number only. The categories and entries contain no commentary or description, which would at times be useful, for example, in clarifying the political orientation of the think tanks. This handbook, nevertheless, contains a large array of names arranged in a straightforward format at a very reasonable price.

520. D'Aleo, Richard J. **FEDfind: Your Key to Finding Federal Government Information: A Directory of Information Sources, Products, and Services.** 2d ed. Springfield, Va., ICUC Press, 1986. 480p. illus. index. $17.95; $9.95(pbk). LC 85-27267. ISBN 0-910205-03-5; 0-910-205-02-7(pbk).

Starting with the admonition that "information is power," the author has designed this reference guide for the general public interested in obtaining information produced by or about the federal government. The book identifies and describes more than 700 publications and services that could serve as tools for obtaining additional information from the sources cited or through contact with the appropriate agencies.

The handbook is divided into three sections. The first covers the organization of the federal government and its personnel. Many directories and biographical works are listed. The second section covers the three branches of the federal government, with information on the legislative and budget processes and on statistical and mapping services. The last section focuses on major agencies as information sources, such as the Government Printing Office and the National Technical Information Service.

This extremely useful guide ends with a series of appendixes that provide information on doing business with the federal government, information on the Freedom of Information Act and the Sunshine Act, and a list of telephone contacts for federal agencies with major statistical programs. Finally, there is a title index to all the publications and services found in the subject sections of *FEDfind*. For another guide to federal information, consult Matthew Lesko's **Information U.S.A.** (entry 525), which emphasizes identifying contact persons and experts.

521. **Elections.** Washington, D.C., Congressional Quarterly, 1976- . biennial. $9.95. LC 86-6817. ISBN 0-87187-387-7 (1986).

The excellent series by Congressional Quarterly both looks ahead and records the past. The 1986 edition, written in early 1986, provided an outlook for the 1986 congressional and gubernatorial elections, with a description of the political forces expected to shape the campaign. Various political trends, redistricting, political action committees, and other factors anticipated to impact on the elections are analyzed in a series of chapters.

The lengthy appendix documents the 1984 election returns for governorships and for Senate and House seats, the 1984 presidential elections, and 1985 campaign finances. The voting records of the individual members of Congress on selected key issues are also documented.

522. Engelman, Thomas S. **The Federalist Concordance.** Thomas S. Engelman, Edward J. Esler, and Thomas B. Hofeller, eds. Chicago, University of Chicago Press, 1988. 622p. index. $60.00; $19.95(pbk). LC 88-10633. ISBN 0-226-20836-2; 0-226-20837-0(pbk).

With the use of a computer, every significant word in *The Federalist* has been indexed, based on the edition of these political writings by Jacob E. Cooke, published by Wesleyan University Press in 1961. This research tool will be of obvious utility for anyone beginning serious study of the Federalist essays.

523. **Federal Regulatory Directory.** 5th ed. Washington, D.C., Congressional Quarterly, 1986. 942p. illus. index. $49.95. LC 79-644368. ISBN 0-87187-362-1; ISSN 0195-749X.

The preface of the fifth edition of this standard guide to federal regulation notes that through the growth of regulatory agencies slowed during the Reagan administration, their importance remains enormous. The main section of this guide provides extensive profiles, as long as nearly 40 pages, of 13 of the major regulatory agencies. Each profile contains sections on the agency's history, powers and authority, personnel, and enforcement activities. Many key officials are listed with phone numbers. Relevant congressional committees and the legislation establishing the agencies are cited. There are very useful segments on regional offices, hotlines, computer databases, publications, and other sources of information.

Ninety other agencies with less important regulatory activities are more briefly described. An extensive introduction covers the history and process of regulation and current issues regarding reform or deregulation. The appendixes contain guides to the use of the *Federal Register* and the *Code of Federal Regulation*.

524. **Freedom of Information Guide.** Rev. ed. Washington, D.C., WANT Publishing, 1984. 116p. $7.95(pbk). LC 81-70749. ISBN 0-942008-030.

This publication attempts to be the citizen's guide to the "vast store of information" (introduction) that may be obtained from the federal government given the right tactics. It offers a step-by-step guide to understanding the Freedom of Information Act (FOIA) and the Privacy Act (PA). There are detailed instructions on how to make initial requests and how to appeal denials of access. There is also a directory of FOIA and PA officers for various government agencies, a discussion of recent developments in FOIA law, and a survey of some recent requests; these requests illustrate the range of information asked for and the responses.

Appendixes include the text of both acts and copies of actual requests and agency responses. This guide is a most useful starting point for the citizen who wishes to take advantage of the opportunities provided by these acts without professional legal assistance.

525. Lesko, Matthew. **Information U.S.A.** Rev. ed. New York, Viking Penguin, 1986. 1,253p. index. $50.00. LC 85-40628. ISBN 0-670-80972-1.

This guide to government information for the general public is based on the premise that a large portion of the nearly 3 million federal bureaucrats employed by the government are information specialists who can be tapped by the public, the information consumers. The core section of this book, a directory of federal departments, attempts to identify these resource persons. While the profiles vary in length depending on the complexity of the agency or the scope of its services, each profile contains a breakdown of major divisions, a very detailed list of experts with names and phone numbers, and a section labeled "Major Sources of Information," which includes publications, programs, and services. The public has access to this information either by browsing through the agency sections or by consulting the detailed index.

There is also, at the beginning, a "Sampler Section" that offers a miscellany of useful information, including "The Best of the Freebies," and lists of hotlines, sources of free help for family or business, and federal information centers and regional offices of federal agencies. Another guide to federal agencies as information sources is the *Washington Information Directory* (see entry 530), which also includes private sources.

526. **National Party Conventions, 1831-1984.** 4th ed. Washington, D.C., Congressional Quarterly, 1987. 264p. illus. index. $10.25. LC 87-20071. ISBN 0-87187-450-4.

The major political parties and most of the more prominent third parties have met in convention to select their presidential and vice-presidential candidates since the 1830s. The fourth edition provides concise, up-to-date information on the nominating process and political conventions.

The core of the handbook is the convention chronology, which contains a 1- to 12-page profile on each convention since 1831. Democrats, Republicans, and other parties receiving at least 2 percent of the popular vote in any presidential election are included. Brief narrative accounts of each convention, with excerpts from platforms and significant roll calls, are included.

Other sections include the results of balloting for presidential candidates and other major issues; historical profiles of political parties; a biographical directory of presidential and vice-presidential nominees; a description of the nominating process before the 1830s; and an overview of the function and development of the national convention. Most of the sections have bibliographies. There is a detailed index.

527. **A Reference Guide to the United States Supreme Court.** Stephen P. Elliott, general ed. New York, Facts-on-File, 1986. 476p. illus. bibliog. index. $50.00. LC 85-20464. ISBN 0-8160-1018-8.

As a comprehensive reference guide, this title examines a broad range of the Supreme Court's history and activities. Its narration and analysis are presented in six major sections: (1) "The Role of the Supreme Court," (2) "Constitutional Powers of the Branches of the Federal Government," (3) "Division of Power," (4) "Individual Rights," (5) "Landmark

Cases," and (6) "Biographies of the Justices." More than 325 major cases are summarized and analyzed in the fifth section. The last section constitutes a biographical dictionary of every justice who has served on the Supreme Court.

The appendixes provide chronologies of the justices and of landmark cases. A bibliography and thorough indexes to cases, individuals, and subjects complete this handbook.

528. Schapsmeier, Edward L., and Frederick H. Schapsmeier. **Political Parties and Civic Action Groups.** Westport, Conn., Greenwood, 1981. 554p. index. (Greenwood Encyclopedia of American Institutions, No. 4). $49.50. LC 80-1714. ISBN 0-313-21442-5.

Profiles of almost 300 political organizations, parties, civic action groups, or "factions" are presented in this handbook. Coverage includes existing and defunct groups from the colonial period to the present. To be included an organization had to have a formal existence, had to have been involved in political activities, and had to have had national historical relevance. Such diverse groups as Tammany Hall, Common Cause, and the Ku Klux Klan are included, along with all significant American political parties.

Entries vary in length from a short paragraph to over 20 pages. The origins, history, goals, and major contributions of the organizations are highlighted. Official publications and sources of additional information are cited. The appendixes include a list of the organizations by function, a chronology of their founding dates, and a glossary of terms used in the text. There is a name and subject index.

529. **United States Government Manual.** Washington, D.C., GPO, 1935- . annual. index. $19.00. LC 35-26025. ISSN 0083-1174.

The United States Government Manual serves as the official handbook of the federal government and as a directory of chief officeholders. Comprehensive information is provided on the agencies of the legislative, judicial, and executive branches of the government. Independent agencies, quasi-official agencies, and international organizations in which the United States participates are also covered.

Agency profiles include a list of principal officials, a statement of the agency's purpose, a brief history, including authorizing legislation, and a description of its programs and activities. There are extensive subsections for all major agency subunits. Most agency descriptions include a Sources of Information segment which offers information on publications, contact persons, grants, and other matters of general interest. Five appendixes provide (1) lists of abolished or transferred agencies or functions, (2) abbreviations and acronyms, (3) organizational charts, (4) a map of standard federal regions, and (5) a list of agencies with references to the *Code of Federal Regulations*. Name and subject/agency indexes complete this authoritative handbook of the federal government.

530. **Washington Information Directory.** Washington, D.C., Congressional Quarterly, 1976- . annual. index. $39.95. LC 75-646321. ISSN 0887-8064.

This directory is an annual compilation of information sources available in the Washington area. The information is divided into 16 chapters covering various topics such as energy, defense, business, health, individual assistance, national security, and international affairs.

The sources cited for the information fall into three categories: executive branch agencies, Congress, and nonprofit organizations outside the government. For each entry there is a paragraph of information which includes name of principal officer, address, telephone number, and a statement of purpose, responsibility, and activities.

As a guide to official and unofficial Washington this is an invaluable reference work. It contains a very clearly written introductory section on how to use the directory efficiently and a detailed subject index. In addition, the appendixes contain listings for senators and representatives (including offices and committee assignments), foreign and American ambassadors, labor unions, regional offices of federal departments, state officials, and mayors of cities with a population of 75,000 or more. For a similar title, see *Washington: A Comprehensive Directory* (entry 531).

531.   **Washington [year]: A Comprehensive Directory of the Key Institutions and Leaders of the National Capital Area.** Washington, D.C., Columbia Books, 1984- . annual. index. $50.00(pbk). LC 84-649141. ISSN 0083-7393.

This annual directory includes major public, quasi-public, and private institutions in the greater Washington area. It includes 17 chapters or categories of organizations, covering national government, local government, international affairs, national issues, the media, business, national associations, labor unions, the bar, medicine and health, foundations and philanthropy, science and policy research, education, religion, cultural institutions, clubs, and community affairs. Each chapter has an introductory note with background information; the entries cover over 3,400 organizations and 15,000 individuals. A large second portion of the volume is a combined index of all institutions and leaders listed. For a similar title, see the *Washington Information Directory* (entry 530).

532.   Whitnah, Donald R., ed. **Government Agencies.** Westport, Conn., Greenwood, 1983. 683p. index. (Greenwood Encyclopedia of American Institutions, No. 7). $49.95. LC 82-15815. ISBN 0-313-22017-4.

More than 100 articles on United States federal government agencies – departments, bureaus, commissions – are covered in this reference source. Notable defunct agencies and quasi-government entities are also included (but not the Library of Congress).

Historical and critical information is provided in addition to an overview on the origins, development, and missions of the agencies. The contributors paid particular attention to achievements, failures, administrative structures, and "in-house and external squabbles" (preface). At the conclusion of each agency portrait is a brief annotated bibliography of sources of additional information. The appendixes present a chronological compilation of agencies and their dates of establishment, a genealogy outlining the evolution of agency names, a list of umbrella agencies with their subunits, and a list of agencies by broad subject category.

533.   Wolfe, Gregory. **Right Minds: A Sourcebook of American Conservative Thought.** Chicago, Regnery Books, 1987. 245p. index. $16.95. LC 86-20388. ISBN 0-89526-583-4.

William F. Buckley in his foreword states that this sourcebook contains "ninety percent of anything one would ever need" to understand the conservative movement in America. Whether that is accurate or not, this book does include information on many useful elements of American conservatism for reference work, including a bibliography of basic writings, brief biographies of 75 individuals, and lists of key journals, publishers, and collections of private papers. There is also a very interesting chapter that identifies and describes the think tanks and foundations that have become so prominent in recent years in conservative efforts to influence public opinion and political decisionmaking.

Indexes

534. American Public Opinion Index. Louisville, Ky., Opinion Research Service, 1981- . annual. $125.00. LC 83-646386. ISSN 0740-8978.

In addition to pollsters with well-known names like Gallup, Roper, and Harris, there are hundreds of other organizations gathering information on public opinion. This index attempts to include all these major national, state, and local polls in its annual volume.

The entries represent, but do not quote exactly, the questions asked in the surveys covered in this annual. They are arranged by subject with cross-references but no index. Responses are not included. Section 2 provides additional information, including some specifics on sample size, methodology, and universe of the polls cited. The address and phone number of the polling organization are provided for users who wish to make contact for more information or for a copy of the public responses. Opinion Research Service's companion microfiche set containing the responses is called *American Public Opinion Data*.

535. Birch, Carol L., ed. **Unity in Diversity: An Index to the Publications of Conservative and Libertarian Institutions.** Compiled by the New American Foundation. Metuchen, N.J., Scarecrow, 1983. 263p. index. $18.50. LC 82-20552. ISBN 0-8108-1599-0.

The growing prominence of research centers, or think tanks, in recent years has produced a considerable volume of literature intended to influence public opinion or directly impact on the policy decision process. This index concentrates on 15 conservative and libertarian research centers such as the American Enterprise Institute for Public Policy (AEI), the CATO Institute, and the Heritage Foundation. The preface states that the focus of the index is on "the most serious work," avoiding "single-issue propaganda mills."

The index covers the period 1970 through 1981 and includes periodical articles, reports, and books. The 3,021 entries are classified into a subject list adopted from *Public Affairs Information Service Bulletin* (PAIS). There are extensive cross-references and an author index. Much of the material covered here is not indexed elsewhere.

536. Guenther, Nancy Anderman. **United States Supreme Court Decisions: An Index to Excerpts, Reprints, and Discussions.** 2d ed. Metuchen, N.J., Scarecrow, 1983. 856p. index. $52.50. LC 82-10518. ISBN 0-8108-1578-8.

The main section of this index lists over 4,000 Supreme Court cases in chronological order. It provides either the full texts or excerpts of these decisions along with citations to the *United States Reports*, the official source of the texts of Supreme Court decisions. There are also citations to discussions of the cases in nonofficial sources. Nearly 600 such sources in books, anthologies, and periodical articles published between 1960 and 1980 are indexed in this second edition. Titles were selected for indexing that were considered to be generally available in undergraduate libraries. The greatest use of this index will be by researchers and librarians working in libraries that lack the specialized legal digests and indexes found in law libraries or that lack substantial runs of the *United States Reports*.

537. Mitchell, Ralph, comp. and ed. **An Index to the Constitution of the United States with Glossary.** Kenosha, Wis., Ralph Mitchell, 1980. 62p. index. $4.95; $2.95(pbk). LC 79-92545. ISBN 0-9604106-0-0; 0-9604106-1-9(pbk).

Appearing in time for the bicentennial of the Constitution, this index makes it easy to locate specific provisions in the United States Constitution. A very thorough subject index leads the user to appropriate articles, sections, or paragraphs in the Constitution. Numerous cross-references add to the ease of finding terms in this index.

This source includes a glossary of 80 basic, technical, and obscure terms used in the Constitution. It also contains the complete text of the Constitution, including all amendments. This one source conveniently combines index, definitions, and text of the Constitution.

538. **United States Political Science Documents.** Pittsburgh, University of Pittsburgh, University Center for International Studies, 1975- . annual. index. $300.00. LC 77-643165. ISSN 0148-6063.

USPSD, which is published in conjunction with the American Political Science Association, has become since its inception in 1975 a major source for periodical indexing in political science. The 1986 volumes contain 43,000 entries selected from 150 journals.

The first volume of the two-volume set includes the five indexes: author, subject, geographic, proper name, and journal. The *Political Science Thesaurus* was used for the subject index. The proper name index contains many entries for specific organizations, events, ethnic groups, etc. that are not descriptors and therefore not in the subject index. The second part contains the abstracts of the articles indexed in part 1. *USPSD* can also be searched online through the DIALOG-database service (see entry 321).

539. **Who Knows: A Guide to Washington Experts.** Washington, D.C., Washington Researchers, 1977- . irreg. index. $125.00. LC 86-645855. ISSN 0894-8801.

The former title of this publication, *Researcher's Guide to Washington Experts*, was a concise description of its focus. The basic premises are that the federal government is the world's largest producer of information and that this information is available free or at minimal cost to those who know the office or individual to contact.

The directory provides access to this information by leading the researcher directly to the appropriate specialist. More than 11,000 federal experts are listed in the latest edition. These experts are arranged by agency, with subdivisions for the major units. Provided for each individual are title (or description of area of expertise), address, and phone number. A detailed subject index provides access to the experts by topic rather than through the main agency arrangement. Two titles with similar purpose are *FEDfind* (see entry 520) and *Information, U.S.A.* (see entry 525).

Sourcebooks

540. **America Votes: A Handbook of Contemporary American Election Statistics.** New York, Macmillan, 1956- . biennial. $80.00. LC 56-10132. ISSN 0065-678X.

America Votes has long been recognized as the standard source for election statistics. The first section covers presidential races from 1920 to 1984, with total vote; Republican, Democratic, and other vote; and plurality. Percentages are tabulated, and all data are broken down by state. Presidential primaries are also covered, but in less detail. The second, major section presents a state-by-state profile of voting. Each state section provides postwar vote for governor and for senator, congressional voting results by district, and a map of congressional districts. Presidential and senatorial voting for 1984 are also given, with country tabulations.

The compilation is strictly a source of election statistics. It does not provide narrative commentaries or analyze results. There are no tabulations by age, race, sex, or any other variables.

541. **Congressional Quarterly's Guide to U.S. Elections.** 2d ed. Washington, D.C. Congressional Quarterly, 1985. 1,308p. illus. maps. index. $100.00. LC 85-6912. ISBN 0-87187-339-7.

The editors claim that this massive compilation is the "most comprehensive published collection of data on elections for president, governor, senator and representative" (p. xiii). Congressional Quarterly, a preeminent publisher of information about American elections, has prepared this volume, which is packed with election statistics, charts, chronologies, bibliographies, and photographs of politicians.

The data is covered in six major sections, which cover (1) political parties, including conventions; (2) presidential elections, including the electoral college, electoral and popular votes, primaries, and a biographical directory of candidates; (3) gubernatorial elections, including lists of governors and popular vote returns; (4) senate elections, including lists of senators and popular vote returns; (5) house elections, including reapportionment and redistricting and popular vote returns; and (6) southern primaries, including popular vote returns.

The extensive appendix includes a list of sessions of Congress, charts of political party affiliation for Congress and the presidency, and constitutional provisions on elections. Finally, there is a general index and a candidate index covering the entire work.

542. **The Gallup Poll: Public Opinion.** Wilmington, Del., Scholarly Resources, 1978- . annual. index. $55.00. LC 79-56557. ISSN 0195-962X.

The results of Gallup public opinion polls are available in these annual volumes. The arrangement of surveys is by date. For each survey the question asked is cited and the results listed, often with breakdowns by various demographic and socioeconomic variables. In many cases the results from recent past years are also provided. Many of the questions deal with political matters, presidential approval, party preference, and foreign and domestic policy issues. Others deal with social questions, for example, religious preference or attitudes on specific matters such as the public schools or treatment of AIDS victims. A very detailed subject index provides access to the polls. At the beginning of the volume there are notes on sample design.

This series has been an annual since 1978. It continues providing the information published in a two-volume set by Scholarly Resources in 1978 (*The Gallup Poll: Public Opinion 1971-77*) and in a three-volume set by Random House in 1972 (*The Gallup Poll: Public Opinion 1935-1971*). *The Gallup Report* (Princeton, N.J., Gallup Organization, 1981- . monthly. $45.00[academic institutions], $75.00[other subscribers]. LC 83-643597. ISSN 0731-6143) provides current data in a monthly publication.

543. **Historic Documents.** Washington, D.C., Congressional Quarterly, 1972- . annual. index. $25.00. LC 72-97888. ISSN 0892-080X.

As an annual collection of documents, this series provides convenient access to important speeches, reports, statements, and court decisions related to national and international events. The diversity of the documents is evident in the 1986 edition, which includes Reagan's State of the Union address, Gorbachev's address to the 27th Soviet Party Congress, the Vatican statement of Liberation theology, and the Institute of Medicine's Report on AIDS. Some documents are printed in full, while longer items have been excerpted.

Each entry is preceded by a brief introduction containing background information that helps place the documents in perspective. The documents are arranged in chronological order. The table of contents and the name and subject index provide access for those who do not know the approximate date or do not have a specific document in mind.

544.   Johnson, Donald Bruce, comp. **National Party Platforms of 1980: Supplement to National Party Platforms, 1840-1976.** Champaign, University of Illinois Press, 1982. 233p. index. $14.95(pbk). LC 81-10448. ISBN 0-252-00923-1.

This supplement updates with the 1980 party platforms the revised edition of *National Party Platforms* published in 1978. That volume contained copies of the platforms of all major and some minor political parties from 1840 to 1976. The unabridged texts of the platforms appeared arranged chronologically in two volumes. Future revisions of the second volume (which covers 1960-1976) are anticipated to include future party platforms.

In addition to the platform texts, there is a discussion of what constitutes a national party, plus brief summaries of the conventions and the election statistics for each national campaign. There are name and subject indexes. This source is particularly useful for locating the platforms of minor, regional, or defunct parties.

545.   Miller, Warren E., Arthur H. Miller, and Edward J. Schneider. **American National Election Studies Data Sourcebook, 1952-1978.** Cambridge, Mass., Harvard University Press, 1980. 388p. $25.00(spiralbound). LC 79-25632. ISBN 0-674-02634-9.

This compendium of nearly 400 pages of tables and graphs was prepared by the Center for Political Studies. The data are based on information gathered on voter backgrounds, behavior, and opinions collected in 14 biennial studies covering postwar American politics. The introduction discusses the interview process and reliability factors, and provides guidance in using the data.

The data are presented in six chapters, which cover: (1) social characteristics of the electorate, (2) political partisanship, (3) positions on public policy issues, (4) support of the political system, (5) political involvement and voter turnout, and (6) the vote. The behavioral and attitudinal differences are analyzed in terms of selected demographic and socioeconomic variables. All of the data are comparable on a cross-time basis, making possible political interpretations over time.

546.   United States Bureau of the Census. **Census of Governments.** Washington, D.C., GPO, 1957- . quinquennial. LC 57-62053.

The census of governments has been taken every five years (for years ending in 2 and 7) since 1957. It was taken at 10-year intervals from 1850 to 1942; the present series began after a 15-year gap. These extensive statistical compilations provide data on state, local, and municipal governments.

The 1987 census has eight sections: (1) government organizations, (2) taxable property values and assessment, (3) public employment, (4) government finances, (5) local government in metropolitan areas, (6) topical studies, (7) a guide to the 1982 census of governments, and (8) procedural history. The Census Bureau's *Census Catalog and Guide* contains a detailed outline and descriptions of the issues in each of those sections.

UNITED STATES—PRESIDENCY

Bibliographies

547.   **The American Presidency: A Historical Bibliography.** Santa Barbara, Calif., ABC-Clio, 1984. 376p. (Clio Bibliography Series, No. 15). index. $65.00. LC 83-12245. ISBN 0-87436-370-5.

As with other Clio bibliographies, the ABC-Clio databases were searched to compile the 3,489 entries that constitute this bibliography. The entries represent periodical articles from over 2,000 titles published between 1973 and 1982. All aspects of the presidency and the careers and personal lives of individual chief executives are included.

The citations are organized in four large chronological sections subdivided by broad subject categories. For most searches the researcher will need to employ the comprehensive, detailed subject index. Each entry has an abstract of the content of the article. For those libraries with *America: History and Life*, the source of this bibliography (see entry 000), the major asset of *The American Presidency* is the convenience of having 10 years of coverage gathered into one volume.

548. Bohanan, Robert D., comp. **Dwight D. Eisenhower: A Selected Bibliography of Periodical and Dissertation Literature.** Abilene, Kan., Dwight D. Eisenhower Library, National Archives and Records Service, 1981. 162p. index. $3.25(pbk). LC 81-3139. ISBN 0-9605728-0-5.

With the increasing interest in recent years in the Eisenhower presidency, this bibliography, compiled by the staff of the Eisenhower Library, will be of considerable use for scholars and students. The first section includes citations for periodical literature arranged in 10 subject categories. There is an author index and a subject index for detailed subjects and those that overlap the subject categories used. Most of the periodical citations have annotations. The articles selected deal either with Eisenhower the man or with issues and persons closely associated with him. The dissertations in the second section are not annotated. Monographs have been omitted, as the compilers concluded that sufficient bibliographic control of them already existed. Coverage in this bibliography extends through early 1980.

549. Burns, Richard Dean, comp. **Harry S. Truman: A Bibliography of His Times and Presidency.** Compiled for the Harry S. Truman Library Institute. Wilmington, Del., Scholarly Resources, 1984. 297p. illus. index. $50.00. LC 84-20223. ISBN 0-8420-2219-8.

Approximately 3,000 items, including books, periodical articles, dissertations, and documents, were selected for this bibliography covering the literature written during the three decades since the end of Harry S. Truman's administration. The annotated entries, arranged in eleven chapters, focus on Truman's personal life, political life, and the major events and personalities involved in domestic and foreign affairs during his presidency. Each chapter is introduced by a brief essay narrating the major events and discussing the more prominent citations.

In addition to the bibliography, there is a 15-page chronology of Truman's life and adminstration and author and subject indexes. This is a useful reference tool for students and scholars, although manuscript collections and foreign-language materials are not included.

550. Casper, Dale E. **Richard M. Nixon: A Bibliographic Exploration.** New York, Garland, 1988. 221p. index. (Garland Reference Library of Social Science, Vol. 415). $30.00. LC 87-28064. ISBN 0-8240-8478-0.

For over 25 years Richard Nixon was a major figure in American politics, which has resulted in a voluminous literature. The compiler of this bibliography noted that since 1980 there was been an average of over 40 scholarly and popular articles published each year. The introduction discusses this literature and the place in history it assigns to Nixon. The bibliography contains over 1,700 unannotated citations dating from the late 1940s to 1986. Books and journal articles in the English language are included. Government publications and dissertations are not. This bibliography, divided into 10 parts, highlights the major political achievements of Nixon's career. There is an author and a subject index.

551. Davison, Kenneth E. **The American Presidency: A Guide to Information Sources.** Detroit, Gale, 1983. 467p. index. (American Studies Information Guide Series, Vol. 11; Gale Information Guide Library). $48.00. LC 73-17552. ISBN 0-8103-1261-1.

Davison's bibliography, a selective listing of materials on the American presidency, would be a good starting point for research in most cases. Researchers needing comprehensive coverage will want to turn to works focusing on specific eras or individual presidents. This bibliography contains approximately 4,000 citations to books, journal articles, documents, and some source materials. The emphasis is on works published since 1945.

The book is organized in two parts, with the first dealing with various general aspects of the presidency, such as elections, presidential functions, powers, etc. The remaining chapters cover the presidents individually, from Washington through Reagan. There are author, title, and subject indexes. For a more extensive treatment of this subject see Fenton S. Martin's two volumes, *The American Presidency* (entry 557), and *The American Presidents* (entry 558).

552. Gould, Lewis L., and Craig H. Roell. **William McKinley: A Bibliography.** Westport, Conn., Meckler, 1988. 238p. index. (Meckler's Bibliographies of the Presidents of the United States, v.24). $45.00. LC 88-15531. ISBN 0-88736-138-2.

The Meckler series attempts to provide book-length bibliographies on the American presidents, with comprehensive coverage of materials for research. The McKinley effort, the first such compilation for this president, provides 1,700 entries arranged alphabetically by main entry in 13 sections that cover major areas of William McKinley's personal and political life. The bibliography contains manuscripts and archival material as well as books, journal articles, dissertations, and government publications. There are author and subject indexes. This will be an essential reference tool for students and scholars embarking on research on the McKinley administration.

553. Guth, DeLloyd J., and David R. Wrone, comps. **The Assassination of John F. Kennedy: A Comprehensive Historical and Legal Bibliography, 1963-1979.** Westport, Conn., Greenwood, 1980. 442p. maps. index. $37.50. LC 79-6184. ISBN 0-313-21274-0.

"America's most notorious homicide" (preface) is the subject of this extensive bibliography of 5,000 citations. The first of the three sections of the bibliography deals with the evidence and the litigants. The focus here is on unpublished sources, archival material, photographic records, judicial records, and published sources, including government reports. The descriptive and evaluative annotations are extremely useful in this section. The second part is an extensive unannotated bibliography of published books and journal articles arranged by subject. The third section lists every assassination news story by its headline as it appeared in the *New York Times* during the period 1963-1978.

The introduction provides a valuable historical overview of the assassination, the official investigations and reports, and the massive flow of secondary literature it inspired. The compilers label much of the work of this latter category subjective, exploitive, and irrational rubbish. A chronology of the assassination, a chronology of Lee Harvey Oswald, and four maps of places associated with the assassination are included. There is a name index but no subject index.

554. **Lyndon B. Johnson: A Bibliography.** Compiled by the staff of the Lyndon Baines Johnson Library. Austin, Tex., University of Texas Press, 1984. 257p. index. $25.00. LC 83-23264. ISBN 0-292-74107-4.

555. **Lyndon B. Johnson: A Bibliography, Volume 2.** Craig H. Roell, comp. Austin, Tex., University of Texas Press, 1988. 362p. index. $30.00. LC 83-23264. ISBN 0-292-74017-4.

Students of President Johnson will find these bibliographies essential reference tools for studying and researching the life and career of the former leader. The extensive coverage includes books, scholarly articles, signed pieces in popular publications, and dissertations. Selected essays, conference papers, and masters' theses are also included. Most foreign publications, newspaper stories, government documents, and fiction were omitted.

The citations are arranged into major subject classifications, such as Johnson's early life, the senatorial years, the presidency, etc. Some chapters are subdivided into sections for important topics such as the Vietnam War or the media. There are separate chapters for Lady Bird Johnson and family. Additional chapters cover the writings of Johnson and his wife. The entries are not annotated. There is no subject index; access is through the subject classification of the table of contents. There is an author index. The second volume covers recent works, omissions from the first volume, and corrections.

556. Marszalek, John F. **Grover Cleveland: A Bibliography.** Westport, Conn., Meckler, 1988. 268p. index. (Meckler's Bibliographies of the Presidents of the United States, v.22). index. $45.00. LC 88-9096. ISBN 0-88736-136-6.

As the other titles in the Meckler series, this bibliography attempts to provide access to the widest possible range of materials in a book-length treatment. The Cleveland bibliography contains over 1,800 citations drawn from books and periodicals, including primary as well as secondary sources. Eighteen subject sections deal with Grover Cleveland's personal life and presidential administrations. The entries have brief descriptive annotations. There are author and subject indexes. This bibliography admirably fulfills its objective of providing an essential reference tool for research, undergraduate and beyond, on President Cleveland.

557. Martin, Fenton S., and Robert U. Goehlert. **The American Presidency: A Bibliography.** Washington, D.C., Congressional Quarterly, 1987. 506p. index. $75.00. LC 87-445. ISSN 087-874156.

558. Martin, Fenton S., and Robert U. Goehlert. **The American Presidents: A Bibliography.** Washington, D.C., Congressional Quarterly, 1987. 756p. index. $125.00. LC 86-30938. ISSN 0-87187-416-4.

The aim in preparing these companion volumes was to produce "the most comprehensive bibliography on the office of the presidency" (introduction). The volume on the institution of the presidency covers the history, development, and powers of the office and its relations with other branches of the federal government. The volume on the individual presidents deals with their accomplishments, policies, and activities, including their private lives.

These unannotated bibliographies include books, articles, dissertations, essays, and research reports; government documents were excluded. The time period of publication is generally 1885 to 1986. Only English-language materials are included. The emphasis in selection was on scholarly, analytical works generally available in larger libraries. Some descriptive and popular material was included.

The over 13,000 citations in the bibliography on the presidents are arranged by individual, with subdivisions for biographies, private life, public career, presidential years, and writings. The over 8,500 citations in the volume on the office of the presidency are organized in a detailed subject classification. Both volumes have author and subject indexes. For a more selective bibliography on the same subjects, see Kenneth E. Davison's *The American Presidency: A Guide to Information Sources* (entry 551).

559. Menendez, Albert J. **Religion and the U.S. Presidency: A Bibliography.** New York, Garland, 1986. 142p. index. (Garland Reference Library of Social Science, Vol. 334). $30.00. LC 85-29300. ISBN 0-8240-8718-6.

This bibliography will be a valuable reference tool for those interested in exploring presidential religion in some depth. The topic includes two related matters: the personal religious beliefs and activities of the presidents plus their relations with various religions and churches and their handling of church-state issues.

After an initial chapter dealing with the basic literature pertaining to all presidents or to the presidency in general, there are individual chapters on each president. The amount of material cited varies considerably among the presidents. Books, newspaper articles, journal and magazine articles, dissertations, and master's theses are included. Although most of the citations are not annotated, there are very useful headnotes for each president that summarize personal religious beliefs and political activities touching on religion. The notes also offer a bibliographic overview of the literature and recommend titles for beginning research or zeroing in on specific aspects of this subject.

560. Miles, William, comp. **The People's Voice: An Annotated Bibliography of American Presidential Campaign Newspapers, 1828-1984.** Westport, Conn., Greenwood, 1987. 210p. (Bibliographies and Indexes in American History). index. $37.95. LC 87-11969. ISSN 0742-6828. ISBN 0-313-23976-2.

William Miles was able to identify 737 presidential campaign newspapers for this bibliography. The great majority were published in the 19th century before the arrival of radio and television as rivals in getting out the messages of candidates. The compilation does, however, include Jesse Jackson's *Rainbow News* from the 1984 presidential campaign.

For each campaign newspaper the entry includes title, place of publication, frequency, dates of publication, editor, and publisher. OCLC and NUC symbols identify libraries with substantial runs. There are indexes by editor, publisher, candidate, title, and geographic area.

561. Ryan, Dorothy, and Louis J. Ryan, comps. **The Kennedy Family of Massachusetts: A Bibliography.** Westport, Conn., Greenwood, 1981. 200p. index. $25.00. LC 81-6672. ISBN 0-313-23189-3.

This bibliography contains over 4,000 items published between 1950 and 1980 that examine the "folklore and facts" (preface) of the Kennedy family and their role in American life. Most of the citations are from books, journals, or magazines; but letters, photographs, flyers, and reports are also included. The bibliography is based on the compilers' personal collection.

The volume covers John F. Kennedy, his wife, his brothers Robert and Edward, and their wives, plus a final short section on other members of the family. Each section is divided into works by and then works about the Kennedy family member. There are short annotations or quotations for many of the citations. The portion of the bibliography on President Kennedy has many useful subdivisions, such as "Photographic Collections," "Relations with the Media," and "Personal Health." The assassination is covered extensively. This bibliography is particularly strong in its comprehensive coverage of the magazine literature and in the detailed subject breakdowns.

Biographical Sources

562. **Political Profiles.** Nelson Lichtenstein, ed. New York, Facts on File, 1976- . index. $55.00. LC 76-20897. ISBN 0-87196-454-6 (v.5).

This series of profiles began with *The Truman Years* (vol. 1) and continued with *The Eisenhower Years* (vol. 2), *The Kennedy Years* (vol. 3), *The Johnson Years* (vol. 4), and *The Nixon-Ford Years* (vol. 5). A sixth volume for the Carter presidency is planned.

Each volume contains approximately 500 biographies, or profiles, of the men and women who played significant roles in American politics during the administration covered. Many of these persons were in the presidential administration, but others were various officeholders, members of Congress, journalists, activists, and leaders from non-government fields. The articles are signed and vary in length from 400 to 2,000 words. Individuals with long careers can be found in several volumes, with each focusing on their activities or importance during the presidency covered.

In addition to the portraits, each volume begins with an introductory historical essay and concludes with an appendix, which includes a chronology, a list of major office-holders, and a bibliography. There is a subject and name index.

563. **The Presidents: A Reference History.** Henry F. Graff, ed. New York, Scribner, 1984. 700p. bibliog. index. $65.00. LC 83-20225. ISBN 0-684-17607-6.

The 38 men, from Washington to Carter, who have occupied the American presidency, from 1784 to 1980, constitute the subject of this biographical sourcebook. The signed essays are written by professional historians or political scientists. They are generally very readable and more suitable for users seeking an overview rather than those researching specific topics. In addition to the biographical information, the articles focus on the major events and personalities in each administration and their impact on the presidency and on the American political system.

The biographies, which vary from 10 to 30 pages, are followed by fairly extensive annotated bibliographies of sources for additional reading. There is a detailed name and subject index.

564. Southwick, Leslie H., comp. **Presidential Also-Rans and Running Mates, 1788-1980.** Jefferson, N.C., McFarland, 1984. 722p. bibliog. index. 49.95. LC 83-25577. ISBN 0-89950-109-5.

Southwick's focus in this book is on the persons nominated to the presidency or vice presidency whom the electors did not vote into high office but "swept off to remote corners" (introduction). These losers are arranged in chronological order by election. For each election there is a summary of candidates, party platforms, and popular and electoral votes. There are biographical sketches for the unsuccessful candidates, except for those who were subsequently elected president or vice president. The biographical sketches, which average six or seven pages, are preceded by sections of information on date of birth, education, religion, ancestry, family, occupation, public offices held, and personal characteristics. They are followed by a short bibliography.

The author does not hesitate to give very candid personal evaluations of the losers' personalities and political qualifications, which makes this work interesting for browsing as well as a source of facts on individuals who have become rather obscure.

Chronologies

565. Justice, Keith L., comp. **Public Office Index. Volume 1: U.S. Presidents, Vice-Presidents, Cabinet Members, Supreme Court Justices.** Jefferson, N.D., McFarland, 1985. 181p. index. $19.95. LC 84-43216. ISBN 0-89940-137-0.

Frustration at not being able to find basic information about major officeholders led the author to prepare this single-volume compendium. It is identified by him as the first volume without indication of what future efforts might be. The volume begins with an "administrative index," a list of the elected vice presidents and appointed cabinet members who served each president. A biographical section gives date of birth, dates of entering and leaving office, length of service, and date of death. The "cabinet succession" list shows the order in which appointees filled specific cabinet positions. There is another biographical section for the Supreme Court justices, with appointment, confirmation, and resignation dates. There is a name index, especially useful for persons who served in more than one office.

Dictionaries and Encyclopedias

566. **Franklin D. Roosevelt, His Life and Times: An Encyclopedic View.** Otis L. Graham and Meghan Robinson Wander, eds. Boston, G. K. Hall, 1985. 483p. illus. index. $27.50. LC 84-24949. ISBN 0-8161-8667-7.

An impressive 321 articles written by 125 scholars constitute this encyclopedia of the life and times of Franklin D. Roosevelt. A variety of alphabetically arranged topics cover comprehensively the president's personal life and political career. People, pets, events, programs, agencies, and activities are all covered. The various authors provide a spectrum of interpretations and perspectives rather than one unified view. The encyclopedia contains numerous cross-references and valuable bibliographies at the end of the articles. It is richly illustrated with photographs and political cartoons. This is an excellent source for anyone interested in Roosevelt or the New Deal era.

567. **Historical Dictionary of the New Deal: From Inauguration to Preparation for War.** James S. Olson, ed. Westport, Conn., Greenwood, 1985. 611p. bibliog. index. $65.00. LC 84-19729. ISBN 0-313-23873-1.

As a reference tool for students and scholars, this dictionary offers information on the New Deal, "a watershed in the history of public policy in the United States" (preface). The major focus is on domestic policies; foreign policies are not considered unless they directly influenced the domestic situation.

The *Dictionary* offers essays, varying in length from a paragraph to several pages, on people, agencies, legislation, and court decisions. For each entry there is basic background information and an elaboration of that person or thing's role in the New Deal. Cross-references are noted with asterisks. Usually only one citation is given for sources with each entry.

A number of lengthy appendixes, including a detailed chronology of the New Deal and a list of agency personnel for 1933 to 1941, add substantially to the value of this handbook. There is also a list of acronyms and a 12-page selected, unannotated bibliography on New Deal programs.

568. Neely, Mark E. **The Abraham Lincoln Encyclopedia.** New York, McGraw-Hill, 1982. 365p. illus. index. $45.00. LC 81-7296. ISBN 0-07-046145-7.

Neely, the director of the Louis A. Warren Lincoln Library and Museum in Fort Wayne, Indiana, was the author of all the articles appearing in this comprehensive one-volume encyclopedia on Abraham Lincoln. The alphabetically arranged articles concern the personal life and public career of the president. Family, friends, political associates, and enemies are all covered. Events and places associated with Lincoln, as well as topics such as Humor and Psychology, are included in the entries, which vary in length from a paragraph to several pages.

Extensive use was made of primary and secondary sources; these are cited at the end of each entry. The detailed index and the cross-references facilitate access. Libraries with major Lincoln collections are noted. This well-illustrated encyclopedia is a readable volume for the browser or Lincoln fan, as well as a source of reference information for the researcher.

Directories

569. **Federal Staff Directory.** Mount Vernon, Va., Congressional Staff Directory, 1982- . annual. index. $40.00. LC 82-647381. ISSN 0735-3324.

This directory, the companion to the *Congressional Staff Directory* (see entry 594), deals with the executive branch of the federal government. Over 27,000 key executives and their staff assistants are covered, including the office of the president, cabinet departments and their subdivisions, and the independent agencies. A selection of international, nongovernmental, and quasi-official organizations are now also included. Entries provide the names of the chief officers and staff, position titles, addresses, and phone numbers.

There is also a biographical section with brief sketches of 2,400 federal staff members. A detailed keyword subject index and an index of all individuals listed add to the efficiency of using this title as a directory of executive branch personnel.

570. **Federal Yellow Book: A Directory of the Federal Departments and Agencies.** Washington, D.C., Washington Monitor, 1976- . quarterly. $135.00/yr. LC 78-642223. ISSN 0145-6202.

With this title, and the companion volume for Congress, *Congressional Yellow Book* (see entry 595), the *Washington Monitor* has earned a prominent position among the various publishers of reference sources that serve as directories of the federal government. The major advantage of these publications over other titles, such as the official *United States Government Manual* (see entry 529), is their quarterly updating to provide more current information.

The entries in this directory are arranged by agency, with the key officeholders identified along with addresses and phone numbers. The fall 1987 issue contained over 30,000 individuals.

Guides

571. Goehlert, Robert U., and Fenton S. Martin. **The Presidency: A Research Guide.** Santa Barbara, Calif., ABC-Clio, 1985. 341p. index. $28.50. LC 84-6425. ISBN 0-87436-373-X.

This research guide focuses on the institution of the presidency rather than on the particular individuals who have been president. The book is designed to assist students and researchers in investigating the presidency. The information provided is divided into four parts. "The Presidency as an Institution" begins with sections on presidential papers; *The Federal Register*; and statutes, executive orders and treaties. Secondary sources such as dictionaries, bibliographies, journals, and databases are also reviewed extensively. The second part, "The Oval Office," deals with primary and secondary sources on individual presidents. The location of papers and manuscripts and the use of presidential libraries are covered. "Running for Office" deals with campaigns and elections. "Researching the Presidency" offers an overview and advice on designing a research project and developing a research strategy.

This guide provides a valuable annotated listing of sources of information for studying the presidency. In many ways it is also a guide to the operation of the federal government and to key government documents. The 26 appendixes contain a wealth of useful information, especially tables outlining executive and legislative activities, with the corresponding titles of resources for information.

572. **Studying the Presidency.** George C. Edwards III and Stephen J. Wayne, eds. Knoxville, University of Tennessee Press, 1983. 312p. $19.95; $9.95(pbk). LC 82-17472. ISBN 0-8704-9378-7; 0-8704-9379-5(pbk).

This guide to the presidency is intended to help undergraduates writing term papers as well as scholars undertaking advanced study. The guidance is offered in a series of essays that cover many aspects of research, including methodology and quantitative analysis. Other chapters discuss various orientations or approaches to political research.

The second half of this book is a bibliographical guide to information sources, reference books, online databases, and records related to the presidency. Locating legal sources, researching in presidential libraries, and interviewing presidential aides are also considered. For a title with less advice and orientation to research but a more comprehensive listing of published reference sources, see Goehlert and Martin's *The Presidency: A Research Guide* (entry 571).

Handbooks

573. Boller, Paul F., Jr. **Presidential Anecdotes.** New York, Oxford University Press, 1981. 410p. index. $14.95. LC 80-27092. ISBN 0-19-502915-1.

This is a book of anecdotes about 39 presidents of the United States, beginning with Washington's cherry tree story and ending with the remarks Reagan made to the hospital staff after surgery. The author believes that these stories reveal a great deal about the character and personality of the presidents. Some presidents, such as Lincoln, lend themselves to this treatment; others rate only a few anecdotes.

Each section of anecdotes begins with an introduction highlighting the career and character of the chief executive. These portraits are illustrated with many quotations. The anecdotes and quotations are all documented, though often to secondary sources. This is a very readable and enjoyable as well as informative work.

574. Boller, Paul F., Jr. **Presidential Campaigns.** New York, Oxford University Press, 1984. 420p. index. $6.95.(pbk). LC 83-25047. ISBN 0-19-503722-7.

The presidential campaigns from 1789 to 1980 are described in this inexpensive guide. Each campaign is covered in a series of chapters, which vary in length from several pages for the earlier contests to over 10 pages for contemporary elections. The portraits are based on a wide selection of secondary literature, which is cited in the notes. These references form a bibliography on each chief executive suitable for general reading or preliminary research.

Boller not only includes the main issues and highlights for each campaign, but goes on to cover "amusing incidents" and "dramatic happenings" (preface). These anecdotes and quotations, which capture the flavor of the campaigns and the candidates, are the main strength of this volume, which is enjoyable to read through as well as useful to consult as a reference source.

575.   DeGregorio, William A. **The Complete Book of U.S. Presidents.** New York, Dembner Books (distributed by W. W. Norton), 1984. 691p. illus. index. $22.50. LC 83-23201. ISBN 0-934878-36-6.

DeGregorio's fascinating series of presidential portraits complement Joseph N. Kane's *Facts About the Presidents* (see entry 577). Each chapter constitutes a presidential biography, a format that is more narrative than Kane's listing of facts. There is extensive information on political careers, including election results, major appointments, and highlights of the administration. The personal information includes physical appearance, personality, family, religion, marriage, and other categories (such as extramarital affairs) not often found in reference sources. There are sections with quotes by and about each president. Bibliographical notes are included for each chief executive. The chapters begin with photographs or portraits. This work brings the personality of each president alive for the reader.

576.   Frost, Elizabeth, ed. **The Bully Pulpit: Quotations from America's Presidents.** New York, Facts on File, 1988. 282p. bibliog. index. $23.95. LC 87-24381. ISBN 0-8160-1247-4.

Some 3,000 presidential quotations taken from written and spoken sources such as speeches, books, letters, and diaries, and cited in this collection. Selection was based on "historic significance, intrinsic human interest, and colorful or eloquent language" (introduction). Every president from Washington to Reagan is quoted.

The entries are arranged alphabetically by topic. Topics include such themes as honesty and leadership, such headline issues as the Middle East or civil rights, and the U.S. presidents. Within each topic the quotations are arranged chronologically. The source and date of each citation is indicated. In addition to an author index, a subject index provides access to specific subjects within the topical arrangement. Of the many books on the presidents, this is the only one to comprehensively collect quotations from all of them, including those who have become obscure with the passing of time.

577.   Kane, Joseph Nathan. **Facts about the Presidents: A Compilation of Biographical and Historical Information**. 4th ed. New York, H. W. Wilson, 1981. 456p. illus. index. $30.00. LC 81-7537. ISBN 0-8242-0612-6.

As a compilation of biographical and historical information about the American presidents, this handbook has been a standard reference source for many years. The fourth edition covers 39 presidents, from George Washington to Ronald Reagan.

The first part, which provides biographical data, is arranged chronologically with one chapter for each president. The information includes family history, election data, highlights of the administration, and major appointments. Some important documents are excerpted. The second part is in comparative form, with data for all the presidents collected under various subject headings, including personal and political topics and miscellaneous information such as the age at which wives became first ladies.

578.   Veit, Fritz. **Presidential Libraries and Collections.** New York, Greenwood, 1987. 152p. $29.95. LC 86-25732. ISBN 0313249962.

In recent years presidential libraries have become increasingly important resources for presidential material, especially manuscripts, memorabilia, and primary research items.

Unfortunately, these resources are scattered among many sites, each with its own individual characteristics as regards the collections and services.

Fritz Veit's reference tool serves as a useful introduction to these presidential libraries. Based on government publications and questionnaires, he has compiled a guide describing scope, policies, programs, and services. Other institutions that have presidential collections, such as the Library of Congress, are also profiled. In addition to the main section, this work also includes an overview of the historical development and present state of presidential libraries and a short bibliography.

Indexes

579. Meagher, Sylvia, in collaboration with Gary Owens. **Master Index to the J.F.K. Assassination Investigations: The Reports and Supporting Volumes of the House Select Committee on Assassinations and the Warren Commission.** Metuchen, N.J., Scarecrow, 1980. 435p. $20.00. LC 80-17494. ISBN 0-8108-1331-9.

The two major official investigations of the 1963 assassination of President John F. Kennedy were: (1) the Warren Commission, which published its report and 26 volumes of hearings and exhibits in 1963, and (2) the House Select Committee on Assassinations, which in 1979 published a report and 14 volumes of hearings and appendixes. This work by Meagher and Owens is a group of indexes to these 42 volumes.

Part 1 includes individual indexes to each volume of the House Select Committee's works, plus comprehensive, cumulative subject and name indexes. There is also a useful key to names, which lists individuals by categories such as CIA, Dallas police, anti-Castro Cubans, witnesses, etc. For the work of the Warren Commission, part 2 reprints the 1966 *Subject Index to the Warren Report and Hearings and Exhibits*, which contains a name index and a key to names as well as a subject index. With more than 15,000 entries, this meticulously prepared index provides invaluable access to the literature of the official investigations of the Kennedy assassination.

580. United States. President. **Public Papers of the Presidents of the United States.** Federal Register Division, National Archives and Records Service, General Services Administration. Washington, GPO, 1957- . annual. index. price varies. LC 58-61050. ISSN 0079-7626.

Since its inception in 1957, this series has become a standard official source of the public messages of the presidents. These documents include the text of public messages, speeches, addresses, letters, pronouncements, transcripts of press conferences, and other statements. Coverage begins with Herbert Hoover. The material is arranged in chronological order. Proclamations, executive orders, and similar materials are excluded, but references to the *Federal Register* are provided. The material in the annual volumes is based on the *Weekly Compilation of Presidential Documents*, which provides a comparable source of current information.

The annual volumes from the Government Printing Office contain name and subject indexes. Cumulative indexes by administration have been published by KTO Press for all presidents in this official series.

581. Zink, Steven D. **Guide to the Presidential Advisory Commissions, 1973-1984.** Alexandria, Va., Chadwyck-Healey, 1987. 643p. index. (Government Documents Bibliographies). $85.00. LC 87-13196. ISBN 0-85964-122-8.

Although not inexpensive, this new reference tool provides both a directory of presidential advisory commissions and an index to their publications. For both functions coverage starts with January 1, 1973, the effective date of the Federal Advisory Commission Act of 1972 that regulates these agencies. The short lifespan of most presidential advisory commissions and the tendency to refer to them by abbreviated or popular names have often created difficulties in identifying their publications, which general indexes to government publications do not always adequately address. This specialized index now provides in chronological order a listing of presidential advisory commissions with exact name, dates of creation and termination, names of members, dates of meetings, and the titles of their reports with notes on their availability. Personal name, title, and subject indexes provide the access so important in tracing these publications.

Sourcebooks

582. Bush, Gregory, ed. **Campaign Speeches of American Presidential Candidates 1948-1984.** New York, Frederick Ungar, 1985. 343p. $25.00. LC 85-3362. ISBN 0-8044-1137-9.

The author, a historian of American politics and the communicaton process, asserts that it is difficult to find the full texts of campaign speeches of presidential candidates in these days when campaigns are dominated by television coverage that features brief clips. This book seeks to redress the situation by providing the full text of 52 speeches, from 1948 through 1984. Four of the speeches are by third-party candidates. For each major candidate the nomination acceptance speech and one representative campaign speech is provided.

The work is divided into chapters for each campaign for the period covered. Each chapter begins with a several-page introduction to major issues to place the speeches in historical context. Though highly selective, this is a useful, convenient compilation.

583. Peterson, Svend. **A Statistical History of the American Presidential Elections with Supplementary Tables Covering 1968-1980.** Westport, Conn., Greenwood, 1981. 250p. $37.50. LC 81-6348. ISSN 0-3132-2952-X.

This statistical compendium claims to be "the only publication that gives complete statistics on the American presidential elections" (preface). The statistics in the main part of the book cover the period 1789-1980, and a supplementary section covers 1968-1980.

The 134 statistical compilations include a table of votes and percentages for each presidential election, by state and by candidate; a table of votes and percentages for each state, by election and candidate; a table of votes and percentages, by state and election, for 11 political parties; and other tables highlighting noteworthy elections. The compiler includes an interesting discussion of his difficulty in locating accurate, reliable figures from the various sources he consulted; those sources were apparently replete with discrepancies.

Another useful title for statistics on presidential elections is G. Scott Thomas's *The Pursuit of the White House: A Handbook of Presidential Election Statistics and History* (New York, Greenwood, 1987. 485p. $48.00). LC 87-11968. ISBN 0313257957.

584. **Presidential Elections since 1789.** 4th ed. Washington, D.C., Congressional Quarterly, 1987. illus. maps. index. 235p. $11.95.(pbk). LC 87-10921. ISBN 0871874318.

First published in 1975, this inexpensive title is an excellent source of presidential election statistics from 1789 to 1984. The statistical tables provide total votes and percentages. State and national primaries, nominating convention results, general elections, and electoral college returns are covered. Major and minor party candidates are included. There are breakdowns by state but not by county or city.

In addition to the election tabulations, there are various useful features including the texts of major election laws, a biographical directory of presidential and vice-presidential candidates, and a selective bibliography.

585.   Scammon, Richard M., and Alice V. McGillivray, comps. and eds. **America at the Polls 2: A Handbook of American Presidential Election Statistics, 1968-1984.** Washington, D.C., Elections Research Center, Congressional Quarterly, 1988. 594p. index. $60.00. LC 87-33221. ISBN 0-87187-452-0.

With this title, which provides coverage for presidential elections from 1968 through 1984, Scammon continues his earlier work (*America at the Polls*) published in 1965, which covered from 1920 to 1964. This volume provides totals for counties and states, Republican, Democratic, and minor party votes, and pluralities and percentages for major parties. There are also national summaries of popular and electoral votes for presidential elections from 1920 to 1984 and for primaries from 1968 through 1984. This is one of several recent titles reviewed in this book dealing with statistics of presidential elections. Check the subject index for these reviews.

586.   **Speeches of the American Presidents.** Janet Podell and Steven Anzouin, eds. New York, H. W. Wilson, 1988. 820p. index. $60.00. LC 87-29833. ISBN 0824207610.

This convenient source for primary materials relating to the American presidency brings together 180 speeches by 40 U.S. presidents. Many of the selections are well known, such as Lincoln's "Gettysburg Address" and Franklin Roosevelt's "Nothing to Fear but Fear Itself" speech, but others are certainly less known and less readily available, such as Eisenhower's "Don't Join the Bookburners" address. Each president is covered by a chapter containing from 4 to 10 speeches, most reproduced in full. There are comments on the circumstances surrounding the composition and delivery of each speech and an account of key events in each administration. There is also an introductory essay on the history of presidential speechmaking. The extensive subject index facilitates comparing the treatment of recurring themes over various administrations.

UNITED STATES—CONGRESS

Atlases

587.   **Congressional Districts in the 1980s.** Washington, D.C., Congressional Quarterly, 1983. 632p. $90.00. LC 83-18988. ISBN 0-87187-264-1.

After the redistricting mandated by the 1980 census, there appeared a number of reference publications focusing on congressional districts. The government's *Congressional District Atlas, 100th Congress of the United States* (see entry 588) provides detailed maps of current districts, while *The Historical Atlas of United States Congressional Districts 1789-1983* (see entry 588) provides a history of the evolving districts over the years. This volume, *Congressional Districts in the 1980s*, is extremely useful for the statistical and demographic information provided for each of the 435 districts based on the 1980 census.

Each state section includes cumulated statewide information and a review of recent redistricting. There is also a discussion of the political and social climate of each district. The profile for each district also includes election results from 1976 to 1982 for president, Congress, and governor. Media, military installations, major industries, and educational institutions are noted. Statistical data include age of population, racial composition, income and occupation, education, and housing and residential patterns. The appendix contains a history of reapportionment and redistricting.

588.   Martis, Kenneth C. **The Historical Atlas of United States Congressional Districts 1789-1983.** Ruth Anderson Rowles, assistant ed. New York, Free Press, 1982. 302p. maps. bibliog. index. $150.00. LC 82-70583. ISBN 0-02-920150-0.

The main section of this atlas, the second part, contains 97 national maps of the United States showing in chronological order the congressional districts as they changed from 1789 to 1983. For each map there is an accompanying list of members with an indication of their state and district. There is also a comprehensive index to all members of Congress. Part 3 provides the complete legal description of the exact boundaries of each district for each Congress.

The first part of this atlas is an extensive introduction to the history of congressional districts and their mapping. There is a bibliography of 258 items for additional information. This massive atlas is an important reference resource for research on the American Congress and the evolution of the districts during the first 97 Congresses.

589.   Parsons, Stanley B., William W. Beach, and Michael J. Dubin. **United States Congressional Districts and Data, 1843-1883.** Westport, Conn., Greenwood, 1986. 225p. maps. $65.00. LC 85-675782. ISBN 0-313-22045-X.

The first volume of this series, *United States Congressional Districts, 1788-1841*, covered the first 27 Congresses. This volume continues the coverage to 1883. In comparison to the first volume, the second has eliminated all references to individual members of Congress, as such biographical information is readily available for this latter period in such standard sources as the *Biographical Directory of the American Congress*. The emphasis is on statistical data, reflecting the expansion of data collecting by the Census Bureau.

The data are presented in four sets: 1843-1853, 1853-1863, 1863-1873, and 1873-1883. For each period there is a state map showing the counties forming the districts. For each district there are data on the total population, population per square mile, and the percentage of blacks in the population. Other data, included as available, relate to agricultural statistics, the value of manufacturing, and the percentage of Catholics and foreign born.

The intent of the series is to facilitate research on legislative behavior and election analysis by supplementing the data found in such other resources as *Congressional Quarterly's Guide to U.S. Elections*, and the roll-call data available from the Inter-University Consortium for Social and Political Research.

590.   U.S. Bureau of the Census. **Congressional District Atlas.** U.S. Department of Commerce, Bureau of the Census. Washington, D.C., GPO, 1960- . irregular. price varies. LC 84-643169. ISSN 0748-4828.

This series of atlases of the United States congressional districts is produced by the Bureau of the Census. The atlas includes maps of each state, the District of Columbia, Puerto Rico, and other dependencies. The maps, which are arranged in alphabetical order by state, depict the boundaries as revised, of the congressional districts for the United States House of Representatives. Each county, state capital, and municipality with over 25,000 inhabitants is indicated. Shaded areas on these principal state maps refer to insert maps, which provide more detailed boundary information as needed. For each state three tables list the district in which each municipality and each county falls and the counties within each district.

Bibliographies

591. Goehlert, Robert U., and John R. Sayre. **The United States Congress: A Bibliography.** New York, Free Press, 1982. 376p. index. $50.00. LC 81-19526. ISBN 0-02-011900-6.

The aim of the two authors was to provide a comprehensive bibliography of the United States Congress, specifically on the history, development, and the legislative process of Congress. The attempt was made to include all scholarly research material published in English since the beginning of the American Republic. Books, edited volumes, essays, journal articles, dissertations, theses, and selected government documents have all been included, for a total of 5,600 citations. Biographical titles and works on national politics and government in general have been excluded.

The unannotated entries are arranged in 14 topical chapters, which cover the history and development of Congress, the powers of Congress, committee structure and work, and legislative analysis and case studies. There are author and subject indexes.

592. Kennon, Donald R., ed. **The Speakers of the U.S. House of Representatives: A Bibliography, 1789-1984.** Baltimore, Johns Hopkins University Press, 1986. 323p. index. (Johns Hopkins Studies in Historical and Political Science, 103d Series, No. 1). $37.50. LC 85-45047. ISBN 0-8018-2786-8.

The United States Capitol Historical Society's bibliography of the 46 members of Congress who have served as Speaker of the House of Representatives begins with Frederick Muhlenberg in 1789 and ends with Tip O'Neill in 1984. The main body of the work focuses on the 46 Speakers. For each there is a brief biography of personal and career information. The accompanying bibliographies include manuscripts, speeches, eulogies, biographies, journal articles and dissertations as well as books. Works by the Speakers are also noted, for a total of 4,280 citations. Though not comprehensive, "all significant references" (preface) were sought through the end of 1983.

In addition to the bibliographies on individual speakers, works on the office of Speaker of the House are covered in the first section, which provides an overview of the office. There are author and subject indexes.

Directories

593. **The Almanac of the Unelected 1988: Staff of the U.S. Congress.** Charles C. Francis and Jeffrey B. Trammell, eds. Washington, D.C., Almanac of the Unelected, 1988. 749p. illus. index. $250.00. LC 88-17171. ISBN 0-8191-6979-X.

The unelected are the congressional staffers—legislative aides, personal assistants, staff directors, administrative assistants, counsels—who work for representatives and senators or legislative committees. This directory lists 600 of the most important. For each staffer the directory includes photograph, address, telephone number, educational background, employment record, fields of expertise, accomplishments, and political orientation. There is a subject index to topics of interest or expertise such as AIDS, China, or disarmament.

This rather expensive title would be most useful to those, such as government officials, lobbyists, or journalists, who need to contact individuals directly involved in specific issues. For many, the long-established, and modestly priced, *Congressional Staff Directory* (see entry 594) would be sufficient. That directory provides access to a larger number of staffers but contains much less biographical information than *The Almanac of the Unelected.*

594. Congressional Staff Directory. Mount Vernon, Va., Congressional Staff Directory, 1959- . annual. index. $45.00. LC 59-13987. ISSN 0069-8938.

This resource provides biographical and directory listings for members of Congress and their staffs in a series of color-coded sections, including: (1) brief biographies of members of Congress, (2) their staffs with titles, office addresses, and phone numbers, (3) membership roles of committees and committee assignments of all members, (4) a list of 9,900 cities with congressional district and representative identified, and (5) biographies of key congressional staff.

This title covers much of the same ground as the government publication *Official Congressional Directory* (see entry 597), which, however, also covers the judicial and executive branches. Each title has certain categories of information not found in the other. The list of cities and the staff biographies are important elements found only in the *Congressional Staff Directory*. This directory has a keyword subject index and an individual name index. A prepublication supplement, the *Congressional Staff Directory Advance Locator*, provides for most sections the latest biographical and directory information about three months before the main volume appears.

595. Congressional Yellow Book: A Directory of Members of Congress, Including Their Committees and Key Staff Aides. Washington, D.C., Washington Monitor, 1976- . quarterly. $112.00/yr.(pbk). LC 85-642859. ISSN 0191-1422.

This directory provides a comprehensive survey of senators and representatives, their committee assignments, and key staff aides. Each senator and representative has a profile page, which includes a photograph, a brief biographical sketch, office address and phone number, committee assignments, and key assistants. After this profile section, the House and Senate committees are listed and described with all members listed in order of seniority. Congressional leadership, party organization, and congressional support agencies, including the Library of Congress, are also delineated.

This directory contains basically the same information as the *Congressional Staff Directory* (see entry 594) and the *Official Congressional Directory* (see entry 597). Its major asset is the quarterly updating, which gives it a real advantage in reference situations requiring very current information.

596. Members of Congress since 1789. 3d ed. Mary Ames Booker, ed. Washington, D.C., Congressional Quarterly, 1985. 186p. bibliog. $9.95(pbk). LC 84-27504. ISBN 0-87187-335-4.

The major portion of this directory consists of an alphabetical list of all senators, representatives, resident commissioners, and territorial delegates who served in the first 99 Congresses, from March 1789 through January 1985. For each member of Congress these few but essential points are covered: name, party affiliation, home state, birth and death dates, and dates of incumbency. Family relationships to other members and service in other high offices are also noted as applicable. The major source for this data was the congressional publication *Biographical Directory of the American Congress, 1774-1971*.

An introductory section profiles Congress, with information on average age, occupation, and religion of members. There are also lists and statistics on women and black members. A final section lists the dates and leadership for each congressional session and the strength of the majority and principal minority parties.

597. Official Congressional Directory. Washington, D.C., GPO, 1809- . annual. index. $15.00(pbk); $20.00(bound); LC 84-755. ISSN 0160-9890.

As one of the best-known government publications, this directory continues its tradition of providing biographical and organizational information about the federal government. While it emphasizes the legislative branch, there is considerable coverage of the executive and judicial branches as well. There are paragraph-length biographical sketches of all members of Congress, cabinet-level secretaries of departments, and major judges of the federal judiciary.

The *Directory* is primarily a listing of officeholders and staffs. Attached to the alphabetical listing of all members of Congress are lists of important staff, with their titles, office addresses, and phone numbers. Another major section identifies the members of all committees and the committee assignments of each member. The executive and judicial sections similarly list key staffs, as do the extensive sections on international organizations, the diplomatic corps, the press, and the media. There is a detailed table of contents and a name index of organizations and individuals.

598.   Stubbs, Walter, comp. **Congressional Committees, 1789-1982: A Checklist.** Westport, Conn., Greenwood, 1985. 210p. index. (Bibliographies and Indexes in Law and Political Science, No. 6). $35.00. LC 85-10007. ISBN 0-313-24539-8.

As the introduction of this very useful reference work points out, congressional committees have had an important role in American government since the establishment of the Republic. Now most of the work of Congress is done at the committee level. There have been 1,500 committees in existence since 1789, with many changes of names and transferrals of responsibilities.

This single source identifies committees—standing, select, special and joint—in existence between 1789 and 1982. The core of the work consists of an alphabetical listing of the committees. Each short entry gives date of establishment and date of termination. The legal sources for both actions are cited. Reference is made to changes of names and to any predecessor and successor committees. The volume also includes a subject index, a list of congressional sessions, and a chronological list of committees established during each Congress.

Handbooks

599.   Bosnich, Victor W. **Congressional Voting Guide: A Ten-Year Compilation of the 99th Congress.** Washington, D.C., Congressional Voting Guide, 1987. 630p. index. $19.75(pbk). LC 87-91609. ISBN 0-9618958-0-2.

Over 200 House or Senate resolutions and bills are tracked for the 10 years from 1977 to 1986 in this handy reference tool. The vote on each item of proposed legislation is recorded for individual representatives and senators. In addition to these voting records, this guide provides a brief biography of each member of Congress covered and summaries of the issues. Support of the President by members of Congress is also indicated in percentage terms. For a study of congressional treatment of major issues of the last decade, or for an overview of particular members of Congress, this is an invaluable resource. Similar information is available for shorter time periods in *Congress and the Nation* (see entry 000).

600.   **CEA Congressional Ledger: Rating Congress on Black and Hispanic Issues.** Washington, D.C., Congressional Education Associates, 1981- . annual. $8.00. LC 85-64124. ISSN 0737-3007.

While many publications attempt a comprehensive coverage of congressional activity, this inexpensive annual zeros in on matters of special interest to blacks and Hispanics. Specifically, the *Ledger* is a record of how each member of Congress votes on selected issues.

The tables can be used by blacks, Hispanics, and others to evaluate the performance of members of Congress on issues impacting these communities.

The main body of this handbook is a tabulation of the votes of senators and representatives on key issues, which are identified and described in the introduction. This review results in a "score" of "right" and "wrong" votes. The percentage of black and Hispanic constituents for each member of Congress is provided. There are also photographs of the black and Hispanic members of Congress.

601. **Congress A to Z: CQ's Ready Reference Encyclopedia.** Washington, D.C., Congressional Quarterly, 1988. bibliog. index. 612p. $75.00. LC 88-20336. ISBN 0-87187-447-4.

Like other Congressional Quarterly publications, for example, the *Congressional Quarterly's Guide to Congress* (entry 604), this title is crammed with information and explanations on the structure and operations of the U.S. Congress. A major part of the material here consists of encyclopedic articles of several pages each on 30 basic activities related to Congress, such as legislation, lobbying, and reapportionment. There are also definitions of 250 terms, biographical sketches of key members, and profiles of committees. The appendixes contain historical lists of members of Congress, historical statistics, lists of vetoes, and much other miscellaneous but pertinent information and statistical data. There is a detailed index of names and topics to all the material presented in this essential handbook of Congress.

602. **Congress & Defense: 1988.** Palo Alto, Calif., EW Communications, 1988. 175p. $85.00(pbk). ISBN 0-918994-19-5.

The role of Congress in supporting defense, the military, and the defense industry is examined in detail in this study. Basically this reference work reviews each member of Congress by means of a series of tables, which reveal such information as the top defense contractors located in each congressional district and state, the key weapons systems produced in each district and state, the major defense PAC contributions, voting records on key defense bills, and the total value of defense contracts received in each district. These and other tables create a defense profile for each member of Congress. There are also 10 appendixes providing similar information designed to permit an evaluation of specific members of Congress, comparisons among members, or an appraisal of the role of Congress as an institution in relation to defense and the defense industry.

603. **Congressional Quarterly's Green Guide.** Washington, D.C., Congressional Quarterly, 1987- . annual. $11.95. LC 87-5321. ISBN 0-87187-435-0 (1987).

The introduction to this paperback handbook states that it was produced to "help you identify members of Congress in committee, in official or informal meetings, or while watching them on C-SPAN." For each senator and representative there is a brief profile and a photograph. The data in the profiles include name, party affiliation, residence, year first elected, date and place of birth, education, military career, occupation, prior positions, family, religion, office and phone numbers, and committee assignments. There follows for each member election statistics for the previous two elections, three voting studies by Congressional Quarterly, and four ratings by interest groups.

This source is in many ways an abbreviated version of the publisher's *Politics in America* (see entry 612), which is published later in the year. For many, depending on specific needs, one of the two titles will suffice.

604.   **Congressional Quarterly's Guide to Congress.** 3d ed. Washington, D.C., Congressional Quarterly, 1982. 1,185p. illus. index. $90.00. LC 82-14148. ISBN 0-87187-239-0.

Unlike Congressional Quarterly publications that focus on the activities of Congress during a specific time period, this guide attempts to examine and explain how Congress developed over the years and how it now functions. The approach is basically narrative, with many tables, fact boxes, bibliographies, and charts interspersed.

The information is organized into seven main categories: (1) origins and development of Congress, (2) powers of Congress, (3) congressional procedures, (4) housing and support of Congress, (5) Congress and the electorate, (6) pressures on Congress, and (7) qualifications and conduct of members.

Several useful appendixes add to the scope of this authoritative, well-organized report on Congress, including a biographical index of members, 1789-1982; a series of documents from the preconstitutional period; congressional statistics; congressional rules; and a glossary of congressional terms. There is a detailed name and subject index.

605.   **Congressional Quarterly Weekly Report.** Washington, D.C., Congressional Quarterly Service, 1945- . weekly. index. $390.00/yr. (includes **CQ Almanac**). LC 84-649232. ISSN 0010-5910.

606.   **Congressional Quarterly Almanac.** Washington, D.C., Congressional Quarterly Service, 1945- . annual. index. $390.00. (includes **CQ Weekly Report**). LC 47-41081. ISSN 0095-6007.

607.   **Congress and the Nation.** Washington, D.C., Congressional Quarterly Service. 1965- . quadrennial. index. $110.00. LC 65-22351. ISBN 0-87187-334-6 (1985).

These three publications by the Congressional Quarterly Service provide authoritative, comprehensive current awareness and retrospective views on the activities and accomplishments of the United States Congress. To follow congressional action chronologically, the first title to use is the *Congressional Quarterly Weekly Report*, which provides a digest in news magazine style. A series of articles provides current information, with photos and the texts of several important documents in each issue. There is also information on legislative action on major bills, including the voting record by individual members of Congress. There is a quarterly index.

The annual *Congressional Quarterly Almanac* provides a compilation and summary of the material reported in the weekly publication. The volume therefore serves as a narrative synopsis of Congress for the year. The opening chapter provides a wealth of information on the organization and personnel of Congress, including a list of all members and their committee assignments. The legislative summary section offers a brief overview of all activity, followed by the major segment of the volume—a series of chapters assigned to the major areas of legislation, including environment/energy, appropriations, health/ education/welfare, and foreign policy. Each chapter covers in detail legislative activity and the provisions of the bills passed. Roll-call votes for the year are also presented. Appendixes provide a number of legislative studies on presidential support, party unity, and such key votes as the Contra aid bill in 1986.

Congress and the Nation began with the volume for 1945-1964, published in 1965, and has continued with an additional summary every four years, one presidential term. This series offers a further synthesis of material from the annual *Almanac*, with the same format of chapters covering major fields of congressional activity. The consistency of coverage among these publications permits research at various levels of detail and chronologically from 1945 to the present. While the focus is on congressional activity, all these publications feature summaries of the major activities of the presidency and the Supreme Court. The comprehensive, systematic coverage of these titles and their excellent indexes make them for many purposes a better starting point for research than the government documents on which they are based.

608. **A Guide to Research Collections of Former Members of the United States House of Representatives, 1789-1987.** Prepared under the direction of the Office of the Bicentennial of the United States, House of Representatives, Cynthia Pease Miller, ed.-in-chief. Washington, D.C., Office of the Bicentennial, 1988. 504p. Y1.1/7:100-171.

609. **Guide to Research Collections of Former United States Senators, 1789-1982.** Kathryn Allamong Jacob, ed.-in-chief; Elizabeth Ann Hornyak, production ed. Washington, D.C., Historical Office, United States Senate, 1983. 362p. U.S. Senate Bicentennial Publication, No. 1). Y1.1/3:97-41.

These two bicentennial publications of the Congress identify the repositories of papers, oral history material, and other archival items such as photographs for some 3,300 men and women who served in the House and 1,800 in the Senate. These guides provide access to primary sources for the study of these individuals and of Congress itself. Both directories are arranged alphabetically by name of the representative or senator. Each short entry identifies the repositories holding their material and very briefly describes the collection. Both volumes list the repositories by state in appendixes. The senate volume also contains a list of all senators by state, with party and dates of service. The Senate Historical Office issued a supplement to its list in 1985; it is included in the Gale reprint published in 1986 (ISSN 0810322242).

610. Library of Congress. Manuscript Division. Compiled by John J. McDonough, with the assistance of Marilyn K. Parr. **Members of Congress: A Checklist of Their Papers in the Manuscript Division, Library of Congress.** Washington, D.C., GPO, 1980. 217p. illus. $9.00. LC 78-606102. ISBN 0-8444-0272-9. S/N 030-003-00019-5.

Of the 11,150 persons who have served as members of Congress from the time of the first Continental Congress through the 95th Congress, wheh this bibliography was compiled, 894 are represented in this work. The checklist covers members' personal papers held by the Manuscript Division of the Library of Congress.

The entries are arranged alphabetically by member. Each entry provides brief biographical data, plus information on the papers held. The collections vary from a single letter or autograph to extensive collections containing several hundred thousand items. The type of materials, the span of dates, and the size of each collection are indicated briefly. Restrictions on access and the availability of finding aids are noted. Two appendixes provide additional access to the members of Congress: the first lists all members by state represented; the second lists each Congress with an attached roll of members.

611. Ornstein, Norman J., Thomas E. Mann, and Michael J. Malbin. **Vital Statistics on Congress, 1987-1988.** Washington, D.C., Congressional Quarterly, 1987. 275p. $16.95. LC 87-30088. ISBN 0-87187-451-2.

The 1987 edition is the third revision of this handbook, which was originally published in 1980. This title is basically a collection of statistics gathered to provide detailed information on Congress.

The more than 100 tables are arranged in 8 chapters on the following topics: (1) members of Congress, (2) elections, (3) campaign finance, (4) committees, (5) congressional staff and operating expenses, (6) workload, (7) budgeting, and (8) voting alignments. The years covered vary from table to table, but usually coverage extends back to the 1940s. In one convenient source there is information on such topics as historical party strength in Congress, the congressional seats lost by the president's party in midterm elections, the size of committee staffs, the number of bills introduced per session, and the voting strength of the conservative coalition. These and many other statistical studies add up to a comprehensive portrait of Congress.

612. **Politics in America: Members of Congress in Washington and at Home.** Washington, D.C., Congressional Quarterly, 1982- . biennial. $29.95. LC 83-7640. ISBN 0-87187-375-3 (1986).

Following an arrangement by state, this guide provides political profiles, with much factual data on the current political situation. The state articles begin with a review of the governor, followed by the senators and each congressional representative. These evaluative reviews consider achievements and failures and all the various political factors involved, such as finances, campaigns, and interest groups. These assessments provide a portrait of the members of Congress in Washington and at home with their constituents. The politics of the states and congressional districts are also briefly described.

Statistical data provided for each member of Congress include election results, campaign finances, voting studies, votes on key issues, and ratings by several interest groups. There is also a directory of committee assignments and a name index. For a similar source, see the *Almanac of American Politics* (entry 517).

613. **Powers of Congress.** 2d ed. Nancy Lammers, ed. Washington, D.C., Congressional Quarterly, 1982. 380p. illus. bibliog. index. $8.95.(pbk). LC 82-14331. ISBN 0-87187-242-0.

This guidebook provides a broad examination of the principal powers of Congress. The study is done in the context of constitutional origins, historical evolution, and contemporary conditions, especially the relationship of Congress to the executive branch. This second edition includes consideration of the long-term effects of events during the Johnson and Nixon administrations, when Congress successfully challenged presidential power.

The powers of Congress are examined under eight categories: powers of the purse, foreign affairs, commerce power, impeachment, investigations, confirmations, amending power, and electing the president. A short introduction offers an overall survey. The manual ends with the text of the Constitution and a bibliography of publications relating to congressional powers.

614. Sharp, J. Michael. **The Dictionary of Congressional Voting Scores and Interest Group Ratings.** New York, Facts on File, 1988. 2v. 1,204p. $125.00. LC 87-9047. ISBN 0-8160-1464-7.

The voting record of each senator and representative in the United States Congress has been highlighted for the years 1947 to 1985 in this useful, if not inexpensive, book. These composite portraits of members of Congress have been created by including scores on several voting scales. These scores reveal a pattern on such matters as party unity and support for the president. The voting of each member of Congress is also rated by 11 interest groups. Brief notes provide background information on the life and political career of each member of Congress. *Politics in America* (see entry 612) contains similar information on voting behavior, but it is not cumulated for long time periods as in this convenient volume.

615. Zwirn, Jerold. **Congressional Publications: A Research Guide to Legislation, Budgets, and Treaties.** Littleton, Colo., Libraries Unlimited, 1983. 195p. index. $22.50. LC 82-18652. ISBN 0-87287-358-7.

While this volume certainly contains a wealth of information on congressional publications as its title indicates, its real focus is broader: the whole legislative process and the information involved in it. Congressional publications are noted within this framework and context of Congress as a "communications network" (p. 18).

The legislative process is traced through the various phases in a series of chapters beginning with the introduction of bills and resolutions. At each stage the appropriate basic documents are discussed. There are bibliographies for additional reading at the end of each chapter. Separate chapters clearly and concisely discuss the budget process and treaty-making. There is a subject index and a document index for access to specific governmental or commercial publications cited in the text.

Indexes

616. Garza, Hedda, comp. **The Watergate Investigation Index: House Judiciary Committee Hearings and Report on Impeachment.** Wilmington, Del., Scholarly Resources, 1985. 261p. $95.00. LC 85-2040. ISBN 0-8420-2186-8.

617. Garza, Hedda, comp. **The Watergate Investigation Index: Senate Select Committee Hearings and Reports on Presidential Campaign Activities.** Wilmington, Del., Scholarly Resources, 1982. 325p. $95.00. LC 82-7353. ISBN 0-8420-2175-2.

The Watergate investigations by the House and Senate committees produced some 40,000 pages of testimony, evidence, reports, and exhibits. The scope of these investigations went far beyond the original burglary to examine fundamental political questions such as presidential misuse of power.

These two volumes index the hearings and final reports of the congressional committees. Access is provided by subject (event, activity, place) and personal and organization name. The indexes are extremely comprehensive and detailed. They include very helpful cross-references and *see also* references. Notes with the entries help identify specific references from among the often long lists. The prefaces contain a brief history of the Watergate affair and guides to the use of the indexes.

UNITED STATES – STATE AND LOCAL GOVERNMENT

Bibliographies

618. Goehlert, Robert U., and Frederick W. Musto. **State Legislatures: A Bibliography.** Santa Barbara, Calif., ABC-Clio, 1985. 229p. index. $35.00. LC 84-24404. ISBN 0-87436-422-1.

According to the authors, this is the first bibliography to focus exclusively on state legislative research. This research includes two categories of literature: studies of single states, and the increasingly common theoretical and comparative works. The bibliography is arranged in two parts, reflecting those two types of literature. The theoretical/comparative/empirical studies section has 25 subdivisions covering such topics as interest groups and legislatures, legislative recruitment and careers, and structures of legislatures. The other part has one chapter for each state.

Coverage is comprehensive, treating all aspects of state legislatures, including their history, functions, organization, structure, and procedures. Books, journal articles, dissertations, research reports, and documents have been included for a total of 2,532 unannotated citations. Chronological limits are 1945 to the first half of 1984. Documents and works not in English have been excluded.

619. Parish, David W. **State Government Reference Publications: An Annotated Bibliography.** 2d ed. Littleton, Colo., Libraries Unlimited, 1981. 355p. index. $25.00. LC 81-788. ISBN 0-87287-253-X.

The second edition of this title includes 1,756 items selected from the 150,000 state publications the author estimated were published between 1974 and 1980. Most titles are official publications of the states. Other essential publications by commercial publishers or state university presses are also included.

The entries are arranged by format. Official state blue books, legislative handbooks, statistical abstracts, and the like constitute important elements in this bibliography. In this second edition, specialized bibliographies, financial and statistical databooks, popular publications as tourist guides, and audiovisual sources are also prominently featured. All entries are briefly annotated. Four appendixes provide a bibliography of suggested readings, a bibliography of reference tools, a subject core of state publications, and agency addresses. There are also personal author, title, and subject indexes.

620. **State Bluebooks and Reference Publications: A Selected Bibliography.** Lexington, Ky., Council of State Governments, 1983. 62p. $15.00(pbk). LC 83-622949. ISBN 0-87292-038-0.

The Council of State Governments completed this bibliography based on its collection and supplementary information from a survey. The result is a comprehensive listing of "blue books," the directories of state agencies, with key personnel identified. These handbooks bear various titles, including official register, directory, roster, and state almanac.

Five additional categories of publications are listed: general reference, legislative manuals, directories, statistical abstracts, and other items. There is a table showing which states have publications in each category. Most of these materials are official documents, though some are commercially published. More than 1,000 titles have been included, with publication information, addresses, and prices.

621. **State Constitutional Conventions, Commissions, & Amendments 1959-1978: An Annotated Bibliography.** Bethesda, Md., Congressional Information Service, 1981. 2v. $350.00. LC 81-3206. ISBN 0-912380-79-9.

This bibliography continues *State Constitutional Conventions from Independence to the Completion of the Present Union, 1776-1959: A Bibliography*, compiled by Cynthia E. Browne (Greenwood Press, 1973). The 3,000 entries for material published between 1959 and 1978 all relate to state constitution revision and related activities such as constitutional conventions and commissions created to consider revisions. The publications of these bodies form the core of this bibliography.

The first volume of the set, the *Research Bibliography*, arranges the entries within states according to the type of revision activity and by time segments. A table of contents lists the items in each state section. The second volume, the *Alphabetical Bibliography*, contains the same material arranged alphabetically by personal or corporate author within state sections. Many entries include brief content annotations. The bibliography is designed for use with the fiche collection of the cited documents provided by the Congressional Information Service, but it may be used independently as a bibliography of materials of constitution revision bodies.

Biographical Sources

622. Holli, Melvin G., and Peter d'A. Jones, eds. **Biographical Dictionary of American Mayors, 1820-1980: Big City Mayors.** Westport, Conn., Greenwood, 1981. 451p. index. $69.50. LC 80-1796. ISBN 0-313-21134-5.

This directory offers signed biographies of the mayors of 15 leading American cities: Baltimore, Boston, Buffalo, Chicago, Cincinnati, Cleveland, Detroit, Los Angeles, Milwaukee, New Orleans, New York, Philadelphia, Pittsburgh, San Francisco, and St. Louis. A total of 679 mayors were covered by 100 historians relying on original sources in local city archives. The biographical portraits all end with a short list of sources of additional information.

Twelve appendixes identify mayors by city, by political party, by ethnic background, by religious affiliation, and by place of birth, and provide population data on the size and rank of the cities represented and the presence of foreign-born and black citizens. This directory can be used as a source of biographical information or could serve as a "rich data base" (preface) for the study of American mayors.

623. McMullin, Thomas A., and David Walker. **Biographical Directory of American Territorial Governors.** Westport, Conn., Meckler, 1984. 353p. $75.00. LC 84-9095. ISBN 0-9304-6611-X.

With the enactment of the Northwest Ordinance in 1787, the United States created a system of government for territories. Territorial jurisdiction was the first stage of the process leading to statehood. This directory provides short biographies of one to two pages on the governors of territories that later became states (excluding Puerto Rico, the Philippines, and the like).

The directory is arranged alphabetically by territory and then chronologically by the terms of the governors. There is a name index for easy access to specific governors. All the biographical portraits were written by the editors. They include personal and family information as well as an analysis of political careers and administrations. There are also bibliographies of sources of further information.

624. Raimo, John. **Biographical Directory of American Colonial Revolutionary Governors, 1607-1789.** Westport, Conn., Meckler, 1980. 521p. $60.00. LC 80-13279. ISBN 0-9304-6607-1.

In this biographical directory, the term "governor" has been interpreted to include all who held executive power in the British colonies in America, which in 1776 became the original 13 American states. About 400 individuals met this criterion.

The directory is arranged alphabetically by colony and then chronologically by the terms of the governors. There is a name index for easy access to specific governors. All of the brief biographical portraits, which range from about 250 to 600 words, were written by the author. They include personal and genealogical information as well as an analysis of political careers and administrations. There is also a bibliography of sources of information. Each colony chapter also has a bibliography of related historical works for research.

625. Solomon, Samuel R., comp. **The Governors of the American States, Commonwealths, and Territories, 1900-1980.** Lexington, Ky., Council of State Governments, 1980. 79p. bibliog. $4.00(pbk). LC 80-624452.

More than 2,000 persons have served as state governors since the American Revolution. Many who became prominent as governors or in other capacities have become obscure, especially with the passage of time. This handy compendium offers basic biographical information in an easy-to-access format.

The arrangement is first by state (or territory or commonwealth). For each state there is a chart listing the governors by dates of term of office. Provided for each governor are party affiliation, residence, birth date, birthplace, and date of death. There are also brief notes on other positions held and family relationships to other governors. At the head of each state table is information on the number of governors, the term of office, and inaugural date. The volume concludes with a short bibliography on state governors.

Dictionaries and Encyclopedias

626. Elliot, Jeffrey M., and Sheikh R. Ali. **The State and Local Government Political Dictionary.** Santa Barbara, Calif., ABC-Clio, 1988. 325p. (Clio Dictionaries in Political Science, No. 12). $35.00; $15.00(pbk). LC 87-18722. ISBN 0-87436-417-5; 0-87436-512-0(pbk).

Among the growing number of titles in the *Clio Dictionaries in Political Science* series, this one is a lexicon of state and local government. As all titles in this series, the entries are grouped in chapters that parallel chapter topics in leading textbooks. There is a detailed index that provides direct access to the entries. Another series feature is the use of two paragraphs for each term: the first provides a definition, and the second, on significance, provides information on historical roots and contemporary usage.

In addition to the definitions of the terms, there is a considerable amount of factual information about state and local political institutions, processes, and policies, so that this reference source can serve as a comparative handbook for political knowledge about American cities and states as well as a dictionary of terms.

Directories

627. **The Book of the States.** Lexington, Ky., Council of State Governments, 1935- . biennial. $42.50. LC 35-11433. ISSN 0068-0125.

628. **State Elective Officials and the Legislatures.** Lexington, Ky., Council of State Governments, 1977- . biennial. $17.50. LC 77-647973. ISSN 0191-9466.

629. **State Administrative Officials Classified by Function.** Lexington, Ky., Council of State Governments, 1957- . biennial. $17.50. LC 78-640949. ISSN 0561-8630.

630. **State Legislative Leadership, Committees, and Staff.** Lexington, Ky., Council of State Governments, 1979- . biennial. $17.50. LC 79-644269. ISSN 0195-6639.

631. **National Organizations of State Government Officials Directory.** Lexington, Ky., Council of State Governments and the National Conference of State Legislatures, 1984. 152p. $15.00. LC 84-623562. ISBN 0-87292-051-8.

The Council of State Governments is an association committed to strengthening state government in the United States. The provision of in-depth, timely information about all aspects of the work of the state governments is a major means employed to accomplish this goal. *The Book of the States* and its related publications provide authoritative information on the structure, functions, finances, and personnel of each state government.

The Book of the States provides, in tabular form with brief narrative discussions, a wide variety of information on state constitutions, gubernatorial campaigns, the powers of governors, cabinet systems, state legislatures, state courts, state government finances, personnel policies, and state services. The emphasis is on providing comparative data, typically the specific legal provisions or statistics for each state. For example, the number of paid holidays or the provisions for removing judges in the various states can be readily determined with this source. At the end of the volume, the "State Pages" provide a half page for each state, with basic facts, the names of key officials, and statistics.

State Elective Officials and the Legislatures is a biennial supplement to *The Book of the States*. It contains for each state a list of the names of elected executive branch officials and of the judges of the court of last resort. There is also a roster of the names and addresses of legislators.

Another supplement, *State Administrative Officials Classified by Function*, consists of the major state administrative officials, elected or appointed, arranged by their functions. Names, addresses, and phone numbers are provided for the state officials listed under more than 100 areas of responsibility (liquor control, ombudsman, tourism, etc.).

State Legislative Leadership, Committees, and Staff has two sections. The first names the legislative leaders, staffs, and the chairs of standing committees in a state-by-state arrangement. The second section has three lists drawn from this material. The first lists the major legislative leaders by office (president of the Senate, House and Senate majority and minority leaders, etc.). There follows a list of selected important committee chairs and, finally, a list of selected staff in administration or such functions as bill drafting or legal research. Addresses and phone numbers are provided for all these officials.

The Council has also published the *National Organizations of State Government Officials Directory*, which provides information on over 100 organizations that serve state officials. For each entry there is a brief description of the function, structure, membership, and publications of the association, as well as addresses, phone numbers, and the names of key officials.

Taken as a group, these publications of the Council of State Governments provide comprehensive, authoritative, and up-to-date directory and handbook information on the state governments in the United States.

632. **County Executive Directory.** Washington, D.C., Carroll Publishing, 1984- . semi-annual. index. $125.00/yr. LC 84-645032. ISSN 0742-1702.

633. **Municipal Executive Directory.** Washington, D.C., Carroll Publishing, 1984- . semi-annual. index. $125.00/yr. LC 84-644939. ISSN 0742-1710.

634. **State Executive Directory.** Washington, D.C., Carroll Publishing, 1980- . triannual. index. $125.00/yr. LC 81-641216. ISSN 2076-7163.

With these three titles Carroll Publishing Company is providing extensive coverage of state and local officials. The *State Executive Directory* lists senior officials in all 50 states. The *County Executive Directory* has entries for those counties with populations over 25,000. The *Municipal Executive Directory* covers cities and towns of more than 15,000.

While each volume has individual features, the basic formats are similar. In all three there are organizational listings based on the governmental structure of the state, county, or municipality. The various departments, agencies, boards, committees, etc., are listed with the names, titles, addresses, and telephone numbers of key officials. There are also alphabetical lists of the officeholders. Keyword, subject, and geographical indexes are provided as appropriate. Though expensive, these directories provide the most complete and up-to-date information on state and local officials throughout the United States.

Two inexpensive directories are listed below. Both include the name, address, phone number, and date of expiration of term for the chief elected official of cities with a population of 30,000 or more.

Directory of Local Chief Executives. Washington, D.C., National League of Cities. LC 86-232393. ISSN 0898-5286.

The Mayors of America's Principal Cities. Washington, D.C., United States Conference of Mayors. semiannual. $10.00. LC 86-15706.

635.   **National Directory of State Agencies.** Bethesda, Md., National Standards Association, 1975- . annual. $95.00. LC 74-18864. ISSN 0095-3113.

This directory, which has expanded its format and is now revised annually, provides comprehensive and up-to-date coverage of the myriad of state activities and the resulting official and agencies. The directory contains five sections: (1) "State Locators," a state-by-state listing of telephone numbers for assistance in locating information not in this volume; (2) "State Elected Officials and Agencies," a listing for each state of key officials, including all legislators, with addresses and phone numbers, plus a listing of state agencies arranged by function (aging, consumer affairs, etc.) with addresses and phone numbers; (3) "State Agencies by Function," a listing by 102 functional areas of the state agencies listed above by state; (4) "Associations of State Government Officials," a listing by function of national associations that represent government officials, with principal contacts, addresses, phone numbers; and (5) "All-State Telephone Directory," an alphabetical list of all the names in this directory, with phone numbers.

636.   **State Government Research Directory: A Descriptive Guide to Basic and Applied Research and Data Collection Programs and Activities.** Kay Gill and Susan E. Tufts, eds. Detroit, Gale, 1987. 349p. index. $175.00. LC 86-27101. ISBN 0-8103-1591-2.

This title by Gale, which will be updated with new editions, now does for the research agencies of the 50 states and the territories what the publisher's *Government Research Directory* (see entry 000) has long done for the federal research agencies.

This directory is arranged by state with listings for 865 agencies, including research organizations, units that oversee or coordinate research programs, and units providing financial support for research. Each entry furnishes information on name, address, and phone number; size of staff; and research facilities, and describes research activities, publications, and information services. There are two indexes: name/keyword/agency and subject.

Handbooks

637.   Hellebust, Lynn. **State Legislative Sourcebook 1987: A Resource Guide to Legislative Information in the Fifty States.** Topeka, Kans., Government Research Service, 1986. $95.00. ISBN 0-9615227-1-2.

For research on state politics and legislation or for lobbying state legislators, this looseleaf guide is extremely useful, especially if updated annually as planned. The main section is arranged by state. Each state segment contains a description of the legislature, including the length and frequency of sessions, leadership and committee membership, procedural rules, and sources of information on the status of bills. Financial disclosure information for legislators and lobbyist registration requirements are also covered. The availability and cost of publications and services are indicated.

The appendixes contain a list of telephone numbers for obtaining information on the status of bills and a bibliography on state politics, legislation, and lobbying.

638.   Mullaney, Marie Marmo, comp. **American Governors and Gubernatorial Elections, 1979-1987.** Westport, Conn., Meckler, 1988. 101p. bibliog. $35.00. LC 88-13248. ISBN 0-88736-316-4.

By reporting on the period 1979 to 1987, Mullaney extends gubernatorial coverage beyond that provided by an earlier work, by Roy R. Glashan (*American Governors and Gubernatorial Elections, 1775-1978.* Westport, Conn., Meckler, 1979. 370p. $45.00. LC 79-15021. ISBN 0930466179). Both of these titles offer election statistics and biographical information about the American state governors. The election statistics provide dates of elections; vote counts for Democratic, Republican, and other significant candidates; total vote; and percentages. The following information is given for each governor: date and place of birth, age at and date of becoming governor, party affiliation, occupation, residence, age at and date of death. While other publications, such as *Almanac of American Politics* (see entry 517) or *America Votes* (see entry 540) provide much the same information, and in some instances more, this volume and its predecessor offer the convenience of concentrating exclusively on information relating to American governors.

639.   **State Information Book.** Washington, D.C., Potomac Books, 1973- . biennial. $75.00. LCSN 85-22757. ISBN 0933937031. (1987/88).

A tremendous amount of directory information is available in this handy single volume concerning state officeholders, state agencies, and services. The data is arranged in state chapters, which include the following sections for each state: (1) state profile (nickname, motto, state bird, etc., plus a short narrative description); (2) key state executives, with addresses and telephone numbers; (3) state agencies, with chief executive, addresses, phone numbers; (4) members of the state legislature and judiciary; (5) information for obtaining vital records; (6) a statistical profile with demographic and economic data; (7) multistate and intrastate agencies; and (8) information on the federal presence in the state, including congressional delegations, U.S. courts, and military installations, all with addresses and phone numbers.

This directory is very well organized for quick reference use. Much of the information is also available in the Council of State Governments' *Book of the States* (see entry 627), which has the advantage of annual revision. Names, addresses, and phone numbers of state agencies and officials are also included in the annually revised *National Directory of State Agencies* (see entry 635).

640.   **Worldmark Encyclopedia of the States: A Practical Guide to the Geographic, Demographic, Historical, Political, Economic, and Social Development of the United States.** 2d ed. New York, Worldmark Press, Wiley, exclusive distributor, 1986. $89.95. LC 85-26455. ISSN 0-4718-3213-8.

Each state in this handbook has a chapter that contains a wide range of political, economic, and social information. Each state section begins with a map and a headnote with brief information on the state name, date of entry into the Union, state flower, legal holidays, etc. The state flag and seal are illustrated. There follows a series of about 50 topics, which are standard across all states. These sections range from a paragraph to a page and include: location, size, and extent; topography; climate; ethnic groups; history; state government; economy; agriculture; education; libraries and museums; tourism, travel, and recreation; etc. Each state profile also includes a list of famous persons and a bibliography for further reading. The concluding chapter is a 50-page overview of the United States as a whole, using the same format.

Yearbooks

641. **The Municipal Yearbook.** Washington, D.C., International City Management Association, 1934- . annual. index. $68.00. LC 34-27121. ISSN 0077-2186.

The subtitle for the 1987 edition, "The Authoritative Source Book of Urban Data and Developments," accurately describes the intent and scope of this yearbook. The first two chapters contain articles which, over the years, have examined various issues of importance to city government, ranging from the problems in the liability insurance industry to a review of major relevant Supreme Court decisions. The remaining chapters present statistical data and directory information gathered through surveys conducted by the association. Long-standing elements of these chapters have included profiles of individual cities and counties, with information on revenue and form of government; directories, including key officials for all counties and all cities over 2,500; statistics on staffing and compensation for municipal and county officials; and an extensive bibliography of books, periodicals, documents, and data files that serve as sources of information on all municipal or urban matters. The 1987 edition contains a cumulative index covering 1983-1987.

5

Political Science –
Topical Fields

INTERNATIONAL ORGANIZATIONS

Bibliographies

642. Baratta, Joseph Preston, comp. **Strengthening the United Nations: A Bibliography on U.N. Reform and World Federalism.** New York, Greenwood, 1987. 351p. (Bibliographies and Indexes in World History). $45.00. LC 87-134. ISBN 0-313-25840-6.

The focus of this bibliography is on world federalism, especially its impact on the United Nations. The over 3,000 citations were selected from books, periodicals, dissertations, nonprint media, and archival and other primary materials. Most of the entries, which cover from the 1940s to 1985, are English-language titles. The bibliographies are divided into chapters on topics such as universal federation, the peace movement, diplomacy, and the union of democracies. This is a valuable resource for those interested in studying the United Nations or world federalism.

643. **International Bibliography: Publications of Intergovernmental Organizations.** New York, UNIPUB, 1973- . quarterly. index. $60.00/yr. LC 85-643416. ISSN 025601042.

This bibliography began in 1973 as *International Bibliography, Information Documentation* (IBID). It is a major resource for the publications of major intergovernmental organizations such as the World Bank or the Council of Europe and of other lesser-known organizations such as the Committee for Whaling Statistics. Many United Nations documents are also included. Approximately 3,000 items are currently indexed annually. Entries are divided into the "Bibliographic Record," where monographs are arranged in broad subject categories, and "Periodicals Record," where the entries are arranged alphabetically by the name of the periodical. There are subject and title indexes to all citations. There is also a useful list with addresses of all the organizations whose publications are indexed.

644. Kuehl, Warren F., and Nancy M. Ferguson. **The United States and the United Nations: A Bibliography.** Los Angeles, Center for the Study of Armament and Disarmament, California State University, 1981. 59p. index. (Political Issues Series, Vol. 7, No. 2). $3.50(pbk).

This bibliography focuses exclusively on one aspect of the United Nations: its relations with the United States. Within this topic the author has included various types of studies on

U.S./UN relations: historical or contemporary descriptions, future-oriented speculations about possible developments, and analytical studies of actions, policies, trends, or specific themes.

The 363 unannotated entries begin with guides to the basic literature, including handbooks for basic United Nations documents. There follows a subject arrangement of entries planned around various themes such as the creation of the United Nations, economic aid, and peacekeeping activities. There is an author index.

Directories

645.   Schiavone, Giuseppe. **International Organizations: A Dictionary and Directory.** 2d ed. Chicago, St. James Press, 1986. 400p. index. $45.00. LC 86-4944. ISBN 0-912289-68-6.

For the purpose of this book the author defines the term "international organization" to cover bodies with sovereign nations as members, such as the Commonwealth, the Benelux Economic Union, and the African Development Bank. The dictionary part contains encyclopedic articles in alphabetical order which describe the history and purpose of some 100 international agencies. These sketches, which run from a paragraph to over 20 pages, also include the name of the chief officer, the headquarters address, a list of publications, and references to literature concerning the organization.

There is a second directory list of less influential agencies with abbreviated information: purpose, membership, headquarters, and publications. There is also a table of members of major agencies, an index of foundation dates, and an index covering both agency sections. The introduction reviews the history of international organizations. The cross-references from abbreviations to the full names of agencies are particularly useful.

Encyclopedias

646.   Osmanczyk, Edmund Jan. **The Encyclopedia of the United Nations and International Agreements.** Philadelphia, Taylor & Francis, 1985. 1,059p. index. $160.00. LC 85-3368. ISBN 0-85066-312-1.

This encyclopedia contains concise articles, varying in length from a paragraph to several pages, on many thousands of topics, persons, events, organizations, and treaties. Most of the entries deal with the United Nations, its specialized agencies, international agreements, or international relations. The text of some major agreements, such as SALT II or the Helsinki Final Act, are quoted in full.

While in some cases some of the entries seem to be only slightly related to the main topics of this encyclopedia, it is nevertheless a valuable compendium of information on the United Nations and international relations, especially activities promoting international cooperation. The volume also includes an essay of projected population growth, a list of acronyms, a subject index, and an index of agreements, conventions, and treaties.

Handbooks

647.   Baer, George W., comp. and ed. **International Organizations, 1918-1945: A Guide to Research and Research Materials.** Wilmington, Del., Scholarly Resources, 1981. 260p. index. (Guides to European Diplomatic History Research and Research Materials). $17.50. LC 80-53893. ISBN 0-8420-2179-5.

This handbook, which focuses on international organizations for the period 1918-1945, is part of a series of research guides on European diplomatic history by Scholarly Resources. As a tool to assist researchers, it will be an indispensable map through a maze of organizations, activities, and publications.

The first part contains a brief overview of international affairs. Part 2 describes the archives of the League of Nations, the United Nations, and other international organizations such as the Permanent Court of International Justice. Part 3 describes archival material in the United States, as well as in Great Britain, France, and other European countries. The remaining chapters are bibliographic surveys of the literature on various related topics such as disarmament and minorities. Altogether there are 1,603 entries, many with short annotations on content.

648. **Everyone's United Nations.** 10th ed. By the Department of Public Information. New York, United Nations, 1986. 484p. index. $14.95; $9.95(pbk). ISBN 92-1-100273-7; 92-1-100274-5(pbk). S/N E.85.I.24.

This basic reference source for the United Nations and its related intergovernmental agencies has now been updated after seven years. As an official handbook it outlines the structure, work, and functions of the United Nations, focusing on events of the period between 1978 and 1985. Earlier editions, especially the eighth and ninth, are important for the years 1945-1978.

Part 1 of this handbook deals with the purpose and principles of the United Nations and its membership and principal organs. Part 2 deals with its role in political, economic, social, and legal questions. For each topic, such as the UN operations in Cyprus or freedom of information, there is a historical summary with references to major decisions and documents. The final part deals with the intergovernmental agencies related to the United Nations, e.g., the World Bank and the International Atomic Energy Agency. Appendixes contain the texts of the United Nations charter, the statute of the International Court of Justice, and the Universal Declaration of Human Rights.

649. Finley, Blanche. **The Structure of the United Nations General Assembly: An Organizational Approach to its Work, 1974-1980.** White Plains, N.Y., UNIPUB/Kraus International, 1988. 2v. 1,051p. index. $160.00. LC 87-3554. ISBN 0-527-91618-8 set.

This work, which updates the author's previous effort published by Oceana in 1977, is a valuable source of information about the many bodies and activities of the General Assembly of the United Nations. The information is arranged under 13 topics (peace, politics, economics, social issues, human rights, international law, etc.). The entries cover specific bodies, committees, commissions, conferences, seminars, and conventions. They include information on such matters as origins, membership, current concerns, and recent actions. Many include references to specific documents and bibliographies of related publications. For a less specialized introduction see *Everyone's United Nations* (entry 648).

650. Hovet, Thomas Jr., and Erica Hovet. **A Chronology and Fact Book of the United Nations, 1941-1985.** 7th ed. Dobbs Ferry, N.Y., Oceana, 1986. 384p. $25.00. LC 86-2427. ISBN 0-379-20693-5.

The chronology section of this historical handbook lists by date from 1941 through 1985 the major events and decisions in the history of the United Nations. Very brief annotations highlight these entries. The handbook section contains the United Nations Charter, the Statute of the International Court of Justice, and the Rule of Procedure of the General Assembly.

Twenty-one tables form the most useful section of this book. These include various data on such matters as membership, principal officers, Security Council vetoes, and budget. Membership and purpose of the specialized agencies of the United Nations are also covered.

For a convenient historical overview this handbook is a useful supplement to the more detailed *Annual Review of United Nations Affairs* (see entry 651) or the *Yearbook of the United Nations* (see entry 653).

Yearbooks

651. **Annual Review of United Nations Affairs.** Dobbs Ferry, N.Y., Oceana, 1949- . annual. index. price varies. LC 50-548. ISSN 0066-4340.

Somewhat more timely in publication, this annual closely resembles in format and content the *Yearbook of the United Nations* (see entry 653). Most of the material in it is derived from the *UN Chronicle*, a UN account of activities published 11 times a year. The *Review* begins with the annual report of the secretary general and proceeds to outline the work of the United Nations under six chapters: "Political and Security Questions," "Decolonization," "Economic, Social and Human Rights Questions," "Legal Questions," and "Other Questions."

There is a lengthy annex section in which speeches delivered during the annual general debate period are summarized or quoted in part. There is an index by subject and speaker. The activities of the UN specialized agencies are not covered in this yearbook.

652. **United States Participation in the UN: Report by the President to the Congress for the Year [year].** U.S. Department of State. Washington, D.C., GPO, 1948- . $10.00. LC 80-12547. ISSN 0083-0208.

The president, as required by law, reports annually to Congress with this publication on the activities of the United Nations and its specialized agencies. The focus is specifically on American involvement in these activities. Recent volumes have divided coverage into five categories: political and security affairs; economic, social, scientific, and human rights; trusteeship and dependent areas; legal developments; and budget, administration, and institutional management. Each topic is subdivided into many specific issues. The 1986 volume for example, included discussions of Lebanon, the U.S. bombing of Libya, chemical weapons, drug abuse, apartheid, the World Weather Watch, and the UN budget. For each entry there is a summary of events, of UN actions, and of American policy and participation. The votes on resolutions are recorded. The appendixes contain rosters of United States representatives at the UN.

653. **Yearbook of the United Nations.** New York, Department of Public Information, United Nations, 1946- . annual. index. price varies. LCSN 87-19677. ISSN 0082-8521.

Despite the three- to four-year publication lag, this yearbook is the major reference source for current information on the activities of the United Nations. It updates the basic information found in *Everyone's United Nations* (see entry 648).

The proceedings and activities of the year are reviewed in considerable narrative detail, with documentary citations. Part 1 covers the United Nations itself with some 50 chapters reviewing political and security matters, disarmament, economic and social questions, trusteeship and decolonization, legal questions, and administrative and budgetary matters. The second part reviews in a similar manner the activities of the UN specialized agencies, that is, the intergovernmental organizations related to the United Nations, such as the World Bank and the International Atomic Energy Agency.

Appendixes include a roster of the United Nations, the Charter of the United Nations and the Statute of the International Court of Justice, the structure of the organization, and a list of UN information centers and offices. There is a detailed subject index, which facilitates using this essential tool as a source of information about the United Nations.

INTERNATIONAL RELATIONS

Atlases

654. Young, Harry F. **Atlas of United States Foreign Relations.** U.S. Department of State. Washington, D.C., GPO, 1985. 98p. maps. index. $5.00(pbk). LC 85-600628.

This atlas is designed to provide in a graphic format basic information about U.S. foreign relations. Most of the data are based on publications of the U.S. government and international organizations. Because the sources are generally cited, the atlas can serve also as a guide to more detailed studies or statistics.

The contents are divided into six sections: "Foreign Relations Machinery," which examines the organization and operations of American foreign relations; "International Organizations"; "Elements of the World Economy"; "Trade and Investment"; "Developmental Assistance"; and "U.S. National Security," which considers collective defense arrangements and the American-Soviet military balance. There are 90 displays, maps, and charts. The maps are large-scale, black and white. The inclusion of considerable economic and trade data will make this atlas of interest to many beyond those studying foreign relations.

Bibliographies

655. Barrett, Jane R., and Jane Beaumont, comps. **A Bibliography of Works on Canadian Foreign Relations, 1976-1980.** Toronto, Canadian Institute of International Affairs, 1982. index. 306p. $30.00(pbk). LC 82-137239.

656. Barrett, Jane R., comp., with Jane Beaumont and Lee-Anne Broadhead. **A Bibliography of Works on Canadian Foreign Relations, 1981-1985.** Toronto, Canadian Institute of International Affairs, 1987. index. $30.00(pbk). LC 87-166792. ISSN 0919084575.

These volumes, with their two predecessors, which covered the periods 1945-1970 and 1971-1975, provide comprehensive bibliographic access to the literature on Canadian foreign policy and foreign relations. Both Canadian and foreign publications are included. The same basic format has been followed since the beginning of the series, though the last two volumes have added a broad classification scheme with 400 subject headings, which facilitates searching for specific topics. There is an author index.

Students of Canadian foreign relations will find that this bibliography, published by the Canadian Institute of International Affairs, provides a most useful access point to the relevant book, periodical, and document literature.

657. DeLancey, Mark W. **African International Relations: An Annotated Bibliography.** Boulder, Colo., Westview Press, 1981. 365p. index. (Westview Special Studies on Africa). $26.50. LC 80-21254. ISBN 0-89158-680-6.

Nearly 3,000 entries have been assembled in this bibliography of African international relations. Books, periodical articles, and pamphlets have been included. Primary sources, such as documents of governments and international organizations, were not included. Coverage is comprehensive for the period 1960-1978. The bulk of the material cited is in English or, to a lesser extent, French. The brief annotations are usually limited to an indication of content.

The bibliography is arranged in 11 subject chapters, including chapters on inter-African conflicts, African unity, and the foreign policies of individual African states. There is a detailed subject index to names and countries but no author index.

658. Echard, William E., comp. and ed. **Foreign Policy of the French Second Empire: A Bibliography.** Westport, Conn., Greenwood, 1988. 416p. index. (Bibliographies and Indexes in World History, No. 12). $75.00. LC 87-37566. ISBN 0-313-23799-9.

The Second Empire in France encompassed the reign of Napoleon III, which lasted from 1852 to 1879, ending with the defeat inflicted on France and Bonapartism by the Franco-Prussian War. The 4,000 citations selected for this bibliography cover all aspects of this period of French history, including the Crimean War and the short reign of the Archduke Maximilian as emperor of Mexico. This era has recently been of increasing interest to historians and political scientists.

The compiler attempted to include all relevant primary sources as well as secondary books, periodical articles, and dissertations written in English, French, German, Italian, or Spanish. The unannotated citations are arranged in topical chapters. There is an author index and a detailed subject index.

659. Finan, John J., and John Child. **Latin America: International Relations: A Guide to Information Sources.** Detroit, Gale, 1981. 236p. (Gale Information Guide Library, International Relations Information Guide Series, Vol. 11). $62.00. LC 73-17508. ISSN 0-8103-1325-1.

This guide to sources on Latin American international relations contains over 1,400 items. It does not attempt to be a comprehensive bibliography for the specialist, but rather a useful guide for the general student. Accordingly, the emphasis is on recent English-language materials and on books and journal articles rather than on dissertations, documents, and "obscure items" (preface). Coverage includes the Latin nations of Central and South America as well as the Commonwealth Caribbean nations. The United States and Canada are included in terms of their relationships to the hemisphere and to individual Latin American countries.

The annotated entries are grouped in 37 chapters in 3 major divisions: (1) bibliographies and other reference sources, (2) a general section dealing with overall considerations of the hemisphere, and (3) chapters dealing with individual countries.

660. Goehlert, Robert U., and Elizabeth R. Hoffmeister. **The Department of State and American Diplomacy: A Bibliography.** New York, Garland, 1986. 349p. index. (Garland Reference Library of Social Science, Vol. 333). $54.00. LC 86-2107. ISBN 0-8240-8591-4.

The focus of this bibliography is the U.S. Department of State. The 3,818 citations selected cover books, journal articles, dissertations, research reports, and some documents; only English-language materials are included. The chronological limits are basically 1954 and 1984, with a scattering of older important publications.

The unannotated citations are arranged in four broad sections with numerous subdivisions. The first section deals with the Department of State and the diplomatic service. The second part concentrates on the conduct of American foreign policy. The third part contains geographical studies organized by country. The last section surveys biographical material on diplomats and foreign service officers. Henry Kissinger is the star attraction here. The introduction of this excellent bibliography contains a guide to United States documents and State Department publications. There is a detailed subject index.

661. **Guide to American Foreign Relations since 1700.** Richard Dean Burns, ed. Santa Barbara, Calif., ABC-Clio, 1983. 1,311p. index. $87.50. LC 82-13905. ISBN 0-87436-323-3.

More than a bibliography, this selective compilation of over 9,000 citations is an indispensable guide to American foreign relations for all researchers. It updates (but not totally replaces) the earlier standard, *Guide to Diplomatic History of the United States, 1771-1921*, compiled by Samuel Bemis and G. G. Griffin. The new work covers the diplomatic history of the United States and forces, such as public opinion, that have influenced its formation. Books, dissertations, documents, and journal articles are included, with short annotations that evaluate as well as describe the contents. The entries are arranged under 40 main headings that reflect the basic chronological orientation of the editor. Within these chapters there are subsections relating to specific persons, events, and topics.

Especially useful for the researcher are the first chapter on reference works and the introductions to each chapter, which provide an overview of the history and scholarship of a diplomatic period in American history. Each chapter also has listings of research aids, bibliographies, and documents collections. Appendixes contain chronological lists of principal makers of American foreign policy and brief biographies of secretaries of state. Access is facilitated by author and subject indexes, an extensive network of cross-references between entries, and a detailed table of contents.

662. Keto, C. Tsehloane. **American-South African Relations 1784-1980: Review and Select Bibliography.** Athens, Ohio, Ohio University Center for International Studies, Ohio University Press; distr., New York, Harper & Row, 1985. 159p. index. (Monographs in International Studies, Africa Series, No. 45). $11.00. LC 85-4937. ISBN 0-89680-128-4.

Relations between the United States and the Republic of South Africa have long been a matter of considerable interest, generating an extensive literature representing a variety of viewpoints. Although this selective bibliography is not a guide to this literature or a comprehensive listing, it is a useful source for relevant books, periodical articles, reports, and dissertations published before 1983.

Additional useful elements include a list of reference works and periodicals dealing with Africa, and a listing of organizations and research libraries with a focus on American-South African relations. There is an author index. The lack of a subject index is unfortunate because of the broad breakdown into subject chapters that was used.

663. Killen, Linda, and Richard L. Lael. **Versailles and After: An Annotated Bibliography of American Foreign Relations, 1919-1933.** New York, Garland, 1983. 469p. index. (American Diplomatic History, Vol. 2; Garland Reference Library of Social Science, Vol. 135). $60.00. LC 82-49115. ISBN 0-8240-9202-3.

The author has provided a bibliography covering American foreign relations for the period 1919-1933. In addition to the usual secondary literature in books and journal articles, this bibliography covers dissertations, documents, manuscripts, and archival sources. While the extension of coverage to include manuscripts and archival material is clearly very beneficial for any bibliography related to foreign relations, the coverage of periodical articles has been restricted in an unfortunate manner, which will mean that this source cannot be used alone as a basis for research. All citations to several essential titles, including *Foreign Affairs* (see entry 177), have been omitted. The entries have brief descriptive annotations.

664. Kozicki, Richard J. **International Relations of South Asia, 1947-80; A Guide to Information Sources.** Detroit, Gale, 1981. 166p. index. (International Relations Information Guide Series, Vol. 10; Gale Information Guide Library). $62.00. LC 73-17510. ISBN 0-8103-1329-4.

This work is a selected bibliography on the international relations of eight countries of South Asia from 1947 to 1980. The author defines the region of South Asia as India, Pakistan, Bangladesh, Sri Lanka, Nepal, Sikkim, Bhutan, and Afghanistan. Burma is not included. Only English-language publications are listed. Newspaper articles, doctoral dissertations and conference papers are excluded. There are short content annotations for each entry.

There is a chapter on each nation covered and a section on bibliographies and reference sources for the region. An eight-page appendix lists "basic books." The bibliography concludes with author and subject indexes.

665. Leonard, Thomas M. **Central America and United States Policies, 1820s-1980s: A Guide to Issues and References.** Claremont, Calif., Regina Books, 1985. 133p. bibliog. index. (Guides to Contemporary Issues, No. 4). $17.95; $10.95(pbk). LC 85-1765. ISBN 0-941690-14-8; 0-941690-13-X(pbk).

The purpose of this volume is to place the problems of Central America and their implications for American foreign policy in historical perspective. The first half of the book provides a historical overview of political, economic, and social conditions in Central America from the colonial period to the present.

Though the first part of this book can serve as a useful summary of Central American history, the main reference utility will be found in chapter 4, a bibliography of some 450 books and journal articles. The citations include English and Spanish works on Central American history and politics and on United States-Central American relations. There is a chapter on reference sources. The entries are not annotated, but each section is preceded by a headnote with background information and bibliographic recommendations.

666. Lincove, David A., and Gary R. Treadway, comps. **The Anglo-American Relationship: An Annotated Bibliography of Scholarship, 1945-1985.** New York, Greenwood, 1988. 415p. bibliog. index. (Bibliographies and Indexes in World History, No. 14). $49.95. LC 88-7225. ISBN 0-313-25854-6.

This bibliography covers an exceptionally wide range of topics related to the relationships between the United States and Great Britain. Publications cited were all published between 1945 and 1985, but the period covered is from 1783 through 1945. The bibliography is divided into two roughly equal sections, one covering diplomatic relations and the other nondiplomatic relations, which includes social, cultural, and economic relationships. Books, journal articles, and dissertations are included among the 1,000 citations, but primary sources and archival documents are not. There are author and title indexes, lists of ambassadors, and a bibliography of reference sources.

667. Messick, Frederick M., comp. **Primary Sources in European Diplomacy, 1914-1945: A Bibliography of Published Memoirs and Diaries.** New York, Greenwood, 1987. 221p. (Bibliographies and Indexes in World History, No. 6). $39.95. LC 87-186. ISBN 313-24555-X.

European international relations from the beginning of World War I to the end of World War II are the focus of this bibliography. The 636 items included cover primary sources—memoirs, diaries, correspondence, and firsthand accounts—by individuals personally involved in the events of the time. The bibliography is limited to published material, with English-language items predominating. The entries are arranged alphabetically by author, and the short annotations include some information about the authors. There is a subject index, a chronology of diplomatic events, and two appendixes: authors by nationality and an alphabetical listing of selected diplomatic events.

668. Mugridge, Ian. **United States Foreign Relations under Washington and Adams: A Guide to the Literature and Sources.** New York, Garland, 1982. 88p. index. (Garland Reference Library of Social Science, Vol. 58). $16.00. LC 78-68256. ISBN 0-8240-9778-5.

This guide contains 411 entries on American foreign relations during the Federalist period of presidents Washington and Adams. The citations are divided into three categories. Part 1 contains 293 citations to secondary materials, books, periodical articles, and dissertations. Part 2 is a list of published primary sources. Part 3 covers major unpublished primary sources, including manuscripts, correspondence, government records, and private papers.

All of the entries are annotated with brief content notes. These are especially useful for the identification and descriptions they provide of the unpublished primary sources. There is a subject index.

669. Plischke, Elmer. **U.S. Foreign Relations: A Guide to Information Sources.** Detroit, Gale, 1980. 715p. index. (American Government and History Information Guide Series, Vol. 6; Gale Information Guide Library). $30.00. LC 74-11516. ISBN 0-8103-1204-2.

American diplomacy, the foreign affairs process—not diplomatic history of world politics—is the concern of this bibliographic guide. For the serious student or researcher this title provides an overview of the field as well as citations for further reading. Plischke has included books, journal articles, official sources, memoirs, and biographical literature. Many bibliographies and reference sources are cited throughout the subject sections. Entries are generally limited to English-language materials.

This bibliography, following an analytical scheme, is divided into four parts. Part 1 deals with diplomacy in a general or comprehensive sense. Part 2, the largest and most important section, covers the conduct of U.S. foreign affairs, with chapters on the president, Congress, the State Department, and other agencies involved in the foreign affairs process. Part 3 provides information on official sources for the study of American foreign policy. Part 4 lists biographical sources and diplomatic memoirs.

Many of the entries have very brief annotations describing content. There is an author/agency index. There is no subject index, though the table of contents is detailed.

Biographical Sources

670. Parker, Thomas. **America's Foreign Policy 1945-1976: Its Creators and Critics.** New York, Facts on File, 1980. 246p. bibliog. index. $22.50. LC 80-21192. ISBN 0-87196-456-2.

As an overview of three decades of American foreign policy, the main element in this work is the biographical section. It offers about 70 biographical sketches of leading American political figures from the Truman through the Ford administrations. The profiles range in length from a single page to 12, for Henry Kissinger.

An opening essay discusses the main thrust of American foreign policy during the period examined: "the containment of Communism" (introduction). Appended are a chronology and bibliographies for each administration. Although convenient as a ready reference source, the information offered here is for the most part easily available in other sources, including the publisher's *Political Profiles* (see entry 562) series.

Chronologies

671. Brune, Lester H. **Chronological History of United States Foreign Relations, 1776 to January 20, 1981.** New York, Garland, 1985. 2v. 1,320p. maps. bibliog. index. $150.00. LC 83-48210. ISBN 0-8240-9056-X.

American foreign relations from 1776 to 1981 have been systematically summarized in this comprehensive historical reference work. The emphasis is on facts, names, and dates, which makes it handy for quick reference use. The arrangement is chronological, with the articles ranging from one sentence to two pages. The entries have captions that read like newspaper headlines: "Suez crisis caused when Israeli, British, and French forces attack Egypt;" "The Iranian hostages are freed, leaving Teheran just minutes after President Reagan is sworn in." For subject approach there is an excellent detailed index.

In addition to the chronological review of American foreign policy and events related to it, there are four overview essays introducing major topics. There are also 24 maps and a selective bibliography.

672. U.S. Department of State. Historical Office. **United States Chiefs of Mission, 1778-1982.** 2d ed. Washington, D.C., GPO, 1982. index. LC 83-601029. S1.69:14712.

The second edition of this title completes the data through 1982 to become a retrospective list of American chiefs of missions for over 200 years. This list of diplomats, most of whom have the title of ambassador now, is arranged by country, then chronologically from the date of the appointment of the first envoy. Given for each chief of mission is the exact title and date of appointment, date of presentation of credentials, and date of termination of mission.

A series of appendixes includes similar lists for the chiefs of mission to international organizations, a list of ambassadors at large, secretaries of state, and deputy and assistant secretaries of state. There is an alphabetical index of all individuals listed in this volume.

Dictionaries and Encyclopedias

673. **Dictionary of International Relations Terms.** 3d ed. Washington, D.C., Department of State Library, 1987. 115p. bibliog. $5.70(pbk). LC 87-600829. SuDoc S1.2:IN8/30/98.

This brief dictionary does not attempt to be comprehensive but aims to supplement existing dictionaries with foreign affairs terms, acronyms, catchwords, and abbreviations that have proven elusive. More than 200 entries are provided, including such terms as "least developed countries" and "futurism." Also included are many important international organizations (e.g., Club of Rome, Group of 77).

The dictionary is particularly useful for the "Notes" section that follows the definitions. These notes document usage of the terms with bibliographic references and quotations.

674. **Encyclopedia of American Foreign Policy: Studies of the Principal Movements and Ideas.** Alexander De Conde, ed. New York, Scribner, 1978. 3v. index. $120.00/set. LC 78-5453. ISSN 0684155036.

Although now over a decade old, this title remains a standard source for background material and analysis of American foreign policy. Ninety-five essays of original scholarship by distinguished subject authorities explore the major concepts, themes, ideas, theories, doctrines and policies of American foreign policy. The set does not cover major events, such as the Louisiana Purchase or the Korean War, or provide a chronological history of foreign relations. It is not designed for finding quick answers to factual questions. The signed essays vary from 5 to 18 pages in length; all conclude with bibliographies and references to related entries. Its readable style makes this work suitable for general readers as well as for scholars in the field. The third volume contains 150 pages of brief biographical sketches of important persons involved in American foreign policy.

675.   Finding, John E. **Dictionary of American Diplomatic History.** Westport, Conn., Greenwood, 1980. 622p. index. $55.00. LC 79-7730. ISBN 033220395.

The author has attempted to serve several purposes with this dictionary. The primary one was to provide basic factual information on about 500 prominent individuals associated with American foreign policy and to define about 500 nonbiographical terms. These biographies and terms have been placed in historical context. There is also a short bibliography of suggestions for further reading. The period covered extends from the American Revolution to 1978. The entries are usually one-half page or less.

In addition to the name and subject index, there are five appendixes: (1) "Chronology of American History," (2) "Key Diplomatic Personnel Listed by Presidential Administration," (3) "Initiation, Suspension, and Termination of Diplomatic Relations," (4) "Date and Place of Birth of the Biographees," and (5) "Locations of Manuscript Collections and Oral Histories."

676.   Plano, Jack C., and Roy Olton. **The International Relations Dictionary.** 4th ed. Santa Barbara, Calif., ABC-Clio, 1988. 446p. index. (Clio Dictionaries in Political Science). $19.95; $12.75(pbk). LC 87-26943. ISBN 0-87436-477-9; 0-87436-478-7(pbk).

A number of unusual characteristics distinguish this dictionary from most. Entries are grouped into 12 subject chapters, such as "International Law," "American Foreign Policy," and "Geography and Population." To facilitate use in teaching, the subjects were chosen to parallel topics found in most current international relations textbooks. Another unusual format feature is that each entry is divided into definition and significance paragraphs.

The extensive index provides the essential direct access for those interested in locating specific terms. There is also a useful separate "Guide to Countries," tracing references to nations spread throughout the chapters.

677.   Not used.

Handbooks

678.   Aster, Sidney, comp. and ed. **British Foreign Policy, 1918-1945: A Guide to Research and Research Materials.** Wilmington, Del., Scholarly Resources, 1984. 324p. bibliog. index. (Guides to European Diplomatic History Research and Research Materials). $20.00. LC 84-5339. ISBN 0-8420-2176-0.

679.   Cassels, Alan, comp. and ed. **Italian Foreign Policy, 1918-1945: A Guide to Research and Research Materials.** Wilmington, Del., Scholarly Resources, 1981. 271p. index. (Guide to European Diplomatic History Research and Research Materials). $17.50. LC 80-53890. ISBN 0-8420-2177-9.

680.   Kimmich, Christoph M., comp. and ed. **German Foreign Policy, 1918-1945: A Guide to Research and Research Materials.** Wilmington, Del., Scholarly Resources, 1981. 293p. index. (Guides to European Diplomatic History Research and Research Materials). $17.50. LC 80-53889. ISBN 0-8420-2167-1.

681. Young, Robert J., comp. and ed. **French Foreign Policy, 1918-1945: A Guide to Research and Research Materials.** Wilmington, Del., Scholarly Resources, 1981. 242p. index. (Guides to European Diplomatic History Research and Research Materials). $17.50. LC 80-53892. ISBN 0-8420-2178-7.

These four handbooks are part of the Guides to European Diplomatic History series. Although each deals with a different nation, they all follow the same basic format. They open with an introductory essay that surveys the growth, organization, and structure of the foreign ministry and the process of foreign policy formation in the country concerned. The second part of each book describes the principal archives, libraries, and research institutes that hold important relevant collections. Hours, admission policies, and other very practical information are included. The core section of each guide is the selective bibliography of from 900 to 1,500 titles of reference works, monographs, periodical articles, documents, dissertations, and memoirs. Most entries have short annotations.

These handbooks have succeeded admirably in their goal of being not simply bibliographies of relevant literature but guides that scholars will want to take with them when they use the archives and libraries noted. There are also many helpful suggestions and comments to help orient the beginning researcher. The great wealth of materials in this field and the maze of archives and libraries involved makes these guides indispensable research aids.

682. DeLong, Linwood. **A Guide to Canadian Diplomatic Relations 1925-1983.** Ottawa, Canadian Library Association, 1985. 57p. $11.23. ISBN 0-88802-199-2.

This guide to Canadian foreign relations has several components that will serve as useful reference aids to students of Canadian diplomatic history and international relations. The core section lists all nations with which Canada has, or has had, diplomatic relations. For each nation, dates, with sources for these dates, are given for when Canada recognized the government, when diplomatic relations were begun, and when a Canadian diplomatic mission was established in the country. These dates can serve as useful starting points for further research through Canadian official publications and other reference sources.

Also included are an introduction, which provides a brief review of the history of Canadian diplomatic relations, and a selected bibliography of major relevant works.

683. Haines, Gerald K., and J. Samuel Walker, eds. **American Foreign Relations: A Historiographical Review.** Westport, Conn., Greenwood, 1981. 369p. index. (Contributions in American History, No. 90). $35.00. LC 80-545. ISBN 0-313-21061-6.

The purpose of this book is "to provide a comprehensive review of the most significant literature in American diplomatic history" (introduction). This has been achieved through 16 narrative chapters. These essays on American foreign relations cover from the colonial era through the origins of the cold war. In addition to these chronological chapters, four focus on U.S. relationships with Asia, Africa, the Middle East, and Latin America. The final chapter surveys the availability and arrangement of source material for the study of American foreign relations, including Department of State records, presidential libraries, congressional material, and the Freedom of Information Act.

Each chapter reviews selectively the relevant literature, with emphasis on historiographical trends and the varying traditional and revisionist interpretations or schools of thought that divide diplomatic historians.

684. Hill, Kenneth L. **A Concise Overview of Foreign Policy (1945-1985).** Melbourne, Fla., Krieger, 1986. 164p. index. $8.45(pbk). LC 86-10254. ISBN 0-89874-849-6.

Included in this handbook are 174 incidents affecting international relations or foreign policy. Each selected incident occurred after World War II and had major foreign policy implications. The entries, which range from Afghanistan to the Yom Kippur War, each has a one-page description. In addition to the chronology of major facts, each article features an analysis of the overall importance of the event for international relations. This work is useful as a handbook for the study of contemporary international affairs and as a reference source for the basic historical facts surrounding major international political incidents of the last several decades.

685.   **The Times Survey of Foreign Ministries of the World.** Zara Steiner, selector and ed. London, Times Books; Westport, Conn., Meckler, 1982. 624p. index. $87.50. LC 82-104557. ISBN 0-7230-0245-2.

Foreign policy institutions, specifically foreign ministries, are the subject of this excellent, if not inexpensive, guide. The principal foreign affairs offices of 24 countries have been examined. Emphasis is on Western European nations, but also included are Canada, Australia, the United States, the Soviet Union, Japan, and China. Despite the title, no Latin American, African, Arab, or South Asian nations are included.

The introductory essay by the editor examines the history and evolution of the management of the conduct of foreign affairs in the modern world. This sets the framework for the studies of the individual states. Each country surveyed begins with a historical introduction followed by organizational charts and a short bibliography.

686.   Weigall, David, with Christopher Catherwood. **Britain & the World 1815-1986: A Dictionary of International Relations.** New York, Oxford University Press, 1987. 240p. maps. $29.95. LC 87-11133. ISBN 0-19-520610-X.

Weigall's book offers a useful, if not comprehensive, selection of terms dealing with British international relations since 1815, the end of the Napoleonic period. The 450 entries vary in length from 100 to 400 words, with a few longer articles dealing with Britain's relations with the major powers. About half of the articles have short bibliographies for further reading.

The entries include diplomatic terms, major events, conflicts, treaties, conferences, etc., and biographical profiles of important individuals involved in foreign affairs. There is no index, as the articles are arranged alphabetically. Asterisks in the text refer to related entries. There is a chronological table of international events and 12 maps at the end of the book.

COMMUNISM AND MARXISM

Bibliographies

687.   Chilcote, Ronald H., comp. and ed. **Brazil and Its Radical Left: An Annotated Bibliography on the Communist Movement and the Rise of Marxism, 1922-1972.** Millwood, N.Y., Kraus International, 1980. 455p. index. $60.00. LC 80-12167. ISBN 0-527-16821-1.

Books, journal articles, pamphlets, and some government and party documents are included in this comprehensive bibliography of materials relating to the communist, socialist, and anarchist movements in Brazil in the half century from 1922 to 1972. The core sections contain 3,000 citations arranged by author. The subject index provides access to these entries. Only about 10 percent of the material cited is in English, with the bulk in Portuguese. Most of the citations have brief descriptive annotations.

The last section of this bibliography is a list of radical left Brazilian periodicals. Many of the citations in all sections have location symbols to Brazilian or American libraries or to private collections. This is a bibliography for researchers interested in source material on the radical left in Brazil.

688. **Communism in the World since 1945: An Annotated Bibliography.** Susan K. Kinnell, ed. Santa Barbara, Calif., ABC-Clio, 1987. (Clio Bibliography, No. 25). $85.00. LC 86-28790. ISBN 0-8743-6169-9.

For this bibliography, based on the *America: History and Life* and *Historical Abstracts* computer databases, ABC-Clio has selected over 4,000 entries for journal articles published between 1974 and 1985, plus selective books and dissertations. Many of the titles are non-English works but have English subtitles.

Of the eight chapters, seven focus on geographic units such as communism in the Soviet Union or communism in Southeast Asia. The last chapter deals with historiography and bibliography. This is not a comprehensive bibliography and, of course, provides no coverage beyond the citations in the databases searched. It is, though, a useful starting point for research and would probably be sufficient for most users. The abstracts with the periodical citations are a strong feature.

689. Egan, David R., and Melinda A. Egan. **V. I. Lenin: An Annotated Bibliography of English-Language Sources to 1980.** Metuchen, N.J., Scarecrow, 1982. 482p. index. $32.50. LC 82-659. ISBN 0-8108-1526-5.

This first comprehensive bibliography of the life of Lenin contains 3,000 sources covering all aspects of the life and career of this first great leader of the Soviet Union. Included through 1979 are books, essays, periodical articles, interviews, addresses, memoirs, and doctoral dissertations. Textbooks, fiction, master's theses, and newspaper and encyclopedia articles are omitted as are works by Lenin. Only English-language material is included. Many of the items, however, were written in English in the Soviet Union or have been translated into English, giving the bibliography an international aspect. The entries reflect no particular creed; they include critical as well as hagiographic works. The most important titles have been marked with an asterisk.

The bibliography is divided into 14 topical chapters covering biography and major political, economic, and social topics related to both Russian and international communism. The annotations are short but sufficient to identify the scope and viewpoint of the works cited. There are author and subject indexes.

690. Eubanks, Cecil L. **Karl Marx and Friedrich Engels: An Analytical Bibliography.** 2d ed. New York, Garland, 1984. 299p. index. (Garland Reference Library of Social Science, Vol. 100). $45.00. LC 81-43337. ISBN 0-8240-9293-7.

Approximately 1,000 new entries constitute this second edition, which appeared only six years after the first. The bibliography attempts to be a comprehensive listing of writings by and about Marx and Engels either written in or translated into English. Books, book chapters, periodical articles, and dissertations are included.

The introduction and the introductory essay reproduced from the first edition provide an extensive bibliographic overview of the literature by and on Marx and Engels. The citations are unannotated. They are divided into various chapters for the works of each author and the works about them. There is an author index of the secondary writings. This bibliography is an appropriate source for the researcher requiring in-depth, comprehensive coverage.

691. Haynes, John Earl. **Communism and Anti-Communism in the United States: An Annotated Guide to Historical Writings.** New York, Garland, 1987. 321p. index. (Garland Reference Library of Social Science, Vol. 379). $47.00. LC 86-25821. ISBN 0-8240-8520-5.

Haynes's bibliography concentrates on two closely related topics: the American communist movement and American anticommunism. Chronological coverage focuses on the founding of the American Communist Party shortly after the Bolshevik Revolution to its loss of prominence in the mid-1950s. Materials published in the 1960s and 1970s and splinter groups receive less emphasis.

Books, essays, periodical articles, and dissertations are included for a total of 2,086 citations. There is a perference for scholarly and historical studies rather than for primary materials or "journalistic works" (preface). The annotated citations are divided into 37 chapters with subsections. The author index and detailed table of contents provide effective access. There is no subject index. The introduction offers background information on the major works and periods of historical writings on American communism.

692. Lubitz, Wolfgang, ed. **Trotsky Bibliography: List of Separately Published Titles, Periodical Articles and Titles in Collections Treating L. D. Trotsky and Trotskyism.** Munich, New York, K. G. Saur; distr., Detroit, Gale, 1982. 458p. $65.00. index. ISBN 3-598-10469-3.

This bibliography of secondary literature contains over 3,000 titles covering Trotsky's life, his work, and his continuing influence on politics and political thought. Only material published between 1917 and 1982 is covered. The editor includes books, journal articles, titles in collections, dissertations, reviews, published speeches, and interviews. Newspaper articles and ephemeral material were excluded. About one-third of the citations are in English; most are in Russian or other European languages. Coverage is provided for all viewpoints regarding Trotsky and his place in history.

The numbered entries are in one alphabetical sequence arranged by author. There are four indexes to provide access: persons and subjects, sources, serials, and a chronological breakdown. The citations are not annotated.

Biographical Sources

693. Bartke, Wolfgang, and Peter Schier. **China's New Party Leadership: Biographies and Analysis of the Twelfth Central Committee of the Chinese Communist Party.** Armonk, N.Y., M. E. Sharpe, 1985. 289p. illus. (A Publication of the Institute of Asian Affairs in Hamburg). $50.00. LC 84-14130. ISBN 0-87332-291-9.

The Twelfth National Congress of the Chinese Communist Party marked the decisive defeat of the Maoist faction by the supporters of Deng Xiaoping in 1982. The Congress elected the members of the Twelfth Central Committee, who in turn elected the politburo, the actual political leadership of China. This reference work contains detailed biographical information on the 348 full and alternate members of the Central Committee. The biographical entries are not portraits, but lists of data. Current position, former positions, and political activities are given for each person. Some of these chronologies are accompanied by photographs.

In addition to the biographies, there are extensive sections that introduce and provide background information about the Twelfth National Congress. Important documents and speeches are summarized. The last part of this work provides various charts and tables identifying the political and military leadership of China as of January 1, 1984. Taken as a whole, this work serves as a reference guide to politics and government in contemporary China.

694a.   **Biographical Dictionary of Marxism.** Robert A. Gorman, ed. Westport, Conn., Greenwood, 1986. 388p. index. $55.00. LC 84-29016. ISBN 0-313-24851-6.

694b.   **Biographical Dictionary of Neo-Marxism.** Robert A. Gorman, ed. Westport, Conn., Greenwood, 1985. 463p. index. $55.00. LC 84-27968. ISBN 0-313-23513-9.

These two companion volumes follow the same format in providing short, one- to several-page portraits of the lives, careers, and thinking of leading personalities who are or were followers of Marx. The 210 subjects in the volume on Marxists are defined as "materialist or orthodox" followers of Marxism (preface). The 205 neo-Marxists, or revisionists, are defined as "nonorthodox or nonmaterialist Marxists" (preface). The introductory essays attempt to clarify these distinctions. The biographies were written by an international group of academics. The sketches are signed. Each portrait has a short bibliography of primary and secondary materials for further study. Each volume has a subject index and two appendixes: a list of biographees by country and a list of contributors.

695.   Lazitch, Branko, with Milorad M. Drachkovitch. **Biographical Dictionary of the Comintern.** new, rev. ed. Stanford, Calif., Hoover Institution Press, 1986. 532p. $44.95. LC 86-7466. ISBN 0-8179-8401-1.

Prominent members of the Comintern, as the Communist International is more commonly called, are included in this biographical directory. The alphabetically arranged sketches, which average two-thirds of a page in length, are unfortunately not followed by lists of sources of the data or of titles for further reading. In addition to the sketches, this volume contains an introduction, a list of pseudonyms, and a list of abbreviations used by international communism.

This 1986 edition follows the edition of 1973. It adds 35 biographies for a total of 753; 229 of the original biographies have been revised.

Chronologies

696.   Rubel, Maximilien. **Marx: Life and Works.** New York, Facts on File, 1980. 140p. index. (Facts on File Chronology Series). $22.50. LC 81-123145. ISBN 0-87196-516-X.

697.   Weber, Gerda, and Hermann Weber. **Lenin: Life and Works.** Martin McCauley, ed. New York, Facts on File, 1980. 224p. index. (Facts on File Chronology Series). $22.50. LC 81-1197. ISBN 0-87196-515-1.

These two chronologies are alike in purpose, content, and format. Each presents a year-by-year summary of the life of its subject: Karl Marx or Vladimir Ilich Lenin. Within the year, events are arranged by month or, in many cases, day-by-day. The authors have attempted to include personal details when they shed light on character or public events. The principal source of information has been the subject's own writings and speeches. The sources are cited.

Both titles could serve as biographies, especially Rubel's *Marx*, in which events are more often summarized by months rather than listed by day as in Weber's *Lenin*. Neither title, however, is a narrative biography; both serve most aptly as reference sources for specific facts. Both volumes conclude with indexes to names, places, subjects, and the writings of their respective subject.

Dictionaries and Encyclopedias

698. Carver, Terrell. **A Marx Dictionary.** Totowa, N.J., Barnes & Noble, 1987. 164p. bibliog. index. $31.50. LC 86-22172. ISBN 0-389-20684-9.

In many ways this title is more of a handbook than a dictionary. It is intended to help individuals who are approaching Karl Marx for the first time. It begins with an introductory essay on his life and works and ends with a bibliography of his works and of secondary sources; extensive notes identify and clarify the usefulness of the titles cited.

The main section of the work consists of 16 chapters, each one of which focuses on one major concept found in Marx's social theories, such as capitalism, class, or revolution. Within these chapters about 100 other important concepts and terms are discussed. An alphabetical entry finder and an index provide access to the terms. Each chapter ends with a list of related terms, writings by Marx, and secondary terms.

For a more traditional dictionary with short definitions of over 2,000 terms, see Jozef's Wilczynski's *An Encyclopedic Dictionary of Marxism, Socialism, and Communism* (entry 704).

699. **A Dictionary of Marxist Thought.** Tom Bottomore, ed. Cambridge, Mass., Harvard University Press, 1983. 587p. $35.00; $9.95(pbk). LC 83-50. ISBN 0-674-2052501; 0-674-20526-X(pbk).

This dictionary provides a comprehensive but concise guide to the basic concepts, ideas, and individuals connected with Marxism. It attempts to take into account the various interpretations and schools of thought within contemporary Marxism. The authors are largely British and American scholars, many prominent Marxists.

The entries are arranged alphabetically, with definitions that vary in length from one to four or five pages. In many cases, especially for major terms such as "capitalism" or "religion," the entries are really short essays or articles rather than simply definitions. They give a historical overview of communist thought and major writings, including current interpretations. The entries all conclude with a brief list of citations for additional information. There is also a bibliography for the works of Marx and Engels and other authors cited. There is a detailed index. For a title with similar coverage, see Terrell Carver's *A Marx Dictionary* (entry 698), which features essay-length definitions of 16 major concepts, such as dialectic and class.

700. Draper, Hall, with the Center for Socialist History. **The Marx-Engels Chronicle: A Day-by-Day Chronology of Marx and Engels' Life and Activity.** New York, Schocken Books, 1985. 297p. (Marx-Engels Cyclopedia, Vol 1). $28.50. LC 84-3013. ISBN 0-8052-3909-X.

701. Draper, Hal, with the Center for Socialist History. **The Marx-Engels Register: A Complete Bibliography of Marx and Engels' Individual Writings.** New York, Schocken Books, 1985. 271p. index. (Marx-Engels Cyclopedia, Vol. 2). $28.50. LC 84-23502. ISBN 0-8052-3975-8.

702. Draper, Hal. **The Marx-Engels Glossary: Glossary to the Chronicle and Register, and Index to the Glossary.** New York, Schocken Books, 1986. 249p. index. (Marx-Engels Cyclopedia, Vol. 3). $28.50. LC 85-25037. ISBN 0-8052-4002-0.

Together these three volumes constitute the *Marx-Engels Cyclopedia*, a comprehensive scholarly reference guide to the lives and works of two of the most influential political philosophers in modern history. This set will be of enormous value to all researchers and serious students. Although the volumes may be used individually, they are most effectively consulted as a unit because of their cross-references and the internal division of information.

The first volume, the *Chronicle*, is a detailed chronology of the lives and activities of Karl Marx and Friedrich Engels, covering the period from the birth of Marx (1818) until the death of Engels (1895). The *Register* volume is an exhaustive bibliography of the writings of these two men. The list is divided into three sections: collaborative writings, writings of Marx, writings of Engels. For each entry the English and original titles are given, with notes on translations and republications. There are no annotations, but there are references to the appropriate sections in the *Chronicle*. The *Glossary* volume contains several hundred alphabetized entries of proper names mentioned in the first two volumes. These include persons, parties, organizations, and places.

703.   Russell, James. **Marx-Engels Dictionary.** Westport, Conn., Greenwood, 1980. 140p. $29.95. LC 80-786. ISBN 0-3132-2035-2.

The author has designed this dictionary to assist readers of the Marxian classics who may have difficulty with terminology. Specifically, this is a dictionary of terms appearing in the writings of Marx or Engels. Difficulties were anticipated because some of the terms used by these writers are no longer in common use. Other terms may have a particular Marxist meaning or may be technical terms drawn from economics or philosophy.

The several hundred terms defined are arranged in alphabetical order. The definitions, which range in length from several lines to several pages, have been based as much as possible on explanations provided by Marx or Engels, whose works are frequently cited.

704.   Wilczynski, Jozef. **An Encyclopedic Dictionary of Marxism, Socialism, and Communism.** New York, Walter de Gruyter, 1981. 660p. $59.00. LC 81-1757. ISBN 3-11-008588-7.

More than 2,300 terms are clearly and concisely defined in this dictionary designed for "quick reference" (preface) use. The ample scope includes Marxism, socialism, and communism. All aspects of these ideologies and political systems—economic, philosophic, political, sociological—are included. Organizations, individuals, events, publications, and concepts are covered as well as terms. The definitions, or explanations, include historical information and a large number of cross-references. This dictionary is an excellent source for scholars or general readers for short, objective definitions of terms related to communism.

Handbooks

705.   Hobay, Charles. **Communist and Marxist Parties of the World.** Santa Barbara, Calif., ABC-Clio, 1986. 529p. bibliog. index. (Keesing's Reference Publication). $70.00. ISBN 0-87436-476-0.

As a reliable, comprehensive, up-to-date survey, this handbook reviews communist and Marxist parties throughout the world, including the nations where they are in power. One very useful strength of this handbook is the clear delineation of the distinctions between communists and Marxists, and among all the various ideologies and orientations that influence the parties, from Trotskyism to Eurocommunism.

The main section discusses individual parties under their respective countries. Entries range from a few lines up to 14 pages for the Soviet Union. For each party there is information of history, membership, party structure, activities, publications, and orientation or international affiliations. Additional sections include a historical overview of the world communist movement, a discussion of international Marxist organizations and conferences, and a chapter on communist front organizations. The appendixes include coverage of party groupings (pro-Soviet, pro-Chinese, etc.), extracts from major historical documents, and a short bibliography. There is a name index but no subject index to the information on the parties.

706.   Staar, Richard Felix. **The Communist Regimes in Eastern Europe.** 4th ed. Stanford, Calif., Hoover Institution Press, 1982. 375p. index. $9.95(pbk). LC 81-84232. ISBN 0-8179-7692-2.

The fourth edition of this handbook presents a review of the countries of Eastern Europe under communist rule. The focus is on the governments, though many aspects of life in these nations are considered. The Soviet Union is not included.

There is one chapter for each country, with information on the governmental structure, constitutional framework, the ruling party, domestic policies, and foreign relations. The economy, minorities, and the churches are highlighted. The remaining three chapters deal with areawide military, economic, and political integration. The data were obtained largely from material published in the various East European languages. Footnotes indicate the sources. There is a selective bibliography and a name index.

707.   Szajkowski, Bogdan, ed. **Marxist Governments: A World Survey.** New York, St. Martin's Press, 1981. 3v. bibliog. index. $27.50/vol. LC 79-25471. ISBN 0-312-51857-9(v.1); 0-312-51858-7(v.2); 0-312-51859-5(v.3).

This three-volume set provides a comprehensive survey of Marxist-Leninist regimes throughout the world. A total of 25 countries on 4 continents are included, with signed articles by scholars. Each country profile includes a history of the Marxist party, a description of the constitution and electoral system, and a discussion of the governmental structure and its major elements. There are biographies of key officials. Domestic policies, opposition groups, and foreign affairs are among the many topics generally reviewed for each nation. The introductory chapters provide considerations of the definition of a Marxist regime and of the diversity found among communist parties. These volumes were designed to be used both as texts and as reference works.

708.   Szajkowski, Bogdan, ed. **Marxist Local Governments in Western Europe and Japan.** Boulder, Colo., Lynne Rienner Publishers, 1986. 216p. index. $25.00; $11.95(pbk). LC 84-62670. ISBN 0-9314-7725-5; 0-9314-7726-3(pbk).

This volume is part of a projected series designed to comprehensively cover Marxist regimes throughout the world. An earlier volume in 1981, *Marxist Governments: A World Survey*, profiled 25 countries in which communists are in power at the national level. This volume focuses on communist parties and local-level governments in 11 countries in Western Europe, plus Japan.

For each nation there is a chapter, or study, that deals with the specific situation. There is typically background information on historical and political developments, plus data on local parties, elections, and institutions. There is a brief introduction with comments on comparative aspects. There are also tables, maps, bibliographies, and a subject index.

709.   Weeks, Albert L., comp. and ed. **Brassey's Soviet and Communist Quotations.** McLean, Va., Pergamon Brassey's International Defense Publishers, 1987. 387p. index. $50.00. LC 86-22664. ISBN 0-08-034488-7.

Although the 2,000 quotations chosen for this collection can represent only a small portion of the potential total, the preface and introduction do not really clarify the criteria used for selection or the scope of this title, which makes it difficult to judge the representatives of the contents. Nevertheless, the quotations chosen provide an interesting array. They are grouped under major subject headings with chronologically arranged subdivisions. This arrangement facilitates scanning a specific topic, such as capitalism or Soviet foreign policy toward Latin America. The subject and author indexes provide good access to the numbered quotations.

Sourcebooks

710.   **Constitutions of the Communist World.** William B. Simons, ed. Germantown, Md., Sijthoff & Noordoff, 1980. 644p. index. $92.50. LC 80-65005. ISBN 90-286-0070.

This volume is the standard compilation of constitutions for the communist states of the world. Fifteen communist nations are included: the Soviet Union and the Eastern European bloc, plus China, North Korea, Mongolia, Vietnam, Kampuchea, and Cuba. For each the constitution has been translated into English. There is a short introductory essay for each constitution providing historical background information. The editor has included a "Systematic Heading Index," which facilitates finding equivalent sections in the various constitutions for comparative purposes.

Yearbooks

711.   **Yearbook on International Communist Affairs.** Stanford, Calif., Hoover Institution Press on War, Revolution, and Peace, Stanford University. 1967- . annual. index. $49.95. LC 67-31024. ISSN 0084-4101.

The main section of this annual provides up-to-date, authoritative profiles of communist parties and governments in all parts of the world where they play a significant role. These profiles are arranged by region and then by country. They contain for each nation the names of communist parties, founding dates, membership, top officials, legal status, and dates of the last party congress and elections. Following this tabulated data there is for each country a several-page article that considers the history, ideology, policies, and activities of the parties.

In addition to the country profiles, recent volumes have provided a bibliography of current publications on communism, a cumulative index of biographies that have appeared in the yearbook over recent years, and lists of recent party congresses. There are detailed name and subject indexes. The introductory essays provide an overview of the world communist movement. This yearbook is the major reference resource for current information on international communism.

HUMAN RIGHTS

Bibliographies

712.   Andrews, J. A. **Keyguide to Information Sources on the International Protection of Human Rights.** New York, Facts on File, 1987. 169p. bibliog. index. $40.00. LC 87-9068. ISBN 0-8160-1822-7.

This "keyguide" contains three rather disparate components. It begins with a series of essays that provide an overview of such topics as the history of human rights and the development of individual rights. It ends with a directory featuring short descriptions of major human rights organizations.

The core of the publication is the bibliography in the middle section. Citations to current books and periodical articles are arranged in subject divisions. There is an index to authors, titles, subjects, and organizations. For a more comprehensive treatment, see *Human Rights: A Topical Bibliography* (entry 713).

713. **Human Rights: A Topical Bibliography.** Prepared by the staff of the Center for the Study of Human Rights, Columbia University, J. Paul Martin, project director and ed. Boulder, Colo., Westview Press, 1983. 299p. index. $30.00. LC 83-6719. ISBN 0-86531-571-X.

As a comprehensive reference source this bibliography contains unannotated citations to 2,500 entries, including books and journal articles. The selection is limited to English-language material published through 1981. The detailed classification with 150 categories provides access to the citations. These categories are organized under seven major headings: "General and Introductory Works," "Philosophical and Theoretical Works," "National and International Perspectives," "Specific Rights," "Related Topics," "Teaching Human Rights," and "Reference Sources." There is an author index.

714. **Human Rights in Latin America, 1964-1980: A Selective Annotated Bibliography.** Compiled and edited by the Hispanic Division, Library of Congress. Washington, D.C., GPO, 1983. 237p. index. $13.00. LC 82-600339. ISBN 0-8444-0415-2. S/N 030-000-00144-3.

Over 1,800 items appear in this bibliography of works on human rights in Latin America, even though several limitations were established. Only material published from 1964 to 1980 is included. Newspaper material was excluded totally. Books, journals, and pamphlets, both popular and scholarly, were selectively included. The resulting extensive bibliography attests to the problem of authoritarian government and human rights violations in Latin America. Many of the items cited are from Latin America and therefore in Spanish.

The annotated entries are grouped in topical chapters, beginning with general treatments of the subject and works covering all of Latin America. Also included are chapters on each nation of the region and chapters devoted to certain major issuing agencies such as Amnesty International, the Organization of American States, and the United States Congress. One chapter is devoted to U.S. policy toward human rights in Latin America. There are also lists of bibliographies, newsletters, and organizations dealing with Latin American human rights.

715. **International Human Rights: A Bibliography, 1970-1975.** rev. ed. Barry O'Conner, comp. and ed.; John A. Scanlan, project director. Notre Dame, Ind., Center for Civil Rights, University of Notre Dame Law School, 1980. 172p. index. $10.00(pbk). LC 80-67763. ISBN 0-268-01148-6.

This revised bibliography lists over 1,408 books and journal articles published in English. The unannotated citations focus on international human rights and human rights in foreign countries. Material about the United States is limited to American foreign policy relevant to human rights and such topics as aliens and immigration. There is an emphasis on works on the legal and moral basis for the defense of human rights. The citations are arranged in one sequence simply by main entry, with subject, country, and area indexes.

Directories

716. **Civil Rights Directory.** Washington, D.C., Commission on Civil Rights, 1968- . irreg. price varies. LC 74-610026. ISSN 0360-1587.

The Civil Rights Commission has revised this directory on an irregular basis since its first publication in 1968. The 1981 revision appears to be the latest. The directory includes both governmental and private organizations concerned with discrimination and denial of equal protection of the laws on the basis of race, color, religion, national origin, sex, age, and handicap.

The directory entries are arranged in four sections, covering federal government agencies, state and local government agencies, private organizations, and research organizations. For each entry the directory provides name, address, phone number, area served, and a paragraph summarizing the purpose and activities of the organization. This information was obtained from the agencies listed. There is no index.

717. **Human Rights Directory: Latin America, Africa, Asia.** Washington, D.C., Human Rights Internet, 1981- . biennial. index. LC 81-194. ISSN 0275-0082.

718. **Human Rights Directory: Western Europe.** Washington, D.C., Human Rights Internet, 1982- . biennial. index. LC 82-645693. ISSN 0732-0906.

719. **Human Rights Internet Directory: Eastern Europe and the USSR.** Laurie S. Wiseberg, ed., with the assistance of Eileen Maloy, Laura Reiner, and Hazel Sirett. Washington, D.C., Human Rights Internet, 1987. 304p. bibliog. index. $30.00. ISBN 0-939338-03-3.

720. **North American Human Rights Directory.** Washington, D.C., Human Rights Internet, 1980- . irreg. index. $30.00. LC 80-647927. ISSN 0270-2282.

These directories are all published by Human Rights Internet, an international clearinghouse and communications network based at Harvard Law School. This organization, which began work in 1976, has maintained its reputation for comprehensive and unbiased reporting.

The directories, which all follow the same basic format, feature a listing of human rights organizations. The length of the entries varies depending on the availability of information. Typical entries include a description of the goals and activities of the organization, data on key personnel, addresses, telephone numbers, and publications. The directories provide extensive coverage, including international and governmental organizations, professional associations, and all types of interest groups that focus on human rights and social justice. The North American directory, for example, includes 500 entries. There are indexes by organizational name, acronym, and subject.

721. **Human Rights Organizations & Periodicals Directory.** 5th ed. David Christiano, ed. Berkeley, Calif., Meiklejohn Civil Liberties Institute, 1983. 247p. $22.00. LC 74-2401.

Now in its fifth edition, this directory identifies and describes organizations and periodicals involved in promoting human rights and social justice. The organizations include governmental agencies, professional associations, and a wide range of interest groups. All are American, but some have an international interest or concentrate on some particular area, such as Central America.

For each entry there is information on the purpose and activities of the group; current subscription information is provided for periodicals. There is also a brief guide to federal agencies involved in protecting human rights, a geographical guide to the location of the organizations listed, and a compendium of materials related to the work of the Meiklejohn Civil Liberties Institute.

Handbooks

722. **Amnesty International Report.** London, Amnesty International Publications, 1962-. annual. $12.00. LC 86-640504. ISSN 0569-9495.

With this publication, Amnesty International provides a comprehensive and highly respected yearly report on human rights violations. These reports are noted for their careful documentation of executions, the use of torture, and the treatment of political prisoners. There is a separate report on human rights violations for each nation for which sufficient data exist. Amnesty International also considers less violent abuses of human rights. Their report, for example, on British judicial practices with regard to IRA prisoners in Northern Ireland is credited with being a factor in influencing the British to change their procedures. These reports also contain information on the organizational activities and publications of Amnesty International.

723. Gastil, Raymond D. **Freedom in the World.** Freedom House, New York, Greenwood, 1978- . annual. $35.00. LC 82-642048. ISSN 0732-6610.

Since 1978, Freedom House, a nonpartisan organization concerned with human rights, has published this yearbook. The main feature each year is the survey of freedom in nations and territories throughout the world. Through the use of tables showing comparative measures of freedom, the states are rated and ranked by the existence of political rights, civil liberties, and the status of freedom. Each year various other indicators of freedom are also reviewed, such as elections, the treatment of minorities, and the process for the selection of political leaders.

In addition to these surveys, the yearbook features each year a series of essays on various specific situations or countries. The last part is a country-by-country summary, which provides some of the information on which the ratings are based. Though the individual ratings may be debated, this title remains a valuable review of freedom as defined by Western notions of individual rights. Charles Humana's *World Human Rights Guide* (see entry 724) provides an alternative rating of countries on human rights.

724. Humana, Charles. **World Human Rights Guide.** New York, Facts on File, 1985. 344p. maps. $35.00. LC 85-27584. ISBN 0-8160-1404-3.

This updated version of the author's original survey assesses 120 countries on their human rights performance. The method used involved a questionnaire based on 40 basic human rights drawn from major United Nations treaties. These rights, which are listed, include, for example, the right to freedom of movement, the right of peaceful assembly, and freedom from torture. Each country was then studied and assigned a rating in the form of a numerical score. If insufficient information was available, a brief description was provided and a generalized rating assigned, such as "poor" or "bad."

The main section of the book consists of a country-by-country review of human rights, with comments on each of the 40 questions, and the assignment of an overall rating. For another system of rating and a few interesting major differences, see Raymond D. Gastil's *Freedom in the World* (entry 723).

Sourcebooks

725. Brownlie, Ian, comp. **Basic Documents on Human Rights**. 2d ed. Oxford, Clarendon Press, 1981. 505p. $37.50; $20.00(pbk). LC 80-49923. ISBN 0-1987-6124-4; 0-1987-6125-2(pbk).

This new edition includes an updated selection of important documents on human rights. All of the sources are preceded by brief introductory notes. Almost half of the volumes are devoted to documents of the United Nations and its related agencies, such as UNESCO or the International Labour Organization. Some of the more important documents in this collection of sources on human rights are the Final Act of the Helsinki Conference, the judgment of the European Court of Human Rights in the *Sunday Times* case, and the UN Declaration on Protection from Torture.

Yearbooks

726. **Yearbook of Human Rights**. New York, United Nations, 1946- . annual. $54.00(1981/82). ISBN 92-1-154062-3(1981/82).

This yearbook began in 1946 and has continued on an approximate annual basis; the current lag in publication is about five years. For an up-to-date survey of human rights activities, *Amnesty International Report* (see entry 722) is more useful, but this title remains valuable for historical information.

While its contents have varied over the years, *Yearbook of Human Rights* typically provides a country-by-country survey of constitutional and legal rights relating to human and civil rights. The focus is not on activities or violations, but on the enactment of legislation and the adoption of constitutional provisions and international agreements to protect specific rights. The texts of these documents are quoted. Sections devoted to the activities of the United Nations consider the progress in drafting and implementing human rights declarations, such as the Universal Declaration of Human Rights, and declarations on other specific topics such as refugees, minorities, and women.

PEACE AND CONFLICT

Atlases

727. Chaliand, Gérard, and Jean-Pierre Rageau. **A Strategic Atlas: Comparative Geopolitics of the World's Powers**. 2d ed., rev. and updated. New York, Harper & Row, 1985. 224p. maps. bibliog. $26.95; $14.95(pbk). LC 84-48143. ISBN 0-06-015387-3; 0-06-091220-0(pbk).

This atlas, the first edition of which was published in France, specifically attempts to fulfill the goal of the authors to provide a strategic atlas with alternative viewpoints to the usual European/American focus. As a strategic atlas it portrays the "geopolitics of the relations of force in the contemporary world" (preface).

In addition to historical maps and maps showing the current global distribution of population and natural resources, there are a large number emphasizing the importance of oceans and the fact that they cover most of the planet's surface. Other maps attempt to graphically portray the security perceptions of various countries from their own perspective. For example, a map centered on the Soviet Union shows the circle of American allies and military bases around the world. There are maps of sea lanes and the deployment of armaments. Others deal with topics related to international strategy in less obvious ways, such as the existence of national minorities and separatist movements. The maps are clearly drawn and use color in a striking manner to effectively communicate their points.

Bibliographies

728. Black, J. L. **Origins, Evolution, and Nature of the Cold War: An Annotated Bibliographic Guide.** Santa Barbara, Calif., ABC-Clio, 1986. 173p. index. (War/Peace Bibliography Series, No. 19). $37.50. LC 85-15032. ISBN 0-87436-391-8.

The Center for the Study of Armament and Disarmament seeks to promote world peace through the War/Peace Bibliography series. This volume focuses on the cold war, that long period of hostility between the Soviet Union and the United States that began at the end of World War II. While all aspects are included, the emphasis is on works examining the nature and origins of the cold war, especially in the 1938-1950 period. Both the foreword and the introduction have valuable discussions of the various schools of thought and periods of revision that characterize this literature.

The entries are divided into 13 topical chapters with many subdivisions. Books, periodical articles, dissertations, and government documents are included. The annotations provide very informative descriptive abstracts of the titles cited. Access is facilitated by a detailed table of contents and author and subject indexes.

729. Carroll, Berenice A., Clinton F. Fink, and Jane E. Mohraz. **Peace and War: A Guide to Bibliographies.** Santa Barbara, Calif., ABC-Clio, 1983. 580p. index. (War/Peace Bibliography Series, No. 16). $42.50. LC 81-4980. ISBN 0-87436-322-5.

The contents of this bibliography of bibliographies on peace and war confirm the observation in the foreword that the rate of publication of literature on this topic is rapidly accelerating. Nearly 1,400 bibliographies are listed, including books, periodical articles, pamphlets, and sections of books published from 1785 through 1980.

The compilers took a very comprehensive view of the subject of peace and war, with an emphasis on concepts such as pacifism, peace research, women and peace, religion and peace, and causes of war, rather than on specific conflicts. The arrangement is under 34 subject chapters. About two-thirds of the bibliographies cited have annotations that provide the number of items, LC classification, and information on the type of citations included. There are author and detailed subject indexes.

730. Cot, Jean-Pierre, Jean-François Guilhaudis, and Chantal de Jonge Oudraat. **Repertory of Disarmament Research.** Geneva, United Nations Institute for Disarmament Research, United Nations; distr., New York, Sales Section, United Nations, 1982. 449p. index. $30.00. ISBN 92-9045-002-9. S/N GV. E. 82.0.2.

This United Nations publications is a bibliography on disarmament, security, the arms race, and other related topics dealing with war and peace. In addition to books and periodical articles, it is particularly strong in government documents and research institute publications from many nations.

The book is divided into three main sections: a bibliography of reference and research works; a bibliography of documents and studies issued between 1970 and 1980, arranged by topic and publication date; and a directory of national and international research institutes, with information on their location, staff, research activities, and publications. This is a very appropriate bibliography for researchers wishing to go beyond secondary literature.

731. Doenecke, Justus D. **Anti-intervention: A Bibliographical Introduction to Isolationism and Pacifism from World War I to the Early Cold War.** New York, Garland, 1987. 421p. index. (Garland Reference Library of Social Science, Vol. 396). $60.00. LC 87-8635. ISBN 0-8240-8482-9.

Although American history from the period leading up to World War I through the cold war has been characterized by major wars and continual conflict, there has been a constant opposition to American overseas involvement by isolationists and pacifists. The 1,600 entries in this bibliography were drawn from books, periodicals, essays, dissertations, and some published primary sources. Popular magazine and newspaper articles, government documents, microform collections, and unpublished sources were omitted. The chapters are arranged chronologically, with the first dealing with the background and nature of pacifism and isolationism. Most of the entries are annotated. There are author, topic, and personal name indexes.

732. Lawrence, Robert M. **Strategic Defense Initiative: Bibliography and Research Guide.** Boulder, Colo., Westview Press; London, Mansell, 1987, 352p. $18.50. LC 86-7811. ISSN 0813372291.

The debate over the Strategic Defense Initiative, SDI or "star wars," began with President Reagan's speech in March 1983 proposing a system capable of defending the United States against ballistic missile attack. The author has gathered some 1,000 citations produced since then in books, periodicals, and government documents. There are three short chapters discussing the general and technical background of SDI and the future prospects of the program. The two main sections consider the cases in favor of and against SDI. Each chapter contains a very useful introductory essay and lengthy abstracts of a short list of major works. The last chapter is a long unannotated general bibliography arranged by main entry.

The text of selected documents, a list of acronyms, and definitions of terms related to SDI are in the appendixes. Unfortunately, this otherwise excellent bibliography lacks both author and subject indexes, which makes access to specific items difficult.

733. Musto, Ronald G., comp. **The Peace Tradition in the Catholic Church: An Annotated Bibliography.** New York, Garland, 1987. 590p. (Garland Reference Library of Social Science, Vol. 339). index. $67.00. LC 86-31950. ISBN 0-8240-8584-1.

As a bibliography this work traces the history and tradition of pacifism within the Roman Catholic church where, with the support of the current pope, John Paul II, it has entered the mainstream of religious thought. The citations to books and periodical articles all have short content annotations. There is an author/title index, but no subject index. This bibliography will be useful for studies of the pacifist tradition, of Catholic thought, and of the relationships of these to the political process.

734. Norton, Augustus Richard, and others. **NATO: A Bibliography and Resource Guide.** New York, Garland, 1985. 252p. index. (Garland Reference Library of Social Science, Vol. 92). $50.00. LC 80-9038. ISBN 0-8240-9331-3.

Approximately 4,000 unannotated citations covering all aspects of the North American Treaty Organization (NATO), have been selected to form this bibliography. Selection has been limited to English-language materials, which are organized into six basic topical sections: (1) "General Section" (subdivided chronologically), (2) "Member States," (3) "Issues in NATO," (4) "Doctrines, Strategies, and Military Issues," (5) "Alliance Politics," and (6) "Warsaw Pact." There is a brief preface and an author index. This is a useful bibliography for students and for advanced researchers, but, despite the subtitle, it has no special features of a "resource guide."

735. **To End War: A New Approach to International Conflict.** 6th ed. Robert Woito, ed. New York, Pilgrim Press, 1982. 755p. index. $25.00. $12.95(pbk). LC 81-15889. ISSN 0-8298-0464-1; 0-8298-0476-5(pbk).

The intention of this book is to introduce the ideas and the resources to further peace research. It is based on the conviction that the problem of war must be studied and that the conditions necessary for a world without war are known.

The first and largest part of this work, "Ideas," introduces concepts such as arms control, territoriality, nonviolence, détente, causes of war, and weapons acquisition. Other concepts deal with crisis areas throughout the world. These topics are grouped into chapters, which begin with introductory essays. The annotated bibliographies follow and point to further reading.

The next two sections discuss various methods of promoting world peace and list resources, including world affairs organizations and periodicals. There are author and title indexes. This bibliography would be useful for students or peace advocates interested in secondary literature. For a more comprehensive approach see Carroll, Fink, and Mohraz's *Peace and War: A Guide to Bibliographies* (entry 729).

Biographical Sources

736. **Biographical Dictionary of Modern Peace Leaders.** Harold Josephson, editor-in-chief. Westport, Conn., Greenwood, 1985. 1,133p. index. $75.00. LC 83-26514. ISBN 0-313-22565-6.

This biographical dictionary attempts to define peace advocacy, to clarify the ideas and approaches employed, and to identify and provide information about individuals who have contributed to the organized peace effort or influenced public opinion through their writings or activities. The 750 biographical subjects, all deceased, were selected from the 19th and 20th centuries. An effort was made to identify peace leaders from many countries, though most of the subjects were American or European.

For each leader there is basic biographical data on birth and death, education, and career. The subject's work, or contribution to the peace movement, is the emphasis of each essay. Each entry also includes a bibliography of key works by the subject and of biographical sources, and information on the location of manuscript collections. This dictionary also includes a historical essay and chronology on the peace movement and an index. This title is cross-referenced to the *Biographical Dictionary of Internationalists* (see entry 338).

Dictionaries and Encyclopedias

737. Waldman, Harry. **The Dictionary of SDI.** Wilmington, Del., Scholarly Resources, 1988. 182p. $35.00; $19.95(pbk). LC 87-12477. ISBN 0-8420-2281-3; 0-8420-2295-3(pbk).

The Strategic Defense Initiative, SDI or "star wars," is the subject of this specialized dictionary intended for the serious examiner of this defense proposal. The author clearly acknowledges his support of this option as a means of arms control reduction. The approximately 1,000 items included cover SDI technology, research developments, arms control, and ballistic missiles. Soviet capabilities and the positions of our European allies are also examined. The alphabetically arranged entries range from one sentence to over a page. There is an abundance of illustrations and *see* references. The concise definitions provide a wealth of specific information but not an overview of SDI.

738. **World Encyclopedia of Peace.** Linus Pauling, Ervin Laszlo, and Jong Youl Yoo, eds. Elmsford, N.Y., Pergamon Press, 1986. 4v. bibliog. index. $375.00/set. LC 86-25520. ISBN 0-08-032685-4.

With the distinguished scientist and peace advocate Linus Pauling as honorary editor-in-chief, and with the dedication by the secretary general of the United Nations, this is a prestigious set, very handsomely produced, on peace research and peace activism. The editors view it as the first comprehensive encyclopedia to present an integrated overview of peace in all its aspects.

The core of this four-volume work is the first two volumes, which contain some 500 signed articles written by more than 300 scholars. These cover topics such as aggression, Buddhism, conscientious objection, East-West conflict, limited war, and peace museums. There are also biographical articles on such disparate persons as Che Guevara and St. Francis of Assisi. There are short bibliographies of major sources appended to these articles, which average several pages in length.

Volume 3 contains the text of 39 major international treaties. There are also a chronology of the peace movement and biographical sketches of Nobel Peace Prize winners through 1985. The fourth volume contains an international directory of peace research institutes, a 60-page unannotated bibliography of peace studies, and a list of peace-related journals. Name and subject indexes cover all the sections of the encyclopedia. The value of this set rests principally in the first two volumes, whose encyclopedia articles provide an overview and analysis of the persons, events, and philosophies involved in the search for peace.

Directories

739. **The Access Resource Guide; An International Directory of Information on War, Peace, and Security.** William H. Kincade and Priscilla B. Hayner, eds. Cambridge, Mass., Ballinger, 1988. 238p. index. $14.95(pbk). LC 88-201405. ISBN 0-88730-260.

Over 600 peace organizations are identified in this directory. Each entry provides for each organization the standard directory information: name, address, phone number, membership, publications, meetings, objectives, and issues of interest. In comparison to the other directories of peace organizations listed in this section, this title is particularly strong for organizations located in the United States and Canada. *The Access Resource Guide* also contains a substantial list of publications, briefly annotated, related to peace organizations and the international effort for peace.

740. Conetta, Carl, ed. **Peace Resource Book 1988-1989: A Comprehensive Guide to the Issues, Organizations, and Literature.** Cambridge, Mass., Ballinger, 1988. 440p. illus. index. $14.95(pbk). ISSN 0740-9885.

The main section of this resource book, part 2, is a directory of the peace movement in the United States. It includes over 300 national peace groups, more than 100 peace-oriented programs at colleges and universities, and some 7,000 local peace groups or local chapters of national organizations. The amount of data provided varies, but all entries contain address, telephone number, and a short note on special interests or activities of each group.

The first part provides an introduction, "Peace Issues and Strategies," to the world military system, arms control negotiations, and the peace movement. Part 3 is a bibliography of approximately 800 books, documents, periodical articles, and pamphlets. The citations have brief descriptive annotations. This work supersedes its predecessor, the *American Peace Directory*, published in 1984.

741. Day, Alan J., ed. **Peace Movements of the World.** Harlow, England, Longman; distr., Phoenix, Ariz., Oryx Press, 1987. 398p. index. (Keesing's Reference Publication). $74.50. ISBN 0-89774-438-1.

With information obtained directly from peace organizations and supplemented by material from published sources, this directory has identified over 800 peace movements, organizations, and groups. Each entry, as the available information permits, contains name, address, aims, history, activities, membership, affiliations, and publications. About one-third of the entries have only name and address.

This volume has 7 sections: 1 for 49 international organizations and 6 for regions of the world, in which the entries are arranged alphabetically by country. There are indexes to publications and to organization names, but no subject or keyword access. This title has much greater coverage than the similar *International Peace Directory* (see entry 743).

742. Green, Marguerite, comp. and ed. **Peace Archives: A Guide to Library Collections of the Papers of American Peace Organizations and of Leaders in the Public Effort for Peace.** Berkeley, Calif., World without War Council, 1986. 66p. bibliog. $7.00(pbk).

The World without War Council has attempted to bring together in this directory information on the "scattered and divers collections" (introduction) that constitute the papers of organizations and individuals involved in the cause of peace. The first part of the directory provides access to major archival collections. Thirty collections are noted, with one or two pages on each. Address, director's name, and a list of services for researchers are provided. Major components of the collections are listed by name with a one- or two-line description of contents and size. More detailed printed guides are cited if available.

The second part of the volume contains short paragraph listings of over 70 individual peace collections. Appendix A includes 27 peace organizations, with information on their records and archives policies. Used in conjunction with other sources with more detailed information, such as the Library of Congress's *National Union Catalog of Manuscript Collections* (annual beginning with 1959/61 volume), this guide is useful in locating peace collections.

743. **The International Peace Directory.** T. Woodhouse, ed. Plymouth, England, Northcote House, 1988. 189p. index. $52.50. LC 87-209099. ISBN 0-7463-0379-3.

This directory lists some 600 peace organizations, with especially strong coverage for the United Kingdom. Each entry provides for each organization the standard directory information: name, address, phone number, membership, publications, meetings, objectives, and issues of interest. It also has two indexes identifying organizations that offer fellowships and those accepting interns. There is very little overlap among the entries in the various peace directories listed in this section.

744. Meyer, Robert S. **Peace Organizations, Past, and Present: A Survey and Directory.** Jefferson, N.C., McFarland, 1988. 266p. bibliog. index. $24.95. LC 88-42515. ISBN 0-89950-340-3.

This directory profiles 92 peace organizations, almost all American and some definitely lesser known. In contrast to the other directories listed in this section, this title provides a short essay, on each entry, varying from one to five pages, rather than simply directory information. These profiles contain information on the history and philosophy of the groups and a review of their activities and goals. The author also includes his own comments on the organizations and their peace efforts and accomplishments.

745. Trzyna, Thaddeus C., ed. **International Peace Directory.** Claremont, Calif., California Institute of Public Affairs, 1984. 63p. index. (Who's Doing What Series, No. 10; University for Peace Information Guides Series, No. 1). $19.95(pbk). LC 84-71214. ISBN 0-912102-72-1.

The editor of this title estimates that there are thousands of peace organizations around the world. This directory is designed to provide detailed descriptions of a selected group of leading international peace organizations. These are the larger major organizations and smaller, lesser-known groups with unusual or innovative approaches. About 100 organizations from 27 countries have been included. The editor expects to expand coverage in future editions. Most of the information included was obtained not from secondary sources but from the organizations themselves or their publications.

The entries are listed alphabetically by name. They represent a wide variety of philosophies and methods within the peace movement. For each organization the directory provides, address, names of directors and contact persons, and telephone numbers. A general description of each group includes information on research projects and publications.

746. **World Directory of Peace Research and Training Institutions 1988.** 6th ed. Social and Human Sciences Documentation Centre and Division of Human Rights and Peace. New York, Berg; distr., New York, St. Martin's Press, 1988. 271p. index. $49.95. ISBN 0-85496-15-9.

Unlike the other directories in this section, which deal mainly with organizations promoting peace or with individuals interested in peace or disarmament, this directory is limited specifically to those institutions, usually academic institutes, dealing with peace research. As such, 650 entries are listed, including national, regional, and international organizations. For each entry, there is information on address, date founded, staff, fields of interest, publications, and scope of activities. Access to specific institutions is provided by a well-developed system of indexes, including an index by research subject, a geographical index, and an index of courses and subjects offered that relate to peace.

Handbooks

747. Abrams, Irwin. **The Nobel Peace Prize and the Laureates: An Illustrated Biographical History, 1901-1987.** Boston, G. K. Hall, 1988. 269p. index. $39.00. LC 88-16313. ISBN 0-8161-8609-X.

The principal section of this reference work consists of profiles on the 86 Nobel laureates selected between 1901 and 1987. These recipients of the Nobel Peace Prize consist mainly of individuals, but organizations also occasionally receive this honor. The profiles range up to 3,000 words, with a record and an evaluation of the peace activities of the Nobel laureates. Each essay also includes an annotated bibliography of primary and secondary sources of further information. In addition to these portraits, this volume includes several introductory essays on Alfred Nobel, the Peace Prize itself, and the work of the Norwegian Nobel Committee. The book concludes with appendixes (which list the prize winners by category and country) and an index.

748. Day, Alan J., ed. **Border and Territorial Disputes.** Detroit, Gale, 1982. 406p. maps. bibliog. index. (Keesing's Reference Publications). $75.00. LC 82-12666. ISBN 0-8103-2030-4.

Publication of this reference guide provides a very useful handbook for information about border and territorial disputes. The conflicts between Britain and Argentina, between

Iran and Iraq, and the century-long dispute between the Arabs and Jews over Palestine draw attention to the importance of and interest in these disagreements.

The handbook presents concise accounts of 70 currently unresolved border and territorial issues. The historical background and current status of each situation are examined. Negotiations, treaties, and hostilities are noted. The longest summary, for the Arab-Israeli conflict, covers 29 pages. Maps are provided for all disputed areas. There is also a one-page bibliography and a subject index.

749.   Larson, Jeanne, and Madge Micheels-Cyrus, comps. **Seeds of Peace: A Catalogue of Quotations**. Philadelphia, New Society, 1986. 276p. index. $34.95; $12.95(pbk). ISBN 0-86571-098-8; 0-86571-099-6(pbk).

Over 1,600 quotations are included in this collection dealing with peace, war, nonviolence, and related topics. The selections are divided into five chapters: "Waging War"; "The Lighter Side of a Serious Subject"; "Patriotism"; "Bumperstickers, Buttons, T-Shirts & Graffiti"; and "Waging Peace." The longer chapters have subdivisions.

As a reference or research tool, this title has numerous limitations. Indexing is by author only, with no access by subject or keyword other than the table of contents. Also, the original sources of the citations are not given. Nevertheless, this specialized collection, which goes far beyond existing general quotations books, is a rich source of quotations for individuals speaking or writing about peace. It can also be recommended for interesting browsing.

750.   Robertson, David. **Guide to Modern Defense and Strategy: A Complete Description of the Terms, Tactics, Organizations, and Accords of Today's Defense**. Detroit, Gale, 1987. 324p. $65.00. LC 87-82651. ISBN 0-8103-5403-2.

This handbook offers definitions and discussions of terms related to defense, strategy, including military and naval affairs. The emphasis is on the last 25 years and on British and American topics. It was originally published in England. There is also a focus on NATO versus the Warsaw Pact, with the Soviet Union assumed to be the opponent against which the various strategies of defense discussed are necessary. The entries average about one-half page and include such concepts as domino theory and strategic superiority, and many acronyms such as INF (Intermediate Nuclear Forces). An extensive list of acronyms includes terms, organizations, and government or military agencies.

Indexes

751.   **Peace Research Abstracts Journal**. Dundas, Ont. Peace Research Institute. 1964- . monthly. index. $150.00/yr. LC 64-9454. ISSN 0031-3599.

Several thousand books, documents, research reports and periodical articles are indexed and abstracted each year in this Canadian publication, which is a major tool for the systematic retrieval of international material on peace-related topics. The abstracts vary in length from a few lines to a page.

The entries are arranged in a detailed classification plan, which includes headings on such topics as ideologies, international organizations, national policies, and crisis areas. These sections are further divided into topical units. The sections of interest may be scanned for citations, or the material may be approached through the author and subject indexes, though the subject index is arranged by classification code number, which requires reference to the code manual.

Yearbooks

752. **Annual of Power and Conflict.** London, Institute for the Study of Conflict, 1971- . annual. price varies. LC 78-640196. ISSN 0307-031X.

Although it is not published in a timely manner, this annual review is an effective means of surveying recent events and their impact of existing political conditions. This series specifically surveys revolutionary, subversive, terrorist, guerrilla, and secessionist movements with a focus on their internal challenge to established political authority. Over 100 countries are considered.

The country-by-country surveys are grouped by world regions. For each nation there is a discussion of the government, the size of the armed forces, and other factors related to the stability of the existing regime. In a similar manner, the activities and strengths of the opposition efforts are evaluated. There is a chronology of revolutionary activities. Levels of violence in each nation are also examined.

753. **United Nations Disarmament Yearbook.** New York, Department for Disarmament Affairs, United Nations, 1976- . annual. $54.00. LC 78-641027. E.87.IX.1 (1986).

The *Yearbook* provides an annual review of the main developments in the field of disarmament, arms control, and such related topics as military forces, the arms trade, and international military expenditures. This narrative overview is arranged in topical chapters, such as "Comprehensive Approaches to Disarmament" and "Nuclear Disarmament." The emphasis is on a factual review of matters related to disarmament dealt with by the various agencies of the United Nations. Resolutions and reports are cited, often with full text. This work is a basic reference source for information on the disarmament activities of the United Nations and its specialized agencies.

754. **World Armaments and Disarmament: SIPRI Yearbook.** Stockholm International Peace Research Institute. New York, Humanities, 1969- . annual. index. $51.00. LC 83-643843. ISSN 0347-2205.

SIPRI is an independent institute in Stockholm organized for research on peace and conflict, especially on disarmament and arms control. Its *Yearbook* analyzes the year's events in relation to peace, the risk of war, and possible progress towards arms regulation.

The examination of recent events and trends is provided through articles on major topics such as military expenditures, the arms trade, and disarmament negotiations. These detailed, comprehensive articles are signed and have extensive bibliographies. The many charts and statistics, such as tables showing the value of weapons exports by countries or Chinese nuclear tests, make this yearbook an excellent sourcebook for specific facts. There is also a brief chronology of major events and a subject index.

TERRORISM, ESPIONAGE, AND INTELLIGENCE SERVICES

Bibliographies

755. Constantinides, George C. **Intelligence and Espionage: An Analytical Bibliography.** Boulder, Colo., Westview Press, 1983. 560p. $75.00. LC 83-3519. ISSN 0-86531-545-0.

The author has used to advantage his many years of experience with the United States government in security and intelligence-related assignments in preparing this bibliography of nearly 500 titles. His familiarity and expertise in intelligence matters is particularly noticeable in the thorough and critical annotations. The work is limited to English-language nonfiction titles. It covers from the 17th century to the present, including American intelligence activities from the War of Independence to the present. Areas that are particularly well covered include the collection and use of intelligence information, espionage and counterespionage, and unconventional warfare.

756. Lakos, Amos. **International Terrorism: A Bibliography.** Boulder, Colo., Westview Press, 1986. 481p. index. $37.50. LC 86-1719. ISBN 0-8133-7157-0.

The publisher describes this title as the "definitive bibliography of the literature describing and analyzing terrorist activities." With 5,622 entries, this seems to be an accurate statement, though the citations are unannotated.

Lakos has included CIA reports, American and United Nations documents, conference reports, and dissertations, as well as books and journal articles. Only newspapers and news magazines were excluded. The focus is on English-language material published after 1960. The 10 chapters of the bibliography cover such topics as theories of terrorism, psychological and social aspects of terrorism, and countermeasures to terrorism. There are also chapters on reference works, general works, and material relating to specific regions or nations. There are author and detailed subject indexes.

757. Mickolus, Edward F., comp. **The Literature of Terrorism: A Selectively Annotated Bibliography.** Westport, Conn., Greenwood, 1980. 553p. bibliog. index. $55.00. LC 80-541. ISBN 0-313-22265-7.

This bibliography was designed to impose some order on the "chaos" (preface) the author found in 1980 in the vast literature of commentary and research on terrorism. Since that time, a fair number of bibliographies on terrorism have been published, but the Mickolus work remains important. Most of his entries are annotated, and he includes some topics not frequently covered, such as media and terrorism and psychological and medical approaches to terrorism.

Books, periodical articles, dissertations and theses, proceedings, speeches, and government documents are all included, for a total of 3,890 entries. These citations are grouped in chapters covering such subjects as tactics, guerrilla war, state terrorism, and responses to terrorism. A separate chapter arranged by geographic area provides works on incidents in specific countries. There are also chapters on fiction and on bibliographies. Author and title indexes are provided, but no subject index. Cross-references by citation number are given to related headings.

758. Newton, Michael, and Judy Ann Newton. **Terrorism in the United States and Europe, 1800-1959: An Annotated Bibliography.** New York, Garland, 1988. 508p. index. (Garland Reference Library of Social Science, Vol. 449). $72.00. LC 88-21848. ISBN 0-8240-5747-3.

The authors have for the purposes of their bibliography defined terrorism as "any resort to violence or coercive action by a group in pursuit of social, economic, or political objectives"(introduction). The citations are grouped in three section: general works; works dealing with Europe, subdivided by country; and works dealing with the United States, subdivided by major topics such as economic violence and racial violence.

The majority of the titles in this volume are not annotated. Chronological coverage stops at 1959. For annotated bibliographies covering more current titles, note the works by Mickolus (entry 757) and Norton (entry 759) in this section.

759. Norton, Augustus R., and Martin H. Greenberg. **International Terrorism: An Annotated Bibliography and Research Guide.** Boulder, Colo., Westview Press, 1980. 218p. index. (Westview Special Studies in National and International Terrorism). $20.00. LC 79-27845. ISBN 0-89158-461-7.

Although there are now more current titles covering the literature of terrorism, this bibliography remains useful for the titles of the 1970s and for the annotations of about one-third of the entries. The almost 1,000 citations cover books, articles, and documents. There is a fiction section with over 100 items.

This bibliography is divided into two main sections: topical and geographic. The topical section includes sections on the philosophic, ideologic, and moral foundations of terrorism, anarchy, and nihilism, and nuclear terrorism. The geographic sections gather all the citations relating to terrorism in a specific region or country. An appendix provides recommended titles for core collections on terrorism. There is an author but no subject index.

760. Rocca, Raymond G., and John J. Dziak, with the staff of the Consortium for the Study of Intelligence. **Bibliography on Soviet Intelligence and Security Services.** Boulder, Colo., Westview Press, 1985. 203p. index. (Westview Special Study). $16.00(pbk). LC 85-3257. ISBN 0-8133-7048-5.

There are over 500 citations to books, periodical articles, and government documents in this bibliography on Soviet intelligence. The authors have experience in American intelligence agencies as well as in academia. The bibliography covers all aspects of Soviet intelligence and espionage, including Soviet domestic politics and world affairs.

The references are divided into five sections: (1) selected bibliographies and other reference works, (2) Russian/Soviet accounts, (3) defector/firsthand accounts, (4) secondary accounts, and (5) congressional and other documents. The entries have brief annotations that contain, in addition to content notes, background information on the author or work and often comparisons with other titles. The availability of English-language translations of Russian works is indicated.

The appendixes contain a short glossary of abbreviations and terms, chronologies of the leadership of the KGB and GRU, and a chart showing the historical development of Soviet intelligence and security services. There are author and title indexes. Rocca is a former senior intelligence official of the Central Intelligence Agency and was an adjunct professor at the Defense Intelligence College.

761. Smith, Myron J., Jr. **The Secret Wars: A Guide to Sources in English.** Santa Barbara, Calif, ABC-Clio, 1980/81. 3v. index. $42.50(v.1); $67.50(v.2); $37.50(v.3). LC 79-25784. ISBN 0-87436-271-7(v.1); 0-87436-303-9(v.2); 0-87436-304-7(v.3).

In these three volumes of the War/Peace Bibliography series, Smith has presented extensive coverage of the literature on clandestine warfare. Volume 1 focuses on intelligence, underground activity, resistance movements, and special forces during World War II. Volume 2 covers similar topics for 1945-1980, the cold war period. The third volume, *International Terrorism, 1968-1980,* concentrates on history, philosophy, tactics, and countermeasures rather than on specific incidents.

There are over 10,000 unannotated citations in this set, although coverage is limited to English-language works. Books, periodical articles, dissertations, and documents are included. In addition to the bibliographies, there are introductory historical essays and extensive chronologies for each volume. The detailed table of contents and the author and subject indexes facilitate access.

Biographical Sources

762.   Payne, Ronald, and Christopher Dobson. **The Dictionary of Espionage.** New York, St. Martin's Press, 1984. 234p. $15.95. LC 85-1790. ISBN 0312874324.

This biographical directory, which was also published under the title of *Who's Who in Espionage*, provides biographical portraits of over 300 individuals active since the end of World War II in espionage or intelligence work. The portraits, while brief, convey the major personal attributes and career activities of spies and spymasters, famous and obscure.

There is also a section outlining the intelligence organizations and activities of 17 countries, a glossary of espionage terms, and a short bibliography on espionage.

Chronologies

763.   Mickolus, Edward F. **Transnational Terrorism: A Chronology of Events, 1968-1979.** Westport, Conn., Greenwood, 1980. 967p. index. $55.00. LC 79-6829. ISBN 0-313-22206-1.

Although terrorism is not new, it is only in the last two decades that it had been adopted by hundreds of groups as a means of political expression. This chronology attempts to identify and list "all unclassified reporting on transnational terrorism that occurred from 1968 through 1979" (introduction). Included are 4,000 incidents, plus another 1,000 from earlier times to illustrate the long history of terrorism. The entries vary from one sentence to several pages, with kidnappings, bomb threats, and aerial hijackings accounting for a large portion of the incidents reported. Names of terrorists and victims, locations, dates, and descriptions of the outcomes of the incidents are provided.

In addition to the chronology of terrorist events, Mickolus has developed a computer program that provides various analyses, including tables on the annual frequency of terrorist attacks, the types of attacks, and the number of deaths and injuries. There is also a list of terrorist organizations with their acronyms, arranged by country. The three indexes provide access by date of incident for countries, types of attack, and groups claiming responsibility.

Dictionaries and Encyclopedias

764.   Buranelli, Vincent, and Nan Buranelli. **Spy/Counterspy: An Encyclopedia of Espionage.** New York, McGraw-Hill, 1982. 361p. index. $24.95.   LC 81-23666. ISBN 0-07-008915-9.

In this alphabetically arranged encyclopedia there are over 400 entries consisting of articles, most of which do not exceed one or two pages. The authors have limited coverage to modern history, beginning with Elizabethan England. The focus is on the 20th century for the United States and Europe. The encyclopedia includes biographical sketches of spies and spymasters, descriptions of historical events, identification of techniques of espionage, and sketches of organizations such as the CIA and KGB. The articles contain good bibliographies for further reading. While this book is written in an entertaining manner, which will appeal to the spy enthusiasts, it also contains much solid historical and reference information.

765. Burton, Bob. **Top Secret: A Clandestine Operator's Glossary of Terms.** Boulder, Colo., Paladin Press, 1986. 127p. $10.00(pbk). ISBN 0-87364-350-X.

The 800 terms defined in this dictionary were culled from a wide spectrum of activities: special operations and unconventional warfare, codes and ciphers, security, and American and foreign intelligence operations. Terminology related to the CIA is emphasized. The definitions, varying from one line to a paragraph, are written in nontechnical terms, often with historical notes.

There are also five rather disparate appendixes of several pages each. The first discusses the criteria and processes used for evaluating intelligence information. The second lists security classifications, such as Secret and Top Secret, in the languages of most countries. The last three appendixes very briefly outline the organization and information-gathering processes of the United States intelligence community.

For another interesting collection of terms defined in popular style see Becket, Henry S. A. *The Dictionary of Espionage: Spookspeak into English.* New York, Stein & Day, 1986. 203p. bibliog. $17.95. LC 85-45003. ISBN 0-8128-3068-7.

766. Thackrah, John Richard. **Encyclopedia of Terrorism and Political Violence.** New York, Routledge & Kegan Paul/Methuen, 1987. 308p. bibliog. index. $35.00. LC 87-4304. ISBN 0-7102-0659-3.

With the prominence in the news of terrorism and guerrilla warfare in recent years, this encyclopedia meets a need for a collection of articles focusing on these topics. The entries cover both specific subjects, such as individual terrorist acts and hijackings, and general concepts. Major events, organizations, individuals, and ideas are all included. A very similar title, George Rosie's *The Directory of International Terrorism* (see entry 769) focuses more on specific events and personalities, while this title has more of an emphasis on concepts and ideologies. In addition to the alphabetically arranged entries, this volume features a useful list of abbreviations and acronyms associated with terrorism, a bibliography, and an index.

Directories

767. Janke, Peter, with Richard Sim. **Guerrilla and Terrorist Organisations: A World Directory and Bibliography.** New York, Macmillan, 1983. 531p. maps. index. $60.00. LC 83-9331. ISBN 0-02-916150-9.

Descriptions of approximately 600 movements that have "attempted to pose a threat to established governments since the end of the Second World War" (preface) constitute this directory. Since, as the author notes, the definition of "guerrilla" or "terrorist" depends on one's point of view, a wide variety of groups is included, ranging from the Mau Mau to the Ku Klux Klan, from the PLO to the Afghan National Liberation Front.

The entries are grouped by region and country. For each country section there is an introduction with background information on terrorist activities and a bibliography of major works on the subject. The paragraph-length capsule descriptions contain information on the history and activities of the organizations. This reference source covers the same subject as Degenhardt's *Political Dissent: An International Guide to Dissident, Extra-Parliamentary, Guerrilla, and Illegal Political Movements* (see entry 767). The duplication in coverage, however, is remarkably slight. The bibliography provided for each nation is a valuable aspect of the Janke work.

Handbooks

768. O'Toole, G. J. A. **The Encyclopedia of American Intelligence and Espionage: From the Revolutionary War to the Present.** New York, Facts on File, 1988. 539p. illus. bibliog. index. $40.00. LC 87-30361. ISBN 0-8160-1011-0.

This work greatly resembles in content *Spy/Counterspy: An Encyclopedia of Espionage* (see entry 764), except that this title focuses exclusively on American intelligence and espionage. The alphabetically arranged entries provide an historical overview and a review of developments and trends in espionage as it has been practiced in the United States. Many of the articles are biographical. Others deal with intelligence activities related to major conflicts such as the Civil War or the Bay of Pigs. There is also a list of abbreviations, a 10-page bibliography, and an index.

769. Rosie, George. **The Directory of International Terrorism.** New York, Paragon House, 1986. 310p. bibliog. $18.95. LC 86-25211. ISBN 0-913729-29-9.

This handbook is a reference guide to terrorist and counterterrorist organizations, major terrorist events, and individuals, whether terrorists or their victims. The entries, in dictionary format, are about a page long and concentrate on assembling the known facts plus some background information. In many cases, the author, a veteran British journalist, found it impossible to establish such seemingly simple biographical details as date and place of birth and date of death for even very well-known terrorists. The information gathered came entirely from published sources—books, reports, and, especially, newspaper accounts.

Although not comprehensive, analytical, or valuable for previously unpublished information, this volume offers up-to-date, basic information on such topics as Yasir Arafat, the *Achille Lauro* hijacking, and the Sendero Luminoso. The introduction has a discussion of the definition, history, and categories of terrorism.

770. Schmid, Alex P. **Political Terrorism: A Research Guide to Concepts, Theories, Data Bases and Literature.** Amsterdam, North-Holland; distr., New Brunswick, N.J., Transaction Books, 1984 (c1983). 585p. bibliog. index. $34.95. LC 86-672072. ISBN 0-4448-5602-1.

This volume attempts to fulfill the promises outlined in its subtitle: *A Research Guide to Concepts, Theories, Data Bases and Literature.* Four major sections deal with these items. The first section contains over 100 pages considering the major concepts and elements of terrorism and political violence. The definitions of major authors are included in this overview. The second section considers the major theories of terrorism and political violence. The third section describes databases on terrorism and includes a very extensive world directory of terrorist organizations with descriptions of their purposes and activities. This handbook concludes with a bibliography of the literature of terrorism, which contains 4,090 entries organized in topical divisions, and an author index.

Sourcebooks

771. Friedlander, Robert A. **Terrorism: Documents of International and Local Control.** Dobbs Ferry, N.Y., Oceana, 1979-1984. 4v. $160.00/set. LC 78-26126. ISSN 0-379-00690-1.

These four volumes constitute a resource for the researcher interested in finding the text of documents dealing with international terrorism. The collection contains about

200 documents from a wide variety of sources. Though the collection is comprehensive in the scope of its treatment of terrorism, hijackings and kidnappings receive considerable attention; many ICAO (International Civil Aviation Organization) and FAA documents relating to air safety are included. There is an extensive collection of United Nations documents beginning in the 1930s. CIA reports, British documents on Northern Ireland, and U.S. court decisions are examples of other materials in this collection. There are detailed tables of content but no indexes to the documents. In addition to the texts, the editor has provided extensive commentaries on the nature, legal aspects, and proposed solutions to terrorism.

6

Public Policy

BIBLIOGRAPHIES

772. Bergerson, Peter J. **Ethics and Public Policy: An Annotated Bibliography.** New York, Garland, 1988. 200p. index. (Public Affairs and Administration Series, Vol. 20; Garland Reference Library of Social Science, Vol. 414). $30.00. LC 87-32997. ISBN 0-8240-6632-4.

This slim bibliography contains 330 citations covering the last 25 years. It does not provide comprehensive coverage of the field chosen by the author but a broad sample of recent literature in this area of considerable current interest. The bibliography is divided into nine chapters, each focusing on one topic such as "Health Care/Medical/Bio-Scientific." There is no subject index for access beyond the breakdown provided by the topical chapters. There is an author index and a useful introduction that provides an overview of the subject and its literature. A strong feature of this bibliography is the lengthy descriptive annotations, some as long as a page.

773. Bowman, Sarah, and Jay M. Shafritz. **Public Personnel Administration: An Annotated Bibliography.** New York, Garland, 1985. 209p. index. (Public Affairs and Administration Series, Vol. 10; Garland Reference Library of Social Science, Vol. 170). $42.00. LC 82-49150. ISBN 0-8240-9151-5.

The chapters of this bibliography cover the fields of public personnel administration, including its traditional functions: recruitment, selection, placement, development, compensation, and such recent issues as equal employment opportunity. The compilers have included both academic publications and sources more oriented to practitioners.

Eleven topical chapters cite 684 items; 55 source periodicals are listed. The longest chapters cover equal employment opportunities, job design, performance appraisal, and productivity. The citations have brief descriptive annotations, often with quotations. The introduction provides an overview of the literature, with comments on selected entries.

774. Cayer, N. Joseph, and Sherry Dickerson. **Labor-Management Relations in the Public Sector: An Annotated Bibliography.** New York, Garland, 1984. 395p. index. $75.00. LC 82-49152. ISBN 0824091531.

The public employee labor relations materials included in this bibliography comprehensively cover from 1962 to 1983. In 1962, the federal government recognized the right of employees to engage in collective bargaining with governmental agencies.

The citations are divided into two major sections, one for articles, the other for books. Within each of these sections, the material is further divided by broad topic. The subject index provides more specific subject access. The entries have short descriptive annotations. There are two appendixes. The first is a short list of periodicals that regularly publish articles on public sector labor relations. The second identifies organizations that offer information, usually publications, on public employee bargaining. The introduction provides a brief historical overview of public employee labor relations since 1962.

775. Dillman, David L. **Civil Service Reform: An Annotated Bibliography.** New York, Garland, 1987. 239p. index. (Public Affairs and Administration Series, Vol. 17; Garland Reference Library of Social Science, Vol. 395). $45.00. LC 87-11887. ISBN 0-8240-8480-2.

This bibliography deals with the literature of civil service reforms, with general coverage for reform throughout the world but with a strong focus on the United States, specifically on the Civil Service Reform Act of 1978. Brief annotations provide information on the contents or viewpoints of the over 500 items selected from books, periodicals, and government publications. The citations are arranged in topical chapters dealing with such matters as the history of civil service reforms, the actual carrying out of reforms, and the effects of reforms that have been implemented. Supplementary features in this volume include an outline of the major provisions of the Civil Service Reform Act and a directory of organizations involved in reform. There are author and subject indexes.

776. Dynes, Patrick S., and Mary K. Marvel. **Program Evaluation: An Annotated Bibliography.** New York, Garland, 1987. 241p. index. (Public Affairs and Administration Series, Vol. 17; Garland Reference Library of Social Science, Vol. 172). $44.00. LC 82-49144. ISBN 0-8240-9146-9.

Program evaluation, a major component of policy analysis, encompasses the processes by which policy is formulated, implemented, and evaluated. Specifically, program evaluation measures the performance of publicly funded programs, to judge their effectiveness against announced goals.

The 440 citations in this bibliography were selected from books and periodicals published between 1970 and 1985, a period that includes "virtually the entire history of program evaluation as we now know it" (introduction). Research design, methodology, and ways to use evaluation results represent the major topics covered. The annotations are brief and descriptive, not evaluative. There is an author index but no subject or title indexes.

777. Goehlert, Robert U., and Fenton S. Martin. **Policy Analysis and Management: A Bibliography.** Santa Barbara, Calif., ABC-Clio, 1985. 398p. index. $55.00. LC 84-16829. ISBN 0-87436-387-X.

The aim of the authors was to produce a comprehensive bibliography of recent policy analysis literature. Dissertations, documents, and foreign-language materials were excluded. While books, research reports, and selected essays are included, the emphasis is definitely on journal articles. Thirty policy journals are listed as the major source of citations.

Over 9,000 citations are included. The unannotated entries are listed in seven topical chapters with numerous subdivisions. The first two sections cover concepts and theories of policy analysis, while the rest focus on such topics as economic policy, including inflation, taxation, and unemployment; political policy, including arms control, elections, and urban management; social policy, including aging, drug control, and poverty; technological and scientific policy, including mass transit and space; and environmental policy, including air pollution, energy, and waste treatment. Most of the citations refer to American policy matters. As the entries are alphabetical by author within the subchapters, the detailed subject index provides direct access.

778.   Grasham, W. E., and J. M. Alain. **Canadian Public Administration: Bibliography. Supplement 4: 1979-1982; Administration publique canadienne: Bibliographie.** Toronto, Institute of Public Administration of Canada, 1985. 269p. index. $20.00(pbk). ISBN 0-919696-30-9.

This bibliography is the fourth supplement to the *Canadian Public Administration* bibliography published in 1972. This supplement, covering only four years, contains 3,779 entries. It includes books and journals in English and in French.

The entries are arranged in 16 topical chapters covering all aspects of public administration in Canada. This supplement added two new sections: "Human Rights" and "Women." Many Canadian government documents, including publications by Statistics Canada and the Economic Council of Canada, are included. There is an author index and a comprehensive, detailed subject index.

779.   Huddleston, Mark W. **Comparative Public Administration: An Annotated Bibliography.** New York, Garland, 1984. 245p. index. (Public Affairs and Administration Series, Vol. 5; Garland Reference Library of Social Science, Vol. 146). $43.00. LC 82-49178. ISBN 0-8240-9182-5.

As a selective bibliography in the field of comparative public administration, this title concentrates on publications from 1962 through 1982. The "User's Guide" explains the author's purpose and provides an overview of recent developments in comparative public administration.

The more than 600 citations in this bibliography include items published as books or journal articles. Dissertations, manuscripts, conference papers, and the like are excluded. The author has defined "comparative" as "non-American." Lesser-known areas receive the highest priority for inclusion in this international survey of public administration. The entries, however, are mainly published in English.

The annotated citations are arranged in nine topical chapters that cover such subjects as administrative history, personnel administration, organizational theory, and budgeting. Each chapter is introduced by a paragraph discussing the nature of the subfield and its literature. There is an author index and a country index; the latter includes references to more than 100 nations or regions.

780.   Lovrich, Nicholas P., and Max Neiman. **Public Choice Theory in Public Administration: An Annotated Bibliography.** New York, Garland, 1984. 122p. index. (Public Affairs and Administration Series, Vol. 8; Garland Reference Library of Social Science, Vol. 167). $27.00. LC 82-49153. ISBN 0-8240-9154-X.

Public choice theory represents a new and growing, if controversial, influence in public administration. Public choice theory is an analytical tool, based on economic forms of reasoning, used to evaluate individual or collective administrative behavior. Two interpretative essays provide background information on public choice theory and an overview of the work cited in this bibliography.

The bibliography contains 200 entries, including books, periodical articles, dissertations, and research reports written in English. The total collection of citations has been divided into two groups; the first dealing with normative works and the second pertaining to empirical studies. Both supportive and critical works of the public choice perspective are included. The paragraph-long annotations provide descriptive and evaluative comments. There are author and subject indexes.

781.   Miewald, Robert D. **The Bureaucratic State: An Annotated Bibliography.** New York, Garland, 1984. 601p. index. (Public Affairs and Administration Series, Vol. 6; Garland Reference Library of Social Science, Vol. 166). $93.00. LC 82-49154. ISBN 0-8240-9155-8.

More than 2,700 items have been cited in this guide to the literature on bureaucracy. The approach has been interdisciplinary and comprehensive, with a broad definition of bureaucracy that includes government, administration, officials, and the whole larger social milieu that surrounds them. This bibliography is generally limited to English-language books and journal articles, with coverage extending back to the mid-19th century.

The entries, which have very brief descriptive annotations, are grouped in 24 topical chapters. Subjects covered include the study of bureaucracy, American bureaucracy, comparative bureaucracy, and national studies. There is also a series of chapters on bureaucracies in specific fields such as education, health care, and the military. There is a final chapter covering humorous treatments of the subject. There is an author index but no subject index to provide direct access beyond the subject classification of the table of contents.

782.   Murin, William J., Gerald Michael Greenfield, and John D. Buenker. **Public Policy: A Guide to Information Sources.** Detroit, Gale, 1981. 283p. index. (American Government and History Information Guide Series, Vol. 13; Gale Information Guide Library). $36.00. LC 80-25872. ISBN 0-8103-1490-8.

As an annotated bibliography of public policy literature, this guide provides a useful source for preliminary research. The over 1,300 citations are devoted exclusively to public policy in the United States. Most of the books cited are contemporary, although some standard titles have been included. The annotations are particularly helpful in identifying the content and focus of the citations.

The eight chapters treat theories and concepts, decisionmaking, state and local policy processes, urban policy, the intergovernmental aspects of public policy, implementation and evaluation, and policy issues in business, education, science, and health. There are author and subject indexes.

783.   Payad, Aurora T. **Organization Behavior in American Public Administration: An Annotated Bibliography.** New York, Garland, 1986. 264p. index. (Public Affairs and Administration Series, Vol. 15; Garland Reference Library of Social Science, Vol. 320). $53.00. LC 85-45111. ISBN 0-8240-8685-6.

This bibliography deals with organizational behavior within the context of public administration. Organizational behavior covers the actions, motivations, conflicts, and leadership styles of individuals and groups, including officials, the bureaucracy, and citizens in general. The organizational development approach was used as a guide to the selection of entries, with four areas of concentration: the organization and its environment, groups within an organization, the interface between the individual employee and the organization, and interpersonal relations.

The 620 citations are grouped in five chapters, each with four or five subdivisions. Books, book chapters, and dissertations written between 1940 and 1984 are included, though this bibliography relies heavily on periodical citations, especially from the *Public Administration Quarterly*. The entries have short descriptive annotations. There is an author index, a subject index, and a short list of professional associations.

784.   **Public Administration Series, Bibliography No. P 1- .** Monticello, Ill., Vance Bibliographies, 1978- . price varies. ISSN 0193-970X.

This series of short, unannotated bibliographies began in 1972. Several thousand titles have now been issued. These brief bibliographies consist of about 5 to 10 pages of citations to books and periodical articles. Each issue is devoted to a specific topic on public administration or political science, such as regulation of mass media, state boards of higher education, or refuse collection. Over the years a wide variety of subjects, American and international, have been covered. Vance has published a number of author, title, and subject cumulative indexes to the series.

785.   **Recent Publications on Governmental Problems.** Chicago, Merriam Center Library, 1932- . monthly with annual cumulations. index. $25.00/yr. LC 85-19905. ISSN 0034-1185.

RPGP, as the editor refers to this publication, is a monthly index to current books, documents, reports of public and private agencies, and articles from approximately 300 periodicals. Annotations are provided only for items that cost more than $20.00.

Citations dealing with public administration are listed under headings that cover such topics as transportation; energy and environment; finance, taxation and economics; housing and architecture; personnel and office management; planning; public works and utilities; public safety, health, education, and welfare; and public administration and law. Each issue also features a brief section on forthcoming conferences and workshops and contains a list of periodicals indexed with addresses.

786.   Robey, John S. **Public Policy Analysis: An Annotated Bibliography.** New York, Garland, 1984. 195p. index. (Public Affairs and Administration Series, Vol. 9; Garland Reference Library of Social Science, Vol. 171). $39.00. LC 82-49149. ISBN 0-8240-9150-7.

As the foreword explains, "Public policy is simply whatever government chooses to do or not to do." The analysis and study of these choices is the subject of this bibliography. Unlike Robert U. Goehlert's *Policy Analysis and Management: A Bibliography* (see entry 777), which is a comprehensive unannotated list with more than 9,400 entries, Robey's work contains 749 carefully selected titles with short but evaluative annotations. The selections are limited to books and articles, to research done between 1977 through 1982, to English-language works, to prominent books, and to the nine journals the author considered the most relevant.

Ten specific policy areas are covered: agriculture, civil rights, the economy, education, energy, military affairs, foreign affairs, sex and drugs, social welfare, and taxation. There are also chapters on policy analysis and policymaking. Author and subject indexes are included.

787.   Stevenson, Hugh A., comp. **Public Policy and Futures Bibliography: A Select List of Canadian, American, and Other Book-Length Materials, 1970 to 1980, Including Highly Selected Works Published between 1949 and 1969.** Ontario, Minister of Education; distr., Toronto, Ontario Institute for Studies in Education, 1980. 413p. index. $6.00(pbk). LC 81-452366. ISBN 0-7743-5231-0.

Public Policy and Futures Bibliography is a guide to the public policy literature of the 1970s. There are 2,665 entries covering books, book chapters, reports, conference proceedings, and government reports. These citations are grouped in the following topical chapters: "Education and the Future"; "General Future Studies"; "Literature"; and "Methodology: Policy, Planning and Future Studies."

While the emphasis is on educational policymaking, other topics, including economics, crime, peace, transportation, and constitutional reform are covered. The future is the major orientation of this bibliography. The emphasis is on Canadian materials, which constitute well over half of the titles cited. There are author, sponsoring agency, and subject indexes.

DICTIONARIES AND ENCYCLOPEDIAS

788. Chandler, Ralph C., and Jack C. Plano. **The Public Administration Dictionary.** New York, John Wiley & Sons, 1982. 406p. index. $17.95; $11.95(pbk). LC 81-12945. ISBN 0-471-09121-9; 0-471-09119-7(pbk).

The authors have attempted to provide in this dictionary definitions of the essential concepts of public administration. Less essential terms can be found within the major entries by using the index. The terms, which encompass concepts, events, strategies, theories, institutions, and individuals, are those that students and practitioners will find fundamental for understanding the field of public administration.

The key concepts are grouped in seven chapters covering the following: fundamentals, public policy, public management, bureaucracy and administrative organization, personnel administration, financial administration, and public law and regulation. These chapters parallel the customary sections of introductory public administration texts. In addition to the definitions, each entry contains a "Significance"paragraph, which comments on the historical and contemporary relevance of the term.

789. Cutchin, D. A. **Guide to Public Administration.** Ithaca, Ill., Peacock, 1981. 159p. $8.95(pbk). LC 80-84211. ISSN 0-87581-272-4.

This dictionary features short definitions of the major concepts, theories, phrases, and terms of public administration. Important specific laws and individuals are also included. While this dictionary is certainly fine for definitions or quick lookups, Chandler and Plano's *The Public Administration Dictionary* (see entry 788) offers more complete definitions that also include information on the historical and contemporary significance of the terms.

In addition to the dictionary, Cutchin's work contains brief annotated bibliographies of major reference sources, periodicals, and indexes and abstracting services.

790. **Encyclopedia of Policy Studies.** Stuart S. Nagel, ed. New York, Marcel Dekker, 1983. 914p. index. (Public Administration and Public Policy, Vol. 13). $99.75. LC 82-22111. ISBN 0-8247-11998.

Although this work does not feature short explanatory articles in alphabetical sequence, the editor considers it an encyclopedia because it embodies "taking a walk around" (introduction) the subject of policy studies. This overview is provided through 34 chapters prepared by 41 contributors, for the most part American academics.

The field of policy studies is defined as the study of the nature, causes, and effects of alternative public policies for dealing with problems facing government. Some chapters focus on problems with a sociological or economic basis, such as poverty, land use, and environmental protection. Others deal with policy problems with a political emphasis, such as American foreign policy and the use and control of military force. Theoretical topics, such as policy analysis and policy formation, are also included. This work may be considered an encyclopedia in the sense that each chapter provides a concise survey of the field and an assessment of the current state of affairs. There is a detailed subject index for those seeking information on topics at a more specific level than provided for by the chapter arrangement.

791. Kruschke, Earl R., and Byron M. Jackson. **The Public Policy Dictionary.** Santa Barbara, Calif., ABC-Clio, 1987. 159p. bibliog. index. (Clio Dictionaries in Political Science, No. 15). $35.00; $12.00(pbk). LC 86-25941. ISBN 0-87436-443-4; 0-87436-460-4(pbk).

As with all other titles in the series, this dictionary employs a thematic approach, grouping the 200 terms defined into topical chapters that could parallel an introductory college course on public policy. The first chapter, which considers the nature of public policy, is followed by others on the processes of public policy, including formulation, implementation, and evaluation.

The scope of this work is limited to terms related to American public policy. The definitions, which are one paragraph long, are followed by "Significance" paragraphs that focus on the historical and current relevance of the terms. There is a comprehensive index for direct access for those not interested in the thematic arrangement of this dictionary.

792.   Shafritz, Jay M. **The Facts on File Dictionary of Public Administration.** New York, Facts on File, 1985. 610p. $29.95. LC 85-27542. ISBN 0-8160-1266-0.

Though a dictionary in format, the inclusiveness of coverage and the care taken by the author to gather information, makes this reference tool an extremely useful handbook for practitioners, students, and researchers in the field of public administration. Entries include individuals, words, phrases, government agencies, professional societies, court decisions, statutes, and much more from the many fields that constitute public administration.

The definitions are brief, but clear and packed with information. For example, the entry for "Act" includes a chart of the path of a bill through Congress; the entry for "Databases" lists and describes 22 computerized information files. Biographical entries include a list of major works. Many entries have short bibliographies attached for further study. Addresses are given for government agencies and private organizations. Cross-references have been liberally provided. The usefulness of the information selected for the entries should make this dictionary a standard reference work for many years.

DIRECTORIES

793.   **Graduate School Programs in Public Affairs and Administration.** Washington, D.C., National Association of Schools of Public Affairs and Administration, 1974- . biennial. $12.50. LC 74-80861. ISSN 0094-6648.

This directory is based on a survey of members of the National Association of Schools of Public Affairs and Administration. It provides information on degrees offered, tuition, application deadlines, admission requirements, financial aid, faculty, and related matters for schools offering graduate degrees in public administration. The *Policy Studies Directory* (see entry 797) covers much of the same information.

794.   **Policy Grants Directory.** Urbana, Ill., Policy Studies Organization, 1977- . irreg. $8.00. LC 78-641048. ISSN 0160-2675.

795.   **Policy Publisher and Associations Directory.** Urbana, Ill., Policy Studies Organization, 1980- . irreg. $8.00. LC 80-648976. ISSN 0272-0671.

796.   **Policy Research Centers Directory.** Urbana, Ill., Policy Studies Organization, 1972- . irreg. $8.00. LC 80-643747. ISSN 0270-1200.

797.   **Policy Studies Directory.** Urbana, Ill., Policy Studies Organization, 1972- . irreg. $8.00. LC 76-644351. ISSN 0362-6016.

798. **Policy Studies Personnel Directory.** Urbana, Ill., Policy Studies Organization. 1979- . irreg. $8.00. LC 81-643479. ISSN 0275-4002.

These five directories are published by the Policy Studies Organization, which was formed to promote the application of political and social science to important public policy problems. It also publishes the *Policy Studies Journal* (see entry 000). The editors are currently planning updates of these directories.

The directory of grants lists 36 governmental and 46 private funding sources. For each source there is information on contact persons, eligibility, size and number of grants, procedures, and the main areas of interest of the agency. The second directory listed identifies publishers, periodicals, and associations concerned with policy studies. The third directory identifies about 100 university and nonuniversity research centers and provides information on their programs, clients, and funding. The *Policy Studies Directory* identifies academic programs concerned with policy studies. It has three lists: doctoral, master's, and interdisciplinary programs. For each program there is information on degrees, research, teaching, funding, and hiring. The *Policy Studies Personnel Directory* identifies political and social scientists active in policy studies. In addition to address, title, and degrees, there is information on each individual's general approach to policy studies, interest in specific policy problems, disciplinary background, special affiliations, and geographical location. The indexes list all personnel by each of these factors.

GUIDES

799. Caiden, Gerald E., and others. **American Public Administration: A Bibliographical Guide to the Literature.** New York, Garland, 1983. 201p. index. (Public Affairs and Administration Series, Vol. 3; Garland Reference Library of Social Science, Vol. 169). $30.00. LC 82-49151. ISBN 0-8240-9152-3.

The intention of this volume is to "winnow out what authorities consider the crucial core of the field" (introduction) of public administration literature. Three areas of publications are covered: (1) abstracts, indexes and continuing bibliographies (103 entries), (2) professional journals (nearly 250 entries), and (3) books (871 entries). The entries in the first two sections are annotated. The bibliography of books includes standard works, anthologies, and the most frequently cited texts. Journal articles and government documents are excluded.

This overview of public administration begins with an essay describing the scope and characteristics of American public administration. There are author and title indexes but no subject index. For a bibliography that includes annotated book citations and journals, see John E. Rouse's *Public Administration in American Society: A Guide to Information Sources* (see entry 802).

800. McCurdy, Howard E. **Public Administration: A Bibliographic Guide to the Literature.** New York, Marcel Dekker, 1986. 311p. index. (Public Administration and Public Policy, Vol. 29). $29.75. LC 85-25436. ISBN 0-8247-7518-X.

As a selective bibliography, this work has a distinctive approach to the subject of public administration. The author concluded that in this field "the bulk of ... knowledge is to be found in books" (preface). With this premise in mind, McCurdy proceeded to identify the most frequently cited books after examining reading lists, textbook citations, and specialized bibliographies.

The result of his study is a bibliography of 181 titles, the most frequently cited books in public administration. For each title a paragraph-long descriptive review highlights that title's particular contribution, focus, or findings. There is also a longer unannotated bibliography of 1,200 books divided into 33 topical areas representing broadly the fields of public administration. These books were also chosen on the basis of citation studies.

There are in addition two essays that trace the development of public administration as a field of study. This bibliography is an appropriate starting point for readers or librarians who require a relatively short listing of prominent titles from recent years.

801.   Nagel, Stuart S. **Basic Literature in Policy Studies: A Comprehensive Bibliography.** Greenwich, Conn., JAI Press, 1984. 453p. $75.00. LC 83-480084. ISBN 0892323671.

The purpose of this impressive bibliography is to promote the application of political and social science to important policy problems. Leading scholars in the various subjects of policy studies have contributed 37 detailed bibliographies for this compilation. Some of the contributions represent updated versions of bibliographies that were previously published in *Policy Studies Journal.*

This comprehensive work contains separate bibliographies on such topics as basic concepts, the research process, and urban policy, and on a large selection of "problem" areas such as foreign policy, economic regulation, racial discrimination, environmental protection, and biomedical policy. All of the bibliographies include only English-language materials. Otherwise, the contributors have set individual standards for chronological limits and the types of materials to include. Most of the bibliographies are unannotated. The editor's introduction provides a definition and overview of policy studies and a discussion of possible future directions for the field.

802.   Rouse, John E., Jr. **Public Administration in American Society: A Guide to Information Sources.** Detroit, Gale, 1980. 553p. index. (American Government and History Information Guide Series, Vol. 11; Gale Information Guide Library). $30.00. LC 80-24633. ISBN 0-8103-1424-X.

According to the author's preface, public administration is not a discipline, probably not even a field. It draws its literature from political science, history, psychology, business, management, sociology, social work, and economics. With this perspective, Rouse has selected from these fields some 1,700 citations; the result is a useful bibliography for academic and governmental contexts.

The bibliography includes books, book chapters, periodical articles, and government documents. The cutoff date is 1980, with the greatest number of entries from the 1970s but with a few standard titles dating back to the 1920s and 1930s. Classics in all subfields of the classified list are identified. All citations are fully annotated. The titles are arranged in a classification designed to show the role of public administration in American life, including such topics as federalism, administrative structure, policymaking, personnel administration, equal employment, and budgeting. This guidebook is a major effort to provide a bibliographic overview of American public administration.

INDEXES

803.   **Sage Public Administration Abstracts.** Beverly Hills, Calif., Sage, 1974- . quarterly. index. $95.00/yr. LC 74-645245. ISSN 0094-6958.

This quarterly publication is the only indexing service focusing specifically on public administration literature. Each issue contains approximately 250 paragraph-length abstracts. These abstracts are drawn from over 150 English-language journals regularly scanned, and from selected books, government publications, significant speeches, and legislative research studies.

The entries are arranged under 14 broad headings, covering such topics as administrative structure, local and state government, public employment, and budgeting and finance. The author and detailed subject indexes of each issue are cumulated annually.

SOURCEBOOKS

804.   Mosher, Frederick C., ed. **Basic Literature of American Public Administration, 1787-1950.** New York, Holmes & Meier, 1981. 314p. $25.00; $12.00(pbk). LC 79-28553. ISBN 0-8419-0574-6; 0-8419-0575-4(pbk).

The editor has attempted to select the basic articles of public administration literature for graduate students and others interested in the development and background of this field. *Basic Literature of American Public Administration, 1787-1950* is an anthology of journal articles and book chapters. A few selections are quoted in full; others are excerpted. The selections are arranged chronologically in four parts: (1) "Heritage," (2) "Birth and Growth of the Public Management Movement," (3) "Maturation of an Orthodox Public Administration," and (4) "Expanding Horizons." Each selection has a short historical headnote that includes information about the author. For a companion volume for official documents, see Richard J. Stillman's *Basic Documents of American Public Administration since 1950* (see entry 805).

805.   Stillman, Richard J. II. **Basic Documents of American Public Administration since 1950.** New York, Holmes & Meier, 1983. 311p. $34.50; $15.50(pbk). LC 82-11726. ISBN 0-8419-0818-4; 0-8419-0819-2(pbk).

For graduate students and others interested in the development and background of public administration, the editor has attempted to select the basic documents of the field. He has provided a convenient set of the major landmarks in two companion titles. *Basic Documents of American Public Administration 1776-1950*, published in 1976, and its sequel, covering the period since 1950, consist of official documents—declarations, the Constitution, charters, laws, and reports. More recent documents focus on personnel management, budgeting, and administrative accountability. A few selections are quoted in full; the others are excerpted. For a companion volume on the general literature of the field, see Frederick C. Mosher's *Basic Literature of American Public Administration, 1787-1950* (see entry 804).

Author/Title Index

Numbers in this index refer to entries, not pages. The letter "n" following an entry number indicates that the author or title is mentioned in the annotation.

Subject Index

Numbers in this index normally refer to entries, not pages. The letter "n" following an entry number indicates that the relevant item is mentioned in the annotation.